Justice for Speedy

A True Horse Story

Judy Berkley

Justice for Speedy: A True Horse Story is a work of non-fiction. All characters are real, but names and descriptions have been changed. The plot and all incidents are true and can be fully documented.

Book formatting and cover art by Jera Publishing
Website and tech support by Maag Consulting

Special thanks to Erin Roof, a professional editor, who reviewed the manuscript and provided excellent advice and encouragement

ISBN: 978-0-692-01518-6

For information:

Justice for Speedy, LLC
P.O. Box 102
Mechanicstown, OH 44651
or
www.justiceforspeedy.com

To Mike
for always having my back

Prologue

"Do you realize you're committing professional suicide?"

The editor-in-chief of the *Oakland Tribune*, David Burgin, was standing behind his desk with my letter of resignation from my job as a daily columnist clenched in his fist. Burgin had been my boss for two years, and we'd had many philosophical tussles. He'd hired me to write five columns per week that were full of happy talk, and that's what he expected.

But, I couldn't ignore the murder and mayhem that were blighting the city of Oakland, California, and claiming the lives of many young African-Americans. After numerous arguments, Burgin had finally allowed me to write one serious column per week. Those commentaries, when they discussed crime and ethnicity, ignited outrage in the community, and, also, in the *Tribune* newsroom, where liberal reporters and editors responded to my columns by conducting a campaign of harassment, shunning, threats, and attempted censorship, which I found shocking in an American newspaper.

Burgin was an old school newsman, who was fond of a quote attributed to the legendary journalist and wit, H. L. Mencken: "The duty of a newspaper is to comfort the afflicted and afflict the comfortable."

But, the duty of the *Oakland Tribune* and many other publications across the country in the mid-1990s, was to observe the prescribed guidelines of political correctness, so as to avoid afflicting any discomfort into the discussion of race. In my view, PC was killing Oakland's kids.

Moreover, that it was impossible to solve problems if you weren't allowed to fully define them.

Despite the difficulties my opinions caused for *Tribune* management, the columns were allowed to run. Then, Burgin reneged on our deal. Unbeknownst to me, he installed a watchdog, an ambitious young woman, who was instructed to dump any of my serious opinion pieces that might ruffle feathers.

Thus, when I wrote a column, which was supportive of the police department's handling of a riot by African-American youth that marred a popular Oakland festival and caused injuries and extensive property damage, the watchdog yanked the commentary and ran something else.

My resignation was on Burgin's desk the next day.

Was I committing professional suicide? I didn't want to get into yet another argument with Burgin. If, with all his experience, he couldn't see that people, who once got their news exclusively from newspapers, now had other sources; if he couldn't see that people were tired of liberal bias and social agendas tainting the news; if he couldn't see that people were angry about suppression of the truth and disrespect for their views, well, there wasn't anything I could say to him.

To me, it was the profession of journalism that was committing suicide. I was just tired of the self-inflicted wounds.

The grinding task of producing five newspaper columns per week had consumed my life and left little time to think about anything other than filling the voracious hole I was responsible for in the newspaper. And the fodder for a daily column was increasingly worrisome, a country and its citizenry losing its moorings and drifting towards anarchy. I was glad that I would no longer have to contemplate that on a daily basis.

Professional suicide? Typical of Burgin, a veteran newsman, to think that life without newspapering was death. I knew I could go back to writing for magazines. Indeed, I thought I might concentrate on writing for the horse industry.

I owned horses, had loved them from my earliest days, and had written for horse magazines when I was a freelancer. While the remuneration wouldn't come close to my *Tribune* paycheck, at least writing for horse publications would not be stressful or contentious.

As I left the *Oakland Tribune*'s offices on June 13, 1994, I felt released from stress and burdensome obligations. I looked forward to the future. I planned a peaceful existence that would be devoted to the things I loved. No controversy. No headaches. No heartbreak.

How does the old saying go? Oh yeah. If you want to hear God laugh, tell him your plans.

Chapter 1

Mares keep things interesting.

Stallions are the stuff of legend and literature. However, stallion behavior is mainly centered on enlarging and protecting their gene pool. Humans, who work with them, must always be mindful of the stallion's primary focus.

Geldings are the preferred workers for most equine endeavors. The alteration of their sexuality makes them compliant, predictable, amenable to training, and dependable. Thus, geldings are in great demand for show, sport, and recreation.

But, mares are multi-taskers. They produce new life. They educate their own offspring and other youngsters in the herd about the meaning of horse-ness. Mares also establish the social hierarchy within wild or domestic herds of horses and constantly monitor the rankings. Mares have a wide range of behaviors. They can be bossy, demure, flirtatious, intrusive, demanding, unpredictable, affectionate, demonstrative, aloof, and creatively emotional.

Mares keep things interesting, and Queenie was interesting from the first moment I saw her. On that occasion, the mare was creating anxiety for her owner during a trail ride by crow-hopping, jigging, side-stepping, and otherwise attempting to avoid doing her job.

Apart from her misconduct, Queenie was a breathtaking sight. She was dark gray, spangled with large white dapples. Her mane and tail were cascades of silver white hair. I could tell she had Arab blood. Her head lacked the elegant sculpting of a purebred, but, she had the *desert eye*, large, soft, and black, and outlined with black skin, which offered protection against the sun. Her ears were small and tipped inward. Her neck was slender and upright. And, she carried herself like royalty.

Instead of giving Queenie a quick firm correction, her owner clung to the saddle horn and reins and began expressing aloud she was going to get rid of the horse at the nearby Badgercreek Auction.

My heart lurched at the thought of Queenie, indeed any horse, going to an auction. Low-end horse auctions are nearly always just way stations on the road to the slaughterhouses. Few skilled horsemen nowadays have the desire to pick a rough-hewn diamond out of an auction pen nor the patience to restore a horse's troubled mind, not when there are plenty of good unblemished horses for sale.

And, unskilled and ill-informed people, who shop for a cheap first horse at auction, are likely to have an unsatisfying, even dangerous, experience that may result in further abuse of the horse, thus, merely delaying the ultimate rendezvous with death.

Badgercreek Auction was mostly frequented by meat-buyers, who scavenge and pay by the pound for aged, outgrown, unused, unwanted, and problem horses, that are the all too abundant detritus of a consumer society, which is easily bored and accustomed to throwing things away.

Queenie deserved better. I knew my husband, Mike, an excellent rider with an uncanny gift with horses, could fix whatever was wrong with Queenie. I offered to buy her on the spot and was accepted.

My impulse purchase became a treasured part of our horse family. Queenie settled into her new life on a twelve-acre farm we had purchased in rural Ohio. She quickly bonded with three horses we had transported from California. Mike soon put things right with Queenie, and she became his favorite riding horse

I rode her occasionally and reveled in the comfort of her gaits. And, Queenie's affectionate and dynamic personality, typical of Arabian horses, set her apart from the reserved, workmanlike temperaments of our Quarter Horses.

As I surmised, Queenie was not a purebred. Mike and I learned our new horse was a Half-Arabian, a paperwork construct for registering the offspring of purebred Arabians, which are crossed with purebred horses of other breeds. The dilution of pure Arab bloodlines to create the Half-Arabian was undertaken to produce horses, which retained Arabian attributes, but had larger size, wider variety of colors, greater performance capabilities—and to stimulate the declining Arabian marketplace.

So, we discovered Queenie, who we purchased out of pity, came with registration papers. Even more surprising, she descended from renowned horses. On the top, equine parlance for the sire's bloodlines, Queenie was descended from *Bask++.

That bay stallion, imported to the United States from Poland in 1963, became the most influential and celebrated Arabian sire of the 20th century. (An asterisk preceding an Arab's name indicates the horse was imported. Plus marks following a horse's name indicate levels of achievement earned in its show career.)

In the dam's lineage, Queenie was again related to *Bask++ via Cognac and Cologne, two notable Arabian Park Horses. Her Arabian heritage was infused with the Stonewall bloodline of the American Saddlebred breed. Her registered name was Bold Impression.

Queenie's rich stew of *Bask++ and Stonewall ingredients boiled up every twenty-one days when she was in season and dominated by Nature's imperative to reproduce. Her heat cycles fueled hormonal antics that became more extravagant as the years went by.

Our geldings could try to ignore her flirtations. Mike and I could look the other way. But the associated noise became intolerable. Queenie's frustration at her motherless state was voiced in a bellow that sounded like the braying of a constipated donkey. And, she vented her frustration frequently for days.

Mares keep things interesting.

Finally, we couldn't stand the clamor any longer and decided to accommodate her fervent desire for a foal. But, we gave it considerable thought. If we were going to add another horse to an already abundant equine population, there had to be a rationale for doing so. Too many horses are bred with no thought given to their prospects in life or their ability to perform useful service for an owner.

Our first inclination was to breed Queenie to an Andalusian or Warmblood stallion like a Hanoverian or Trakehner. The resultant foal would likely have been a horse with superior athletic ability, but could not be registered with any breed association, and could only be exhibited in open shows.

However, we decided to stay within the Half-Arabian registry by breeding Queenie to a purebred Arabian stallion. Our decision was influenced, in part, by the Arabian's storied past. As a freelancer, I'd published many articles about horses and had always been intrigued by the exotic history of the Arabian horse. Thus, I had some basic knowledge about the breed's origins and development.

The Bedouins of the Arabian Peninsula were the first stewards of the Arabian horse. They knew bloodlines and preserved pedigrees even before the advent of writing. According to Bedouin tradition, Allah fashioned the Arabian horse from the desert winds. So prized were Arabian mares, they lived in the Bedouins' tents with the family, a practice that was thought to have contributed to the breed's particular fondness for people.

Owing to the isolation of the Middle East and the nomadic life of the Bedouins, Arabian horses, the most ancient of breeds, were virtually unknown to the rest of the world for centuries. Muslim invaders in the

8th century introduced Arabians into Spain and France. But, wider exposure to Arabians probably occurred when the Crusades brought Europeans to the Middle East.

The Crusaders, who were mounted on heavy, big-boned horses bred in Europe to accommodate the weight of armed knights, must have been astonished at the fleet, beautiful horses of their adversaries. The acquisition of Arabian horses as spoils of war began with the First Crusade in 1095.

The captured Arabians were taken back to Europe and used to upgrade local stock by adding refinement, speed, and stamina. The ability of Arabian blood to enhance the offspring of other breeds is legendary, and nearly every recognized modern breed had an infusion of Arabian blood at some point.

The incursions of the Ottoman Turks into Europe in the 16th century introduced a greater number of Arabians to Poland and Hungary. Horses taken after the defeat of the Ottoman Empire laid the foundation for Arabian breeding facilities in Eastern Europe. A number of studs (breeding facilities) were established elsewhere in Europe by royal decree owing to the rise of light cavalry and the need for swift, agile horses with stamina, qualities the Arabian possessed.

In the 18th century, the Thoroughbred was created in England following the importation of the Godolphin Arabian, the Byerly Turk, and the Darley Arabian.

Horses came to the New World in the 16th century with the Conquistadors. It's likely their mounts were Andalusian-type horses, along with Barbs from North Africa, and horses with Arabian blood. The wild mustangs of North America are supposed to have originated from vestiges of Conquistador horses.

Arabians had a presence in America from Colonial times. English immigrants in the 18th century brought Arabians with them. George Washington owned two Arabians he rode in the Revolutionary War.

The first breeder of purebred and cross-bred Arabians was operating prior to the Civil War.

At the 1893 World's Fair in Chicago, an exhibit of desert Arabians stirred interest in the breed. Major importations began in the early 1900s. The U.S. Army Remount Service fostered breeding by offering quality Arabian stallions to the public at reasonable rates. By the modern era, all types of Arabians, Egyptian, Polish, Spanish, Crabbet, Russian, and Domestic, were represented in the U.S.A.

In shopping for an Arabian stallion to breed to Queenie, Mike and I were on unfamiliar ground. From horses we previously owned, we had some knowledge of Quarter Horse, Tennessee Walking Horse, and Saddlebred bloodlines, but Arabian bloodlines were new to us. While we wanted to create a well-bred horse and would search for a special sire, the decision ultimately would come down, not just bloodlines, but also to Mike's uncanny ability to evaluate horses, a talent that began very early.

When Mike was eight years old, his parents divorced. He was sent to live with his uncle and aunt, Elwood and Winnie Stern, who owned and share-cropped a large farm in southern Alabama. The Sterns were childless and viewed Mike as another farmhand, who had to earn his keep despite his youth. Whatever affection the older couple developed for the dispossessed child during the six years Mike lived with them, was restrained and seldom expressed.

The grueling work routine on the farm was relieved for Mike in the spring when truckloads of wild horses gathered from Colorado, Utah, and Idaho, were shipped to the Sterns' farm for breaking. The horses came off the stock trailers and were herded into corrals for assessment.

Elwood Stern, who hired twenty cowboys to break the mustangs, would make the rounds of the holding pens, giving instructions to the wranglers on how each horse was to be handled. Elwood had a keen eye for horses. With a glance he could read a horse and make a decision without sentiment. The meat man was there at the Stern farm to take away the culls that Elwood indicated.

Just as Mike was expected to work in the fields, he had to participate in the annual rodeo. The quiet, lonely boy was among the cowboys, who followed Elwood from pen to pen as the boss swiftly decided the fate of every horse. Then, the cowboys began the process of *hard-breaking.*

They'd enter the pens, lasso a horse, snub the roped horse to a post set firmly in the ground, throw a saddle on the frightened animal's back, cinch it tight, and climb aboard. At first, Mike had to be tied to the saddle because of his inexperience and small stature. But, he soon learned to ride a bucking horse and developed fearlessness about riding that never left him.

Mike didn't adopt Elwood's ruthless practicality. Perhaps those sessions around the holding pens where fate was so casually dispensed, reminded Mike of his own broken family and disjointed childhood. Life is a tenuous situation unless someone sees a glimmer of your potential and gives you a chance. Thus, Mike was always drawn to a hard luck horse whose heart could still be touched.

My efforts to find a suitable mate for Queenie, which also met with Mike's approval, were not going well. None of the stallions we saw sparked Mike's interest. In addition, clocks were ticking.We knew Queenie's biological clock was already on overdrive. But, we wanted to time the breeding for the foal to arrive in the spring, so the youngster's first experience of life was what Nature intended, growing strong and learning about life at its mother's side in the warm and carefree months of the year.

However, another clock, which Mike and I didn't even consider, was also ticking, that being, the artificial time frame imposed by the world of registered horses. The designation *yearling* applies to the period between a horse's birth until it reaches twelve months old. For paperwork purposes, January 1st is the official birthday for registered horses. So, professional breeders plan foal births for January or February to get the most maturity for their yearlings.

Not being professionals, Mike and I didn't have that foresight. Out of consideration of hardship for a foal, we probably would have opted for birth during warmer months anyway. But, the point was moot. We still couldn't find a stallion we liked.

Mike and I were almost resigned to listening to Queenie's lovesick caterwauling when a neighbor, Gretchen "Gigi" Greiko, offered to introduce us to McKenna Jamison, who might be able to recommend a stallion. Gigi and McKenna had been friends since high school. During their teenage years, they worked as stable hands and grooms at various Arabian horse farms. Three decades later, they were still involved with Arabians. Except for their shared interest, the two friends were very different.

Gigi was a blonde, gregarious, squeaky-voiced free spirit, who knew everyone in the small town where we lived. Whenever a new blonde joke came along, it was gleefully related to Gigi, and she took the ribbing with good humor. The Ditzy Blonde persona masked Gigi's insight and experience. She had a keen eye for horseflesh and had bought and sold some excellent horses.

McKenna was a slim, attractive brunette, who was knowledgeable, focused, and soberly efficient. From her high school days onward, McKenna single-mindedly pursued horseshowing. For thirty years, she set goals for herself, accomplished them, set the bar higher, and moved up through the ranks of amateur Arabian exhibitors competing at Class A, the highest level. McKenna's ambition was to win a national title in Western Pleasure.

Her partner in that endeavor was a stunning purebred Arabian gelding named Imperial Echo+. McKenna had purchased Imperial Echo+

when the horse was a four-month-old weanling. She gambled on her ability to see potential in a very young horse and bought the bay colt when the price was most affordable.

McKenna was right. Imperial Echo+ proved to have a sweet disposition, a quick and receptive mind, the physical ability to do his job, and the beauty to wrap around the whole package. The two of them were formidable competitors, who traveled thousands of miles together on the horseshow circuit. McKenna was utterly besotted with Imperial Echo+ . He seemed to reciprocate. His favorite trick was to take the zipper of McKenna's jacket in his teeth and slide it up and down the track while gazing soulfully at her face.

Because of her longtime connection to the Arabian show world, McKenna had contacts and information a newcomer like me could never access. When I related our frustrations in locating an exciting stallion, McKenna made one firmly stated recommendation: Queenie should be bred to the sire of her horse, a stallion named Imperial V.

The *vee* in Imperial V signified the stallion was a product of the breeding program of Sheila Varian, an esteemed California horsewoman and internationally-known Arabian horse-breeder. In creating Imperial V, Varian had incorporated the blood of two of the most celebrated stallions of modern times, Huckleberry Bey++ and Khemosabi++++.

Varian sold Imperial V to Gordon Meriwether of Ohio, who was quietly building a breeding program around his Varian-bred stallion.

By and large, stallion promotion in the big leagues is a time and money-consuming activity. The stud has to be shown in-hand and under saddle at prestigious shows where it will be seen by mare owners and by other horse enthusiasts. Ideally, the stallion will garner championships and awards to bolster its reputation. The promotion extends to highlighting the outstanding progeny of the stallion. The expenses are considerable, trainers, grooms, hauling, stabling, publicity, photographs, brochures, and advertising, advertising, advertising. The process resembles the hullabaloo associated with Hollywood starlets, but, it gets results.

Among horse-lovers, great stallions can generate fascination, which borders on idolatry. The appeal is part physical and part historical. A stallion, after all, is a charismatic sexual being, imbued by Nature with fire and beauty, presence, and procreative power. But, a stallion is also a torch that has been handed from one generation of horse breeders to the next. The dreams and ambitions of horsemen long dead have a sort of immortality through the bloodlines of horses.

The linkage of horsemen across time is understood on a gut level by true horse-lovers. A contemporary horseman, wearing a ball cap and T-shirt, who is transfixed at the sight of an Arabian stallion today, is connected across the centuries to the same sense of wonder felt by a helmeted, red-crossed knight on a crusade to Jerusalem. No other creature can compel such complicated feelings in humankind.

However, not all quality stallions receive fanfare. Gordon Meriwether was not promoting Imperial V with expensive hoopla. He was just breeding good horses and making it possible for others to do so, too. His approach had earned him a coterie of loyal clients, which was growing as Imperial V's offspring proliferated and began appearing in showrings

Meriwether's breeding operation was off the beaten path, and he appeared to live a rather solitary life devoted to horses. He was slim, handsome, elegantly reserved, and treated Mike and me, two self-admitted newcomers to Arabian horses, with measured courtesy when we came stallion shopping.

First, Meriwether showed us a gray stallion that was attractive and well-bred, but again, the horse failed to spark anything in Mike. Then,

Meriwether escorted us to the stall of the horse we'd come to see, Imperial V.

Mike looked through the grate of the stall door. Looking back at him through a long swag of black forelock were two luminous eyes set wide apart in a chiseled head. Small inward-tipped ears cocked towards Mike. The delicate skin of the bay stallion's nostrils flared. Imperial V was assessing his visitors with sight, sound, and scent, the primal sources of equine information-gathering. After a brief moment, the stallion's breath was slowly exhaled through shuddering nostrils. In kingly fashion, Imperial V had decreed the present company was acceptable.

But, what did my husband think? I knew from experience Mike had probably made up his mind at first glance. However, nothing in my husband's body language gave me a clue.

When Mike was around horses, he focused on projecting a reassuring but sovereign presence to creatures that are bound to the pecking order of the herd, and always look for leadership in their relationships. Mike's imperceptible communication with horses always took precedence over human chitchat.

Gordon Meriwether put a halter on Imperial V and led the horse to a large paddock to show the stallion at liberty. Imperial V trotted boldly across the ground. The sunshine on his bay hide shot off scintillations of red and gold. He flagged his long black tail. His luxuriant black mane floated aloft with each stride.

The stallion performed with a kind of professional *gravitas*, as though he knew it was his job to look good and secure another breeding fee.

I tried to assess Imperial V in my own mind. At that time, I'd only been involved with horses for a decade, which had begun when I was forty years old. Though I'd longed for a horse throughout my childhood, the dream didn't come true until relatively late in life. Therefore, I didn't have the same experience and intimacy with horses as people, who've had them as lifelong companions.

Nevertheless, I'd tried to close the gap with research. I'd spent nine years in college chasing various interests, and I'd been a published writer for many years, so I was used to studying and investigating. But, the fulfillment, late in life, of my childhood dream and the need to mentally catch up meant I was always a bit mechanical in evaluating horses.

So, as I watched Imperial V cavort around the paddock, I could not see him as a complete, functioning whole, as great horsemen do, but had to mentally click through a checklist of attributes:

Laid back shoulders allowing for long strides with the front legs, yes.

Hind legs reaching well under the body providing the power to propel the horse forward, yes.

Strong straight legs with good bone, yes.

Nice length of neck with a clean throatlatch, yes.

Level croup and triangular hip in accordance with Arabian type, yes.

Forequarters, mid-section, and hindquarters properly balanced, yes.

And good hooves with straight walls and good angulations, yes, because, as horsemen have always said, "No hoof, no horse."

Imperial V looked good to me. And, Mike was ready to let me know what he thought. He nodded.

Chapter 2

Meriwether's stud fee for Imperial V was $1,000. At that time, spending one thousand dollars on a non-essential was an extravagance for Mike and me. We had moved to Ohio from California three years earlier and were struggling financially. The rundown farm we purchased proved to be a more daunting money drain than we anticipated. And, only one of us was bringing in a real paycheck.

I was writing articles for two monthly horse publications, but, the pay was negligible. My plan to work on a book full time was constantly interrupted by farm necessities. And, Mike, who'd spent his whole working life as a long-haul trucker, couldn't find a local job that would pay the bills and allow him to be home every night as he longed to do.

So, shelling out one thousand dollars to get Queenie bred and to enjoy the peace and quiet of her eleven-month gestation period, seemed to run counter to our economic situation. But, we reasoned, the sale of Queenie's offspring would easily recoup our money down the road.

The combination of Queenie's Bask-rich bloodline with Imperial V's illustrious ancestry suggested a foal that would be highly attractive to Gordon Meriwether's clients and to the growing number of Imperial V admirers. Meriwether himself sweetened the deal by offering to let us make payments on the breeding fee during the course of Queenie's pregnancy. We signed the contract.

Imperial V and Queenie had a modern equine romance. They never met. With stallions valued at hundreds of thousands of dollars, horse-to-horse breeding, what is called *live cover*, was increasingly rare owing to the potential hazard of an unreceptive mare injuring a valuable stallion. Except in the Thoroughbred racing industry, where live cover is required, artificial insemination (AI) is commonly used.

The technology of AI has created a borderless world for horse breeding. A stallion can breed a mare wherever FedEx delivers.

The breeding of Imperial V and Queenie was handled by Dr. Penelope Kean, who was the veterinarian for Gordon Meriwether's facility. Dr. Penny, as she was known to her clients, grew up on a farm in Jersey County, Ohio. She was one of countless rural American youngsters whose hearts and minds were formed by the values of 4-H clubs, county fairs, church activities, small town life, and the harsh demands of farming.

Initially, Penny's career plans were modest. She wanted to be a schoolteacher, to marry and have children. However, when Penny went to college, she entered a curriculum, which led to vet school. The young woman from a small Ohio town performed brilliantly, winning awards and national recognition both as a student and a teacher.

By 1989, Dr. Penny had achieved what many would consider the pinnacle of success, a tenured position as an assistant professor performing large animal surgery at an esteemed veterinary college. But, the former farm girl, who had been imbued with the virtues of honesty and hard work, became disillusioned with the gossip and backstabbing of her peers, with the political maneuvering for advancement that often trumped merit, and with serving under less-talented bosses.

So, in 1995, Dr. Penny left the comfort zone of tenure to return to Jersey County to become her own boss. She surveyed the area, which was largely rural, and saw the need for a large animal practitioner. That was a professional move, which ran counter to the national trend.

Veterinarians, who specialize in treating large animals, generally horses and cows, are something of a disappearing breed owing to the demanding nature of the profession.

Except for the fact drugs are better these days, the physical hardships are not much different from those experienced by Dr. James Herriot, the Yorkshire veterinarian whose memoirs made him famous worldwide. And, when Dr. Penny relocated to Ohio, she knew that would be the case.

Restraining powerful animals for exams, castrations, vaccinations, and difficult births, are all activities, which can result in sudden injury, even death. She would constantly be on the road. Her pickup truck, with an insert full of equipment and drugs in the truck bed, was her mobile office, and the vehicle constantly criss-crossed the countryside regardless of the weather and road conditions.

Emergency calls are no respecter of dinner dates, personal plans, or private lives. At times, it seemed animals' problems coincided with the worst conditions. During a lightning storm, Dr. Penny was asked to attend a cow that was calving while stuck in a creek bottom. In the dead of winter, she did field surgery where the stainless steel instruments froze to her hands, and space heaters had to be utilized to keep the internal organs of the animal from freezing.

Frightened animals in pain can be dangerous. Dr. Penny was attacked by a stallion, which pinned her to the ground and broke her collar bone. Her ribs were fractured by animals that slammed her into walls. Despite the hazards posed by large animals, Dr. Penny was comfortable with cattle and horses and fond of them. She said, "I understand them."

The woman, who opted for such an arduous career, was about 5' 4" tall, with delicate features, blue eyes, and a cap of blonde hair, which fell into tendrils, a look that reminded me of the faces of fairies and pixies in the illustrations of old children's books.

But, Dr. Penny was no pixie.

Her wardrobe consisted of green coveralls and muck boots. Her primary office was her truck. She was undaunted by the rigors of her profession. She lived simply and structured her off-duty time to be available for emergencies.

When Dr. Penny's work day was done, there was paperwork to take care of. State licensing required that medical records be kept up-to-date and carefully stored. Veterinarians also had to attend regularly-scheduled continuing education seminars.

In an era that encouraged the pursuit of pleasure and self-indulgence above all else, Dr. Penny was a rare example of service to others.

In preparation for Queenie's breeding via artificial insemination, Dr. Penny paid several visits to our farm to ascertain Queenie was in good health and to determine the optimum time for AI.

When the signs were right, Gordon Meriwether was called, Imperial V was collected, and a cooler of semen arrived. Dr. Penny inserted plastic tubing into Queenie's uterus, drew the semen out of its plastic bag into a syringe, and sent it through the tubing.

The success rate of AI is somewhat less efficient than Nature's method and mares like Queenie, who've never been previously bred, sometimes require repeated AI breedings. But, Queenie conceived the first time. When Dr. Penny examined her a few weeks later, the ultrasound showed Queenie was in foal.

My acquaintance with Dr. Penny, brought about by Queenie's breeding, came at a good time. The vet I'd been using, a nice local man, had broken his back in a tractor accident. Thankfully, he recovered, but fearing another injury, he gave up his large animal practice. Therefore, I was grateful to meet Dr. Penny soon after she established her practice and, moreover, to again have a woman veterinarian.

Wherever Mike and I had lived, we'd been fortunate to have access to good veterinarians and horseshoers. But, in my experience, even the best male vets cannot empathize with the level of affection women can have for their horses.

The beginning of that affection goes by the term *horse crazy* and mostly applies to young girls. Those of us, who were afflicted with horse crazy, can't remember a time when we weren't drawing horses, reading horse books, riding broomsticks, collecting plastic horses, dreaming of horses, and begging parents for horses.

I'm not aware any sociologist has ever studied horse crazy. But, a male friend, who liked to tease me, said, "Well, Judy, you know what Dr. Freud said about women and horses, don't you?"

I replied, "Given what Freud said about nearly everything else, I think I can fill in the blanks."

Snarky insinuations aside, horse crazy remains a mystery. But, no explanation seems to be necessary between women veterinarians and women clients.

During Dr. Penny's visits to our farm to prepare Queenie for breeding and to handle the artificial insemination, we established the same kind of rapport I'd had with other female vets. I was grateful for her service and for the opportunity to learn more about horses. Dr. Penny was professionally courteous and efficient. I admired her quiet confidence and calm manner in handling Queenie.

Often a mare that's going to be poked, probed, and penetrated from behind by medical instruments, plastic tubing, and the entire length of a human arm, will need to be tranquilized. Many vets would do so routinely before standing in back of the hindquarters of a hormonal mare. But, Dr. Penny's philosophy was no drugs unless necessary.

Occasionally, the AI process elicited a bit of female locker room humor from both of us, and I would see Dr. Penny's usually reserved demeanor erupt into merriment. But, her professional detachment would quickly return. I didn't anticipate we would ever have anything other than a doctor-client relationship.

Our personalities, it seemed to me, were too different to generate deep friendship. Dr. Penny was serious, intent, and committed to her demanding profession. I was irreverent, unfocused, and derelict of my talent. When Queenie's first breeding took place in 1998, I was fifty-two years old. What did I have to show for fifty-two years?

I didn't regret my decision to leave the *Tribune*. Yet, I had many second thoughts. Had I cut-and-run? Had I succumbed to a secret part of myself, which had always been fearful and insecure? Was I supposed to be doing something? Did life have a purpose? Or was I just maudlin and menopausal?

In any case, I found myself at a dead end on a small rundown farm in Ohio, with only the solace of my husband and our horses. It was highly unlikely I would ever face my insecurities or do anything worthwhile. I'd just be sleepwalking through what remained of my life.

Yes, Dr. Penny and I were very different, not exactly gal pal material. But, what developed between us was something more rare than friendship. The events, which followed the breeding of Queenie and Imperial V, led to devastating heartbreak, dark and difficult years, and profound disappointment. The simple life I had sought as a refuge from my shortcomings became a complicated and exhausting search for justice.

Along the way, I discovered widespread animal abuse, institutionalized veterinary malpractice, unresponsive bureaucracy, unethical lawyers, a flawed legal system, ruinous greed, and an apathetic citizenry. The journey allowed me to assess the condition of my country, and I came away alarmed. As a people, we were unprepared for the tough times the pendulum swing of time inevitably delivers.

Through years of fear and frustration and defeat, Dr. Penny provided steadfast integrity. Her calm professionalism, as I grappled with frightening events, renewed my spirits when I faltered.

My husband's patience and loyalty were also unwavering.

But, dark journeys ultimately make us solitary travelers. And, when I felt lost and forsaken, I found comfort and guidance from an unexpected source.

On the evening of June 27, 1999, Queenie was again keeping things interesting. The calendar indicated her foal was due, and Queenie's body indicated signs of impending birth.

I was spending hours in the barn awaiting the event. Despite a decade plus around horses, I had yet to witness a foaling. Mares are famously finicky about where and when they foal. And unlike human females, the equine mother has considerable control over the timing. According to an old saying, the foal chooses the day of its birth, but the mare chooses the time.

About 11 p.m., I decided to take a break. Queenie wasn't acting unusual, so I went into the house to brew a cup of coffee and to update Mike, who was going to bed. When I returned, I heard Queenie emitting soft guttural sounds from an outside paddock that adjoined the foaling stall. Had I left the door open or had Queenie let herself out? I was too excited to think.

Through the door, I could see the gray mare, looking ghostly against the dark night sky and bending her neck over something in a corner. I entered Queenie's stall and approached her with care. Would she be aggressively protective or allow me near? She was solicitous of her task, but didn't object to my presence.

Wedged in a corner where the paddock fence adjoined the barn was a heap of thrashing legs and wet red horsehair. The normal struggle of a newborn foal to get to its feet was complicated by the confined space where Queenie had given birth.

I wrapped my arms around the foal and tried to remove it from the corner. It was greasy with amniotic fluid. At roughly eighty pounds, slippery and struggling, the foal was more than I could manage.

I rushed to the house and woke Mike, who flew with me to the barn. Between the two of us, we extracted the foal from the corner, hauled it into the lighted stall, laid it on the deep bedding of straw, and watched the marvelous bonding of mare and foal take place

Queenie's delight with her baby brought tears to my eyes. It was wondrous to see how instinct overtook Queenie and infused her with maternal knowledge.

When the foal managed to stand on its own and found Queenie's udder, Mike and I relaxed. The scuffle by the fence had not injured the baby. The umbilical cord had dropped away. The foal, smacking its tiny lips on Queenie's teats, was ingesting the life-enhancing colostrum of the mare's first milk.

With all the excitement, we almost forgot to ascertain the foal's sex. Mike lifted its tail and looked underneath. One hole. We had a colt.

Chapter 3

On a Sunday morning in the fall of 2000, the phone rang shortly after dawn. Though I was exhausted from the weekend's activities, I thought it must be important and climbed out of bed to answer the call. I heard Gigi Greiko's high-pitched voice screaming excitedly.

"I can't believe it! I can't believe it!" she yelled, "You beat the big name trainers! You beat the millionaires! You beat the system! Ohmygawd!"

I was trying to wake up and couldn't respond. Gigi brought her enthusiasm down a notch and said, "You are so new to all this, I don't think you really understand what you've done."

Mike and I had just returned a few hours earlier from the Jubilee Arabian Horse Show. I could scarcely believe Gigi, even though she was so plugged into the hotline of horse gossip, had already heard the news. Indeed, she had heard, and, gleeful about the outcome, she continued her squeaky outpouring.

"Little people like you, little people like us, we just don't take a backyard horse to the Jubilee Show and win everything. That just doesn't happen. I don't know if it's ever happened. Ohmygawd, ohmygawd, it's wonderful, wonderful. Unbelievable!"

After Gigi's congratulatory call, I was fully awake. I put on the coffee pot and sat at the kitchen table thinking back over the past fifteen months that had led to what was, as Gigi said, wonderful and unbelievable.

The morning after the red colt's birth, the youngster was gaining mastery over his long legs, and I couldn't get enough of watching him. He was a chestnut, the color of a bright copper penny, with three high white stockings and a wide blaze. The short baby hairs in his mane and tail contained a few white hairs, which eventually grew out long, silky, and flaxen, a shade I called Heather Locklear Blonde.

Dr. Penny came to see the new arrival and to inspect Queenie's afterbirth to insure no part of it was retained, which might cause infection. She checked out the foal and expressed satisfaction with his appearance and health. Assisting in the creation of new life was obviously a satisfying part of Dr. Penny's job.

Mike was a frequent visitor, and the colt was intrigued with him. As Mike entered the stall, he would assume a crouched position, so the baby felt superior in size. When the colt left the security of his mother's side to investigate, Mike would scratch his chest and withers, two places the baby couldn't reach himself. After those initial pleasurable experiences, the colt was soon welcoming all his new admirers.

Before long, the amiable youngster and Queenie were turned out into a large paddock where the colt's sudden swift sprints earned him the nickname "Speedy."

"Well, what do you think?" I asked Mike, "Did we get a good one?"

"Oh yeah," he replied, "He's special. But remember, we bred him to sell. Don't go getting attached to him."

Although I'd have to work at it, I was sure I could remain detached from Speedy. I knew Mike and I would only sell to someone, who was a kind, knowledgeable horse-lover. The colt would have a good home with a buyer, who had the money and means to train, show, and promote, the great showhorse we expected Speedy could be. And, we might get some relief from our increasingly worrisome financial situation.

After Speedy's birth, I set about updating the paperwork for the colt. Speedy had to be registered with the International Arabian Horse Association (IAHA), the organization, which, at that time, kept registration records for Half-Arabians and had its headquarters in Aurora, Colorado, a suburb of Denver.

Speedy needed an official name for his registration papers and an incentive fund called the Breeders Sweepstakes. By tradition, a registered horse may draw its name from its sire, dam, or a significant ancestor. And, I wanted to concentrate on featuring Imperial V, as McKenna Jamison had when she named her horse Imperial Echo+.

The red-gold colt, I felt sure, was going to be a credit to Imperial V and the more horses successfully competing on the show scene that referenced Imperial V, the better it was for Gordon Meriwether.

During Queenie's pregnancy, I kept Meriwether apprised of the mare's progress and sent him numerous checks to pay the breeding fee whenever I could divert small sums from the financial drain of the farm. Meriwether never complained about the additional bookkeeping or pressed for payment. With so many other expenses piling up, I was grateful for Meriwether's gentlemanly restraint.

Finally, I came up with a name, which acknowledged Speedy's daddy, and that Mike and I both liked: Imperial Marquis.

I filled in the registration forms for Imperial Marquis and sent them off to IAHA with the filing fee. Meriwether's breeding fee was paid. The vet bill was paid. Sweepstakes was paid. All with monies scrimped from here and there. Once I managed to get an expense paid, I was relieved and moved on. It wasn't until later, after three years of investing in Imperial Marquis, that I had occasion to calculate the full amount Mike and I had sacrificed for our dream. I would be shocked.

But, that was later.

At home, Imperial Marquis was rarely referred to by his official moniker. He was always Speedy, and he was the center of Queenie's world and mine. We both began training him immediately. Queenie initiated her foal in the language of horse, the subtle body movements of pinned ears, snaky necks, and cocked hooves, which convey so much information within the herd.

As with most foals, Speedy was energetic and self-absorbed. When his behavior became too rambunctious, Queenie applied firm but motherly corrections. Even though Speedy was destined to be a gelding, and most likely a pampered showhorse that would spend little if any time in a herd setting, it was still important for him to know how to be a horse.

While Queenie gave Speedy a horse education, I took care of the human side of Speedy's training: Putting a halter on him, teaching him to lead, grooming him in the cross-ties, loading him in and out of the horse trailer, and picking up and handling his feet in anticipation of the horseshoer's work that would be a regular feature of his life.

To preview the show world Speedy would be entering, I attended the Ohio Buckeye Sweepstakes Horse Show. Generally referred to as The Buckeye, the annual Memorial Day weekend horseshow at the Ohio Exposition Center in Columbus was the third largest show of Arabian and Half-Arabian horses in the country, following Scottsdale, Arizona's show and the U.S. Nationals.

The Exposition Center was an accumulation of concrete structures set amidst acres of asphalt-paved parking lots. It's adjacent to the campus of Ohio State University and within shouting distance of OSU's College of Veterinary Medicine.

The ground floor of a multi-story parking garage served as stabling for the horses. Rows and rows of portable stalls were erected on the concrete floor with enormous amounts of wood shavings loaded into the stalls to cushion legs and hooves from the effect of unforgiving surfaces.

Numerous professional training facilities reserved blocks of stalls, which were lavishly decorated with heavy cloth drapes, attractive furniture, photo displays, promotional materials, rows of potted flowers and shrubs banked with dyed mulch. Cloth draperies provided privacy for trainers, horseowners, and participants, and some measure of security for valuable show saddles, bridles, and personal property. But, stall drapes also served to conceal other less benign activities.

To my surprise, the bleacher seats in the Main Ring stadium were rather sparsely populated given the prestige of The Buckeye. But, that didn't seem to dampen the enthusiasm of the attendees, a mixture of breeders, professional trainers, big wigs, wannabes, groupies, and amateur exhibitors whose ages ranged from tiny tots in lead-line classes to senior citizens, all operating in an atmosphere that partook of Old Home Week, class reunions, show-and-tell, horse-trading, family outings, and business wheeling and dealing.

While I had been to a fair number of horseshows in my life, I'd never paid much attention to the divisions for younger horses that are referred to as halter or *in-hand* classes, where horses are shown from the ground not the saddle. As this was to be the next stage in Speedy's life, the halter classes were the focus of my visit to The Buckeye, and my initial reaction was perplexity.

The weanlings, young horses that have recently been separated from their mothers, seemed too young and traumatized by the horseshow experience. I felt sorry for the frightened little creatures. The yearlings seemed slightly better able to handle the sights and sounds of a major show.

But, in both age groups, the young horses had been robbed of their charming adolescent looks by over-zealous grooming. They were body-clipped. Their little hooves had been sanded and coated with polish. Their ears were shorn of all hair except for little tufts at the tips. The long hairs of their forelocks were compressed with goop, which kept the forelock in a single greasy strand.

Their faces were closely shaved and lathered with oil to highlight the underlying bone structure. And, there was *balding*. That is the process of shaving the hair around the eye sockets right down to the skin and applying grease to make the eyes look larger. (In fact, the practice of balding creates an unflattering raccoon effect.)

Balding was specifically forbidden by IAHA rules, but, the universal disregard for that rule, it turned out, was a portent of a larger disregard for rules and for the inability of many in the Arabian horseshow world to deviate, even in the smallest ways, from How Things Are Done.

Other troubling issues were the weight and musculature of the young horses. Many of them looked like miniature versions of full-grown, well-conditioned performance horses. It seemed unwise to me that youngsters, whose bones were still developing, should be carrying an unnatural amount of weight and be exercised so hard.

Speedy was immature and slim, and despite someone's suggestion that I double his grain ration and exercise Speedy vigorously, I declined to bulk him up and to endanger his still-growing bones and muscles with excessive training. If Speedy's slim physique counted against him in the showring, as I was told it would, then so be it. I planned to take the long view in making decisions for Speedy. The quality of his whole life was more important to me than short-term goals.

I made my way from the stabling area of The Buckeye to the Main Ring and took a seat in the bleachers to watch numerous classes and to try to get a general impression of showing in-hand. Those classes featured a professional trainer or an amateur handler, who carried a lead line in one hand and a whip in the other. The lead was connected to a chain called a shank, which ran through the show halter, under the horse's head, and across the jawbones. The whip was not supposed to be applied but used to give directions.

Each handler paused at the in-gate with their horse and awaited a signal to enter the ring. Then, the exhibitor trotted the horse briefly for a length of the rail to show its movement to the judge, and took their place at the far end of the arena to await their individual inspections. At that point, some handlers began practicing the *hard stand-up*, the pose young horses had been taught, which was supposed to show conformation to best advantage.

In other breeds, a halter horse is allowed to assume a fairly natural pose, front legs together under the forequarters, back legs together under the hindquarters. In the Arabian halter pose, the hind legs are offset and further behind to show off the level *croup*, which is a distinctive feature of the breed. The length of neck, which Arabian fashion has bred to be longer and swanlike, was shown off by asking the horse to stretch the neck upwards then extend its head forward.

As the individual judging began, each entry was walked toward the judge so the straightness of its front legs could be evaluated. Then, the horse was asked for the hard stand-up. After posing in front of the judge, the entry was trotted away in a straight line to check for the quality of its hind legs.

Each handler and horse generally had a fan club of friends, family members, and equine connoisseurs in the bleachers. They emitted war whoops to signal their support and to try to influence the judging. Occasionally, a horse was deemed so exceptional, the partisan spirit was set aside, and general whoops of appreciation rang out through the coliseum.

On the entertainment scale, watching innumerable halter classes ranked with watching cars rust. As a novice, I couldn't decipher why one horse or handler generated so many more whoops than others. Nor was I privy to the inner workings of training and showmanship that had a bearing on which horses won the prizes. It just seemed to me each halter class went on interminably, and I wondered how the participants endured the tedium.

Besides observing the halter classes, I had another mission at The Buckeye. I planned to seek out a woman Arabian trainer, whose facility was within an hour's drive of our farm, to inquire about getting Speedy trained to show in halter classes. Proximity was important because I was becoming attached to Speedy and wanted to be able to readily visit my horse and keep tabs on his welfare.

After walking through seemingly endless rows of stalls, and envying those with golf carts and motorized scooters, I located the stalls of the woman trainer. I pulled aside the heavy curtains that shielded her stalls from public view, entered, and found the trainer and an assistant *twitching* a horse.

A twitch resembles a pair of long-handled pliers.The fleshy upper lip of a horse is placed between the handles and pressure is applied. Twitching is done to make a resistant horse compliant for procedures like medical exams and grooming.

One theory is twitching is not painful, but releases endorphins, which calm the horse. Clamping down on my own upper lip didn't release endorphins, and, though I had a twitch in my tack box for medical emergencies, I'd never used it. It just seemed better to train the horse to be a willing partner in necessary procedures.

The twitching, which was going on behind the Arabian trainer's stall drapes, went beyond anything I'd ever seen before. The device was torqued down so intensely the captured portion of the horse's upper lip resembled a softball. The trainer and helper were applying the twitch so as to use electric clippers on the horse's face, which already appeared completely devoid of hair.

The trainer looked over her shoulder at me and said, "We're kinda busy here. Could you come back later?"

I backed out through the curtains—and never returned.

My scouting trip to The Buckeye revealed some things I didn't like. My own philosophy of horse management was averse to the excessive weight and muscling of young horses, the garish grooming practices, and twitching. But, I figured those were things I could control where Speedy was concerned. When I found a reputable trainer, I would mandate how my horse (my property, after all) was to be handled. I believed I could safely navigate the unfamiliar world with Speedy, get him trained and shown, and safely delivered to an appreciative buyer.

Unbeknownst to me, the world of major Arabian horseshows was already being navigated by people with considerable experience and knowledge, and they were keeping secrets. What a newcomer like me couldn't possibly comprehend in a single visit were the layers of abuse, the averted eyes of the in-crowd, and the complicity of those entrusted with the well-being of Arabians.

I couldn't have imagined the full extent of the activities, which went on behind the stall drapes. I had not read the notifications printed in show programs that said:

"Competition management shall place…at least one sharps container per fifty occupied stalls for the disposal of needles and other sharps instruments in convenient locations in barns housing competition horses."

I didn't know the use of performance-enhancing drugs on showhorses was so pervasive it was called *chemical warfare*. I didn't know that, in the shadow of the Ohio State University College of Veterinary Medicine, an institution chock full of vets, The Buckeye show managers brought a veterinarian from Florida all the way to Ohio to be the official show vet.

And, I wouldn't have believed so many people, who called themselves horse-lovers, knew and tolerated what was going on. But, I would learn. I was at the beginning of a long, painful education.

In the spring of 2000, McKenna Jamison had two horses in training with a professional horse trainer named Tyler Wragge. They were her beloved Imperial Echo+ and his half-sister, Kiss Me Kate. While McKenna was a veteran of Class A amateur showing and quite capable of training horses by herself, she had collaborated with several professional trainers over the years.

The reasons why even accomplished amateur exhibitors in the Arabian show world employed trainers, were varied. Trainers were up-to-date on the complex and ever-changing rules, which govern how and when horses can be shown. They had staff to perform the menial tasks of feeding, watering, stall cleaning, grooming, and doing the heavy lifting involved in transporting horses and equipment. And, trainers were thought to have special training methods that could bring out the best in horses.

A trainer with a barn full of horses also provided a built-in social scene for his clients. They had the backstage pass to go through the stall drapes, into what, in the case of the preeminent training facilities, might be lavishly appointed lounges with well-stocked bars and catered buffets. The clients could hang out in the lounge, chat obsessively about horses, and engage in the gossip, which is always a feature of insular and elite societies.

In conversation, clients frequently referred to *my trainer* this, *my trainer* that. The words carried a certain cachet, rather like saying *my butler* or *my gamekeeper*. However, top tier trainers, those who are referred to as BNTs (short for Big Name Trainers) didn't think of themselves as servants and might reveal themselves to surprised clients as self-interested tyrants.

Thus, a client, who had been paying a hefty fee all year for board and training in anticipation of seeing their horse compete at the national championships, might find themselves tossed aside at the last moment if their trainer opted for a different horse that had a better chance of winning.

The clients might find their monthly board and training bill padded with unexpected extras and inflated fees for services like braiding, bathing, and body clipping. And, clients, who had a butler/gamekeeper view of their trainers, might have the rudest surprise of all, that the trainer's control over and independent decisions about their property exceeded anything they could have imagined.

Perhaps the most compelling reason for hiring a professional trainer was the belief only the pros could produce horses, which would perform faultlessly in the demanding show world of Class A. That level of perfection was especially sought for two groups of participants, youth riders and amateurs.

The term *youth rider* encompassed kids so small they have to be lifted into the saddle, all the way to experienced riders in their late teens.

For the tiny tots, all decked out in expensive show clothes, perched atop silver-encrusted saddles, and accompanied by parents in lead line classes, perfect horses were needed because the kids are too small to control a horse if it were to bolt and run amok. Teenagers, often the biggest know-it-alls in the horse world, needed perfect horses, because any screw-ups that occur in the showring are frequently blamed on the horse and immediately followed by demands to parents for another more perfect horse.

In some instances, youth riders don't even get to ride their own horses regularly. They might live in another state and commute to shows to meet up with their horse and trainer just prior to a class where the trainer hands over the perfectly groomed and tuned-up horse to the kid for a few minutes in the spotlight.

Less fortunate kids, who have a pony in a backyard shed that's always available to be hopped on, ridden around, pull a plastic toboggan in the snow, consume carrots, and get its forelock braided, probably have a more fulfilling experience with horses than rich kids whose every move with their horses is dictated by a trainer.

The other group of amateurs, who sought perfect horses, range in age from eighteen-year-olds to advanced geezerhood.

In all age brackets, the designation *amateur* is quite elastic. Given the high cost of competing at the Class A level, most amateurs have considerable riding and showing experience, but, an amateur, who is training their own horse, often competes against other so-called amateurs, who have all the advantages and none of the expense of professional training, those being, the wives, children, and other relatives, of professional trainers. (It is just one of many inequities genuine amateurs endure to be part of the scene.)

Finally, employing a trainer is especially useful for horseowners, who are trying to accumulate a winning record either for their own personal satisfaction or to enhance the appeal of a horse intended for sale. The trainer can ride the client's horse in *open* classes, and the owner can also show their horse in amateur classes, thereby giving the horse double exposure at each show.

The open classes are the only place where the professionals show, and, while amateurs were not restricted from the open classes, the competition is thought to be too tough for *ammies.*

In McKenna's case, she chose to employ a trainer in the spring of 2000 because she was working full time. She was also hoping to find a buyer for Kiss Me Kate, the second horse she had in training with Tyler Wragge. Since recommending Imperial V as a sire and stopping by the farm twice to see Speedy, McKenna and I had little interaction. But, Gigi occasionally mentioned McKenna's adventures on the show circuit and the ribbons accruing for Imperial Echo+ and, increasingly, the young mare, Kiss Me Kate.

Gigi also told me that McKenna felt she had found an ideal trainer in Tyler Wragge. He was a young man, who had not yet ascended to the top tier of Arabian horse trainers, but not for want of skill. McKenna believed he was patient and kind with horses, unwilling to take shortcuts to produce quick results, and was respectful of the rules she laid down for the care and treatment of her property.

Horseshow results that were published each month in a Midwest newspaper called *Horsemen's Corral,* allowed me to track Tyler Wragge's progress with McKenna's horses. While Imperial Echo++ had the same sire as Speedy, Kate was even more closely related to my horse. She was sired by Imperial V out of Bold Amour, who was Queenie's mother.

Kate was being shown as a Western Pleasure horse, and she was winning, winning, winning. The show record Kate was compiling, I thought, might be a good indicator of how Speedy would do. And, Kate would a harbinger in the marketplace for Speedy and any other foals sired by Imperial V that Queenie might have.

By midsummer, however, my plans for Speedy were frustated. I had sent him to a young trainer whose facility was within twenty minutes from our farm. But, I soon suspected Speedy was being mishandled. The trainer required an appointment to see my own horse. On my appointment times, I'd find Speedy in his stall, hot and wet, as though he'd only been worked in anticipation of my visit—and not cooled down.

Even worse, Speedy was no longer confident and people-friendly. His body language was sending out a signal. When I'd enter Speedy's stall, he would turn away and try to evade me rather than greeting me happily as he used to. Once, while the trainer was teaching me how to show my horse at the trot, Speedy took the opportunity to cow-kick me in the leg. After a couple worrisome incidents, I took Speedy home.

Through Gigi, McKenna became aware of the unsatisfactory experience I was having with the trainer. McKenna phoned to encourage me to remove Speedy from the facility, something I was about to do. She offered to show me how to train Speedy for the hard stand-up.

I counted on that.

But, McKenna didn't follow through, didn't answer my phone messages, and actually seemed to be avoiding me. When McKenna failed to keep her word, I was very disappointed. Her unkept promise became a sequestered grievance. Instead of utilizing McKenna's experience in the show world, I wrote her off as unreliable, and I resolved to make my own decisions.

Speedy's opportunities to show as a yearling were slipping away. I took him to several horseshows but wasn't able to exhibit Speedy to his best advantage. He took home ribbons but not blues. The show season would be wrapping up in a few months, and I hadn't accomplished anything on Speedy's behalf.

So, I called Tyler Wragge.

Chapter 4

Despite my disappointment in McKenna's broken promise, I considered her endorsement of Tyler Wragge an A+ rating. Given McKenna's experience and exacting standards, he must be an ideal young man. Though Speedy would be three hours away from our farm, a long trek I had hoped to avoid, I believed my horse would be in good hands.

Tyler's training business, which was called Tyler Wragge Elite Horses, was located on his parents' property. Tom and Tina Wragge were longtime Arabian horse trainers, and the amenities of their T&T Stables were functional but not high falutin'. The presence of Tyler's parents and their experience gave me additional assurance Speedy would be well cared for.

As I backed Speedy out of the trailer beside the Wragge's barn, Tyler appeared and took hold of the lead rope. On the phone, he'd expressed his interest in training another Imperial V offspring, and it was clear he was pleased with what he saw.

We took Speedy to the covered riding arena inside the stables and turned him loose so Tyler could observe Speedy's movement. After the cramped trailer ride, Speedy happily stretched his legs and demonstrated the long stride and powerful thrust off the hindquarters that bespoke a youngster with athletic potential.

While Tyler checked out Speedy, I assessed him. He was in his early twenties, six feet tall, with a slim build. He was fair-skinned with a sprinkle of freckles across his face. His hair was brown and buzz cut close to his head. Overall, he was an attractive young man with a kind of boy-next-door appeal.

Most importantly, Tyler seemed to know horses. In fact, it was all he seemed to know. He'd been born into and grew up in the horseshow business. He graduated from high school and went directly into the family business with the aim of creating his own identity. He wasn't an articulate conversationalist, but, he seemed to speak to horses with the economy of movement and comforting presence they respond to.

Tyler did not hide his enthusiasm about Speedy. Within minutes of seeing my horse, he was calculating where the Arabian national championships would be in the year 2002 when Speedy would be a three-year-old and under saddle.

On alternate years, the championships, called the U.S. Nationals or Nationals, rotated between Albuquerque, New Mexico, and Louisville, Kentucky. In 2002, the Nationals would again be in Louisville, a much easier commute for Tyler than the grueling westward trip.

Mike and I weren't looking as far ahead as 2002. We hoped to find a buyer for Speedy sooner. But, Tyler made a case for himself with regard to our horse. He explained why he had yet to reach the top of his profession. Trainers must win national titles to achieve success and prominence. Great horses are necessary to win national titles. Clients take great horses to successful BNTs not to second-tier trainers, no matter how talented. To break out of the Catch-22 situation that was holding him back, Tyler needed national quality horses—and he said Speedy was that caliber horse.

I explained Mike and I didn't have the resources to campaign a horse to a national title. Perhaps a new owner might. That proposal put Tyler back at Catch-22; a new owner was not likely to keep Speedy in training with an unproven young trainer.

Tyler offered us a drastic reduction in board and training fees if we would agree to let him train, show, and promote Speedy through the 2002 U.S. Nationals.

Tyler's offer and his vision of Speedy's future validated my secret dreams for Speedy. But, I had decided early on I had to keep my feet on the ground and not be lured into unrealistic expectations. At that point, Speedy had yet to bring home a blue ribbon as a yearling. And, few opportunities remained that year for my horse to begin compiling his show record.

There was only one significant show still on the 2000 calendar, that being, the Jubilee Arabian Horse Show, and there was little time left to prepare. Tyler wanted to show Speedy at the Jubilee, but would only have two weeks to get my horse ready. I agreed to table the matter of a long-term arrangement with Tyler until later.

While Tyler outlined his agenda, I made sure to outline mine to him. I related the bad experience I already had with the young trainer. Tyler knew him and disparaged him as a trainer, saying he was a phony whose rich daddy built him a big barn.

I told Tyler I suspected Speedy had been mistreated. I removed my horse from the previous trainer for that reason and wouldn't hesitate to do so again. Tyler assured me he wouldn't dream of abusing a horse.

Physical abuse and cruel training practices were counterproductive, on that we both agreed. The best training methods take place in steps, as the horse is ready to learn more, the lessons proceed. Again we both agreed.

On one other matter, I was very clear. Because of his late June birthday, Speedy looked immature in classes with other yearlings, which had been born near the first of the year. I had refrained from trying to close the maturity gap with excessive feed, and I told Tyler unnatural measures, including anabolic steroids, were not to be used on Speedy.

His late development would be a factor for a number of years, but, Speedy would eventually catch up, with his health and soundness intact.

I said to Tyler on that occasion and several other times, "I don't want you to train Speedy for the next show. I want you to train him for the rest of his life."

Here again, Tyler was in complete agreement. No steroids or drugs of any kind were used on horses in his training, and a horse intended for a great career, indeed every horse, must develop at its own pace. Tyler did not use written contracts, nor did I feel we needed one when our verbal agreements were in such accord.

I could see why McKenna Jamison was so keen on this young up-and-coming trainer. As hard as it would be to leave Speedy hours away from home, I, too, had confidence in Tyler.

I was assured, not only by his words, but by his vision of a partnership with Speedy that could be so good for his career. Surely, Tyler would have a vested interest in doing what was best for Speedy.

With my horse installed at Tyler Wragge Elite Horses, Mike and I began the countdown to the Jubilee, our first big horseshow, and Speedy's debut. Now and then, Tyler called to report Speedy was responding well to training and he was looking forward to showing our horse. I appreciated those courtesy calls. They relieved the loneliness I felt for my horse and suggested Tyler was bonding with Speedy.

One day, shortly before the Jubilee, I received a phone call from someone I hadn't heard from in awhile. McKenna Jamison called to say she had just learned Speedy was in training with Tyler Wragge. I answered affirmatively and expected to exchange pleasantries about Tyler.

Instead, McKenna launched into a scorching diatribe against Tyler. Words of condemnation came out of her mouth like chunks of loathing. McKenna blurted, "Tyler Wragge is a villain. He's an unethical cheat. A congenital liar. He's an animal abuser. He's ruined horses and he'll ruin Speedy."

She repeated variations of the same accusations over and over until she seemed to exhaust her own emotions. I listened in dazed silence. Throughout my life, I have tended to be tongue-tied in moments of stress, only later thinking of what I might have said. And, I was certainly stressed by what appeared to be a phone call from a parallel universe.

Mere months earlier, Gigi told me McKenna had the highest praise for Tyler Wragge—and now—a complete reversal of opinion. McKenna, always cool and composed when I'd seen her, sounded, well—crazy.

McKenna didn't cite any specifics to bolster her accusations, which left me even more confused and feeling helpless. The Jubilee Show was only days away. I wasn't able to drop everything and drive to Tyler's and, even if I could, what was I to do there and why? Load Speedy in the trailer and bring him home without a reason? Accuse Tyler based on unsubstantiated name-calling? Absent any specifics from McKenna, I couldn't see any option but going forward.

And, frankly, deep inside where I nurtured my grievance about McKenna, I thought, "You said you would help me and didn't. And now, at the last minute, you're dumping on a person who is helping me. Who am I to believe?"

I didn't share my grievance with McKenna, didn't remind her she had failed me. Instead, I stuffed that irritant back down where it continued to fester. However, I couldn't dismiss her frantic phone call, not if there was the slightest chance Speedy was in danger.

Tyler should have the opportunity to rebut her accusations, particularly that he abused animals and ruined horses in his training. When I presented him with the content of McKenna's call, he was surprisingly unperturbed. Indeed, he suggested in some small way McKenna was correct.

He said, "I have made some mistakes in my training. So, I created a journal for myself where I've gone back to basics. I record what works good and consult my journal often."

That slight admission managed to suggest McKenna was grossly embellishing a few minor mistakes on Tyler's part. He followed that up with something I already knew from the horse community, that gossips and know-it-alls are frequently second-guessing what others are doing.

Tyler's explanation and my own *hubris* smoothed things over. While I was a novice in the Arabian show world, I had a lot of experience in the larger world. I had book learnin' and street smarts. I was a convert to country living and fairly well-grounded in horsemanship.

And, I was twice Tyler's age. Surely, I must be wise enough, shrewd enough, savvy enough to read this young man's character. He was a good kid trying to break through the professional glass ceiling of the Arabian show world, surely, I must have that right.

Halter classes are the red-headed stepchildren of horse shows. They generally kick off the schedule early in the morning the first day of the show. On Friday, halter classes began at 8 a.m. at the Jubilee Arabian Horse Show. I left home while it was still dark to make the long trip to the event, nervously changed into show clothes in the restroom at the showgrounds, and sought out Tyler's stalls.

My horse was cross-tied in a stall so Speedy couldn't roll in the bedding or otherwise mar the impeccable grooming job done by Tyler and his assistants. His russet coat gleamed with layers of polish. His flaxen mane and tail shown like white gold.

And, Speedy knew his job.

In the aisle-way between stalls, Tyler demonstrated Speedy's ability to assume the hard stand-up, arching his neck upwards, and stretching his head forward. I practiced several times. Speedy was on auto-pilot, seeming to anticipate what he needed to do.

Speedy's first appearance was Class #25, Half Arabian/Anglo Arabian Colts and Geldings AOTH, shorthand for *amateur owner to handle.* Given I was an amateur in the truest sense of the word and one with middle-aged spread and arthritic knees, that didn't seem like an auspicious beginning for the show.

Tyler was to exhibit Speedy in Class #27. He was handsomely dressed in a dark suit that complemented Speedy's coloration.

The call for the on-deck class came over the PA system. Tyler led Speedy toward the coliseum with me following. I was amazed at Speedy's composure. He was surrounded by unfamiliar sights and sounds, which would usually be alarming to an inexperienced horse, yet, he scarcely seemed to notice.

My composure, however, was completely frazzled. I felt dizzy and disoriented before I realized I was holding my breath. *Breathe, breathe*, I told myself. *Relax, have fun.* At the in-gate to the Main Ring, Tyler handed me the lead and the whip.

With a signal from the ring steward, I walked Speedy to an orange traffic cone, and, then, trotted him along a section of the stadium wall. That was the opportunity to show off one of Speedy's best attributes to the judge, his long stride and fluid, cadenced gaits. I tried to stay in the proper position, behind Speedy's head and next to his shoulder, so the judge could get the optimum profile in the few seconds allotted to us.

Then, I joined the queue at the end of the arena while the other entries made their individual entrances. Suddenly, a horse coming through the in-gate jerked loose from its handler. With the lead line flying, the frightened horse careened around the showring. The gate staff quickly closed the gate.

Reflexively, I put Speedy against the wall and stood between him and the runaway. Later, I thought, "What were you thinking, fool?

Speedy's back end is much better able to deal with a runaway horse than your body."

The loose horse was gotten under control, and the class proceeded. To my surprise, Tyler was on the other side of the solid stadium wall. His head popped up and he gave me a few words of encouragement. When it was our turn, I walked Speedy from the wall straight towards the judge, who nodded affably.

From that point on, things were a blur. *Breathe, breathe. Don't faint. Set the back legs. Set the front legs. Raise the whip. Lift the lead line. Bring the whip stock close to Speedy's nose and ask for the extension. Square up Speedy and trot away. Then, wait in the queue.*

How could I ever have imagined halter classes were boring? A whole mini-drama was packed into just a few minutes.

While the judge tallied his scorecard and relayed the results to the announcer, the handlers and yearlings relaxed. I still had to coach myself. *Breathe, breathe.*

Then, the PA system boomed out the message, "First place—Imperial Marquis, owned and shown by Judy Berkley."

There was scarcely time to appreciate those wonderful improbable words. Another class was gathering at the in-gate, and following that one, Tyler would be showing Speedy. I hurried across the arena with my horse and was met at the gate by Tyler and his father, Tom, who carried a bucket of grooming supplies to restore Speedy's flawless grooming job. I handed the lead to them and scooted up into the bleachers to watch.

Several amateurs from Class #25 were showing against the professional handlers in Class #27, but, the difference in skill levels was obvious. One of the pros was Daniel Strahan, who trained and showed halter horses exclusively. He had been leading a chestnut yearling named Prince Aragon throughout the 2000 show season. The duo was unbeaten and, no doubt, expected to continue that winning streak at the Jubilee Show.

Prince Aragon and the other horses in the yearling class looked all grown up. Against them, Speedy seemed like a pipsqueak kid, who'd wandered onto the big boys' playground. I tried to be objective about Speedy's chances. Yes, he was immature by comparison. But Speedy's gaits set him apart. Most of the other entries had the shuffling trot now typical of many Arabians. Speedy took a long stride in both the walk and the trot. From what I'd heard about politics in judging, I couldn't imagine how much consideration was assigned to conformation, to Arabian type, to movement, and to other factors.

In Class #27, Strahan's showmanship style made the most of his tall slim physique. He kept his torso and shoulders quiet and upright, yet managed a long effortless lope that encouraged Prince Aragon to trot beside him. The chestnut knew his job, showed beautifully for Strahan, and earned whoops from his fans.

Tyler's halter handling ability, I hadn't seen yet. As it turned out, other trainers and regular attendees of Arabian horse shows hadn't seen it either. Since turning pro, Tyler only rode and trained Western Pleasure horses. He didn't show halter horses. He made an exception for Speedy and told me later he had earned praise for his performance.

While Tyler didn't have Strahan's practiced elegance, he showed Speedy with his own style. He ran through the trot sections with Speedy on a long slack lead line, which spoke to mutual confidence between horse and handler. He set Speedy in place for the hard stand-up with a minimum of movement. His hands, the whip, the lead, did not detract the judge's attention from Speedy.

The class consisted of a dozen or so yearlings, but, the contest was between Prince Aragon and Speedy. At the end of the judge's calculations, again came the wonderful improbable words, "First place, Imperial Marquis, Tyler Wragge showing an entry for Judy Berkley."

And, there was more to come on that Friday.

The first and second place winners of the weanling, yearling, and two-year-old classes, were called back for the Half Arabian/Anglo Arabian Colts and Geldings Junior Horse Championships. Since the judge had already viewed those horses individually in their respective classes, the format was different for the championship. Twelve young horses were brought into the ring and arranged in two rows.

The handlers asked their entries for the hard stand-up. By that time, the youngsters had already been through one or two classes, their youthful attention spans were expiring, and their handlers were dealing with fidgety behavior by shanking the horses to get them to perform.

By contrast, Tyler brought Speedy into line, set him up, and stepped back the full length of the lead. Standing six feet away from Speedy, Tyler held the very end of the lead line with two fingers. Speedy stuck his pose and extended his long neck up, head forward, eyes bright, ears cocked towards Tyler. The two of them froze into position. It was a daring, bravura performance.

Amid the other restless youngsters, Tyler and Speedy stood motionless. An aura of stillness and beauty enveloped them. I brushed tears from my eyes in an attempt to see them as clearly as possible. I wanted that image of Tyler and Speedy to stay in my memory forever.

The judge made his way through the rows of contenders, circling each horse to assess its merits again. When he came to Speedy, the spectators whooped their approval. The judge circled Speedy again and the whoops increased. Then, Speedy left the show ring with the Junior Horse Championship sash around his neck. On Friday, Speedy won all three classes he'd been entered in.

On Saturday, Speedy was scheduled for a Half Arabian/Anglo Arabian Futurity. I made the trip all the way home to collect Mike, so my husband could share in the excitement. When we arrived at the Jubilee and made our way to Tyler's stalls, we were surprised to see Speedy had groupies. Tyler had several lamps positioned overhead and directed on Speedy, and he was buffing layers of polish into the coat while half a dozen people watched. The Futurity was likely to be another head-to-head competition between Speedy and Prince Aragon, and that had generated interest among Tyler's clients and some other halter connoisseurs.

But, Speedy was not the same horse he'd been the previous day. He was lethargic and dull-eyed. Tyler said he'd picked up a bug of some kind at the show and was coughing. It wasn't uncommon in large gatherings of horses, stabled in close quarters, for coughs, colds, and other ailments to be passed around. It was a particular risk for young horses that were still building up their immune systems.

Dr. Penny had vaccinated Speedy on a regular basis for the most serious horse diseases, so I hoped it was nothing of concern. But, my heart sank at the change in Speedy. He was going up against mature yearlings with show experience whose handlers wanted the prestige of winning a futurity. And, Speedy was not at one hundred percent.

Great showhorses can overcome minor disabilities. They know their job. They respond to the crowd. They gather themselves up and come shining through. But, Speedy didn't have that experience to draw upon. If the other entries showed the way they had in Friday's classes and Speedy couldn't shake off his malaise, we weren't going home with all the prizes.

Mike and I, and the groupies, and Tyler's parents, Tom and Tina, sat together in the bleachers. We all chatted nervously. Tina said the judge was Dirk Michaels and she said, "There aren't many people who know more about good halter horses than Dirk."

I thought Michaels was the judge, who had already pinned Speedy three times on Friday, but, realized I hadn't paid sufficient attention to be sure.

Tyler and Speedy were the first to enter the ring. Holding the lead at full length, Tyler brought Speedy along the wall for the judge's inspection. After several strides, Speedy emitted a cough that traveled the length of his body. Had the judge seen it? Or were his eyes already on the next entry? I hoped so.

Several amateurs, gripping the lead lines too close to the halter, showed their horses and got poor results. The yearlings fought the constraint to their heads and couldn't balance themselves to trot freely. The professional handlers knew better and swept into the ring with their entries on slack lines. Then came Daniel Strahan and Prince Aragon, again exuding the confidence of a seasoned team.

Tom Wragge leaned over from his seat and said to Mike and me, "It's between those two. Speedy's got him beat on movement. But, it's going to be close."

For the fourth time that weekend, the red-gold yearling from a run-down farm in Ohio, the fortunate gift bestowed upon first-time breeders, took top honors. The blue Futurity Champion ribbon was draped around Speedy's neck.

The reserve champion was Prince Aragon, who seldom, if ever, took second place honors again. He went on to have an illustrious career as a Hunter-under-saddle and was several times Ohio Horse of the Year.

Mike and I were thrilled with the results of the Jubilee Show. We had a memorable experience, but, we were not swept away by the Arabian horseshow world. Our decision to accept Tyler Wragge's proposal to train Speedy for two more years with the aim of competing at the 2002 U. S. Nationals was part business and part love for Speedy.

As a three-year-old with a show record, Speedy would be worth considerably more than a yearling with one successful outing. Having been trained by the admirable trainer we thought Tyler Wragge to be, Speedy would have a good foundation for the rest of his life.

And, I would have Speedy in my life for a couple more years.

However, one sentence from Gigi Greiko's congratulatory call the morning after Speedy's victorious weekend would prove ominously true in a way she didn't intend. That's when she said to me, "You are so new to all this, I don't think you really understand what you've done."

Chapter 5

In 1999, the year Speedy was foaled, International Arabian Horse Association was handed a scorching hot potato. A complaint was filed with IAHA's Ethical Practices Review Board, which accused professional horse trainer, David Boggs, of surgically altering Arabian horses.

To understand how volatile a complaint naming Boggs was for IAHA, it's necessary to review recent history of the Arabian horse in America, that being, the heyday of the breed's popularity in the 1980s. In those days, the Arabian was still considered an exotic breed. Since then, importation of European breeds like Friesians, Dutch Harness horses, Andalusians, and various types of Warmbloods, have stolen much of the novelty of Arabians, as well as diverting many horse-buyers away from the breed.

But, in the 1980s, finely bred Arabians were marketed as status symbols, as tax deductible investments, and as *living art.* Wealthy buyers and celebrities were courted during elaborate horse sales where Arabians were presented with Las Vegas-like pageantry. Handlers leading horses might appear through billowing clouds created by dry ice onto sumptuously decorated stages with music and dramatic lighting heightening the artistic effect.

The horses responded with flared nostrils, startled eyes, and elevated tails, like the Moroccan paintings of Delacroix come to life. The visual ballyhoo, fueled by sumptuous buffets and flowing champagne, swept many would-be investors, often those with little or no knowledge of horses, into the high dollar world of Arabian horse breeding.

The appeal to human greed was successful for a short time. Prices assigned to some Arabians were off the charts. In 1984, a mare named NH Love Potion sold at auction for a record-setting $2.55 million. An $11 million syndicate was formed to promote the Arabian stallion *Padron. Breeding operations came into being or were enlarged with the expectation of cashing in on those astronomical prices.

The bubble burst in 1986 with the passage of the Tax Reform Act, which limited the use of horse farms as tax shelters. The market for high end Arabian horses, which had inflated prices to unrealistic levels and encouraged breeding more horses than there were buyers for, collapsed.

Breeders filed for bankruptcy and sent many purebred horses to slaughterhouses. Old-timers still relate stories of seeing Arabian horses standing in holding pens awaiting death with their registration papers tied around their necks in the unlikely event buyers would suddenly appear to save them from their grisly fate.

Practices from the 1980s continue to adversely affect Arabians, notably halter horses. Because the Arabian was marketed as living art, breeding decisions were made to maximize certain beautiful attributes, for example, sculpted heads, dished faces, and long necks. The emphasis on fashion-over-function eventually changed the physique of horses in many bloodlines and reduced the breed's legendary athleticism.

Thus, there is a distinction today between in-hand/halter Arabians and under saddle/performance Arabians, a difference bemoaned by long-time Arabian lovers, who recall the versatility, natural beauty, and balance of pre-1980s Arabians.

Another legacy of the 1980s boom was the role of professional handlers. Since Arabians were being marketed to buyers, who often didn't have horse-owning experience and didn't intend to acquire it, a trainer was an essential part of the package. The ascendancy of professional trainers within IAHA and the obeisance paid to the professionals by showhorse owners, probably began in earnest during that era and burgeoned to the current state of affairs where many IAHA members complain the organization, which is supported by their dues and show fees, is primarily the handmaiden of the professional trainers.

Besides the emphasis on the handlers' status, the professionals changed the manner in which Arabians were exhibited in-hand. Previously, Arabian halter horses were presented in a way, which emphasized their conformation and tractability and such is the case in most other breeds. Knowledgeable horse-buyers look for animals with good minds and good bodies, that is, calm temperaments and the physical makeup to be able to do a job.

But in the 1980s, Arabians were not being marketed to knowledgeable horse-buyers. Because the object was to make fortunes breeding Arabians, no one asked the question, "Who is going to want to ride horses that appear unhinged?"

The perception of Arabians as beautiful but unrideable lawn ornaments has persisted since the 1980s and spawned sardonic humor such as a bumpersticker parody of an anti-drunk driving campaign that said, "Friends don't let friends ride Arabians."

Despite the damage the halter handling style of the 1980s caused to the breed's reputation, the persistence of the *snort and blow* style continues.Complaints about practices, which support the crazy Arabian image, go unheeded by a contingent of Arabian officials, who appear so stuck in the past, so resistant to change, so disconnected from reality, and so dismissive of criticism, their mindset could be described as "unteachable."

Those who are teachable and want to get in step with the times, decry the abusive practices that are used to achieve the halter presentation unique to Arabian horses, the hard stand-up.

The most visible practice in achieving the hard stand-up is shanking. A shank chain that runs under the halter across the pain-sensitive jawbones, is jerked, and often repeatedly jerked, to get the horse to lift and extend its head forward. A chain behind the ears, which pinches or causes pain, may be used to enhance the look.

While much of that type of training takes place out of public view, it's not unusual to see handlers shanking frightened animals in the showring, even though excessive shanking is expressly prohibited by association rules and often draws booing from spectators.

Another type of training that was forbidden by IAHA rules, is whipping. The whip is carried by the handler in the show ring and supposedly is used as a *directional aid*. But how does the horse learn to take direction from the whip? Why not a lollipop or a feather duster?

In training sessions away from spectators, trainers may give horses a crash course in the hard stand-up by lashing the animals repeatedly. Thus, when a horse sees the whip raised as a directional aid, the animal quickly complies.

Teaching the hard stand-up can be accomplished with time, patience, and rewards, but, time-is-money in the professional horse training business. A trainer with dozens of horses in his barn may only spend minutes per day with each client's horse and fast results are what pay the bills. The effect of fear and abuse on a horse's psyche and the impediments abuse can create for the horse's long-range ability to be trained, well, that's probably not given much consideration when the objective is to make a quick buck.

While the shank and the whip may be used to physically teach the hard stand-up, a horse may still not have the requisite snort and blow charisma to be competitive. For those, who still embrace the 1980s style, the Arabian needs to be pumped up and hyper-alert when it's Showtime. If it doesn't do so naturally, well, trainers have ways of generating the necessary pizzazz.

While veterans of Class A Arabian horseshows may privately relate stories of abuses and heinous late night training sessions they have witnessed, they won't come forward to say so. However, in 1999, someone did come forward to report abuse of a different kind. The object of the allegations was David C. Boggs, who, with his brother, Bob, rose to prominence as handsome blond *wunderkinds* in the heady years of the 1980s.

In that era, David Boggs handled many stellar Arabians, including the $11 million stallion *Padron. From his training facilities, Midwest Arabians in Elk River, Minnesota, and Scottsdale, Arizona, Boggs built a worldwide clientele. He was arguably the most successful and famous trainer in the Arabian horseshow industry with a roster of well-to-do clients and their extraordinary horses.

In the complaint to IAHA's Ethical Practices Review Board (EPRB), Boggs was accused of using liposuction and surgery to conceal genetic defects or undesirable traits on horses in his care. As those were breeding animals, alteration of their appearance would be a misrepresentation of the genetic traits likely to be passed to their offspring. Even the best Arabians are not flawless, but, according to the complaint, cosmetic surgery was utilized to achieve perfection—despite the inherent dishonesty.

The findings of the EPRB were made available to the membership of IAHA. Names of horses, their owners, veterinarians, and others involved, were specifically cited, as were evidentiary exhibits. Documents showed Boggs used the services of two veterinarians to perform surgery to correct a *wry tail*, that is, a tail carried to one side.

Evidence was also presented that Boggs authorized veterinarians to do surgeries to remove fat deposits from the croups of horses to enhance the Arabian attribute of a level line across the back, and that Boggs authorized veterinarians to do surgeries to alter the throatlatch of horses to achieve more slender necks. (The throatlatch is the area under a horse's jaws where the head joins the neck.)

The invoice for one of the throatlatch alterations noted the procedure required three hours under anesthesia for a stallion, despite the dangers to large animals of prolonged anesthesia. The stallion was shown five weeks later at the U.S. Nationals. An eight inch scar discovered under the hair of its throatlatch was further evidence of the surgery.

Additionally, Boggs used veterinarians to tranquilize a horse so a tattoo artist named "Spider" could tattoo and dye the patchy pigmentation of skin surrounding the horse's eyes. Mottled skin of the eyelids is considered a genetic fault that would disqualify an Arabian from a show career. Following Spider's tattoo *artistry*, the horse was shown.

Two veterinarians were named in the EPRB's report as Boggs' accomplices. The alteration of the appearance of breeding stock, as any reputable vet knows, violates the rules of all horse breed registries.

Additionally, one of the veterinarians changed his medical records in an attempt to misrepresent the procedures he performed and to conceal Boggs' identity. The vet undoubtedly knew tampering with medical records is a violation of medical ethics and of law.

The point man for EPRB's case against David Boggs was Michael D. Brown. In the aftermath of Hurricane Katrina in 2005, Brown, who was then head of the Federal Emergency Management Agency, became known to the general public. But, from 1991-2001, Brown was IAHA's Commissioner of Judges and Stewards, the sector of IAHA, along with Ethical Practice Review Board, that was charged with upholding the Code of Ethics and Sportsmanship.

The EPRB hearing took place August 23-30, 1999. Both Respondent Boggs and Complainant Brown were represented by counsel, two lawyers each. Six members of EPRB heard the evidence, deliberated for two days, and pronounced their verdict. The burden of proof was sufficient to show seven of the twelve horses named in the complaint had received unnecessary surgery at Boggs' direction.

David Boggs was suspended from IAHA membership privileges and participation in shows and events for five years, commencing September 15, 1999. At the conclusion of his suspension in 2004, Boggs was to be on probation for another five years.

However, Boggs was not willing to accept his punishment.

In October, 1999, Boggs filed a suit against IAHA in the Arapahoe County Colorado District Court seeking a reversal of EPRB's decision and alleging slander and defamation. Boggs amended his complaint twice to add individual defendants, one of whom was Michael Brown.

Several of Boggs' clients filed lawsuits against IAHA generally alleging product disparagement, intentional interference with prospective business advantage, defamation, and violation of the Colorado Consumer Products Act.

The trainer, IAHA claimed, encouraged multiple lawsuits as a means to intimidate and to bankrupt the Arabian horse organization. But, by suing IAHA rather than Boggs, the horseowners set themselves up for countersuits by IAHA for fraudulent concealment of cosmetic surgeries.

The prospect of financial ruin and the public spectacle of a besmirched icon of the Arabian horse industry caused divisions within IAHA and its membership. One side may have found it offensive that Boggs, who already had such a cream-of-the-crop competitive advantage, still felt the need to cheat. Another side felt the demi-god of halter showmanship should not be jostled from his pedestal by questions of ethics. Others quailed at the prospect of financial ruin associated with lawsuits.

Perhaps there was also an unacknowledged sense the chicanery, animal abuse, and slaughter of the innocents, from the tarnished Golden Era of the 1980s, were fading from public memory, so why, a decade later, revive that shame by making such a fuss about a little nipping and tucking?

Adding to the turmoil within the organization was Michael Brown's desire to create his own legal defense fund with additional monies raised from breeders and IAHA.

Brown, who was an attorney, earning an annual salary of $100,000 from IAHA, wanted an additional financial cushion to protect his own assets. He was doubtful IAHA would stand with him and cover his legal bills.

Indeed, one of the consequences of the flurry of lawsuits was IAHA, as an economic measure, entered negotiations for a merger with Arabian Horse Registry of America to form Arabian Horse Association. The new AHA entity, still headquartered in Aurora, Colorado, became official January 1, 2003.

Despite the litigious pressure brought by Boggs, the Court upheld EPRB's decision to sanction him. Boggs spent his five-year suspension figuratively flipping off IAHA by building lucrative relationships with breeders and buyers in South America, the Middle East, Europe, and Australia, and otherwise demonstrating he didn't need IAHA, AHA, or whatever the association was calling itself, to be prosperous.

When his suspension expired in 2004, Boggs again began showing halter horses at AHA sponsored events. However, the lithe golden boy of the 1980s was succumbing to middle-aged spread, including a couple fat deposits under his chin, which (how ironic!) made him a candidate for throatlatch surgery. Soon, Boggs was again the master of halter showing with the best horses and the richest clients.

Michael Brown, though many admired his campaign to clean up the halter scene, didn't fare as well. The legal tab for Boggs' lawsuit was $1.5 million, a hefty sum for a 45,000-member association that wasn't attracting numerous new recruits to the breed. The financial toll, added to Brown's seemingly self-serving legal defense fund, led to his resignation. Part of Brown's separation agreement with IAHA was to donate $25,000 from his legal defense fund to the IAHA Legal Defense Fund.

In the Hurricane Katrina debacle, many officials, who should have borne more of the responsibility, were able to offload their shares of blame onto Michael Brown. His resume prior to his FEMA appointment was ridiculed in the press, and he was depicted as the inept commissioner of a "small horse organization."

A little journalistic digging might have disclosed the *small horse organization* was a dysfunctional alligator pit of conflicting agendas, egotism, envy, emotion, money, greed, power, and ambition, where the leadership was disconnected from its mission and the people it represented. In short, a place that looked a lot like America.

At the time Boggs' sanction and subsequent lawsuit were going on, I was unaware of the fracas that was Topic One in the Arabian horseshow world. Speedy was only two months old, and my thoughts had not yet turned to his future as a horse that would be involved in AHA shows. Because of the events in Speedy's life, however, I had more contact with the Arabian Horse Association than I anticipated. The impression I formed was troubling.

Based on accounts I read, the countersuit for defamation filed by David Boggs had no legitimate basis. Defamation is the issuance of a false statement about another person to a third party, which causes them harm, either in spoken form (slander) or print form (libel). If the statement is not false, if it is the truth, that is supposed to be an absolute defense against a lawsuit for defamation.

The allegations about Boggs were shown to be true. Someone in a position to know gathered evidence and blew the whistle on him. A preponderance of evidence—not an easy standard to achieve at trial—won the case for IAHA. In a term we don't hear much anymore, Boggs was caught *red-handed.* But that doesn't seem to be a disqualifier nowadays.

Apparently, lawyers can be retained, who will look at the evidence for defamation, thin or non-existent though it may be, and still file a legal action. What do they have to lose? Professionally, there is little in the way of discipline lawyers need worry about. When accused of misdeeds, lawyers are usually brought up before their bar associations where their peers pass judgment with generally predictable outcomes.

The aim of unsubstantiated defamation claims is to intimidate the plaintiff, gum up the lawsuit, and try to divert attention from the evidence of red-handed misconduct. The secondary effect is the suppression of speech. What the false defamation racket does on the legal side is what political correctness does on the media side. Both are pernicious efforts to choke off the right to tell the truth.

The assault on freedom of speech, the most essential right granted to Americans, should be of great concern. Every human enterprise is affected when Truth is strangled. The atmosphere at AHA after the Boggs' lawsuit, where paralysis through fear of litigation had set in, may serve as a warning.

By August 2001, Speedy was back at home after being lightly shown as a two-year-old by Tyler Wragge. Often, rapidly growing two-year-olds aren't shown at all because their appearance can change almost daily. However, Tyler did show Speedy as a two-year-old to continue giving Speedy exposure in the marketplace and to continue associating himself with an up-and-coming quality horse.

That exposure brought about a scary situation for Tyler. He phoned me one day to say a fellow trainer and friend of his was interested in buying Speedy. The friend wanted to add Imperial V-bred horses to his show string, and he'd been tracking Imperial Marquis (Speedy) on the show circuit.

Tyler's voice was nearly quaking when he related his friend's interest to me.

I listened. A thrill of excitement surged in me at that confirmation of Speedy's potential. But, I didn't inquire about the price the trainer friend might be offering or ask to enter negotiations with him. I reminded Tyler of our agreement. In exchange for a reduced rate in board and training, which was making it possible to show and promote our horse, Tyler had an exclusive on Speedy until the 2002 U.S. Nationals. Only after Tyler had his shot at a national title, would Speedy be for sale. I had given my word and that was that.

Tyler's relief was palpable. He knew I needed money and figured I would be tempted. He'd seen himself once again without a ticket to the top. But, I surprised him. Tyler stammered his gratitude and said, "There aren't many people like you."

So, at the conclusion of the 2001 show season, as fall approached, Speedy was home again where I could enjoy him for what might be the last time. One sunny morning in September, after feeding Speedy and the other horses, I walked the short distance from our farm towards the tiny post office of our little town.

As I chatted with the postmaster, someone ran through the post office door and yelled, "We're under attack! New York City is being attacked!"

On September 11, 2001, it seemed impossible life would ever return to normal. It seemed impossible, indeed selfish, to even consider taking up trivial pursuits again. But, soon, shockingly soon, the horrors of that day began to diminish. And, many Americans resumed the pursuit of materialism and pleasurable activities.

In the early spring of 2002, Speedy was, for official purposes, a three-year-old and could begin his campaign for the U.S. Nationals. Dr. Penny x-rayed Speedy's knees to insure the growth plates had closed. She gave Speedy his annual vaccinations, reviewed his overall health and soundness, and pronounced him fit and ready to begin training.

Besides Dr. Penny, the other professional, who was part of what I called Speedy's Home Team, was my longtime horseshoer, John Travis "J.T." Laney, who had been attending to Speedy's hooves since my horse's birth.

A skilled, dependable horseshoer is essential for good horse management, and J.T. was as skilled and dependable as they come. He was a certified journeyman farrier, the highest ranking among horseshoers, who have received formal training and credentials. He regularly attended continuing education seminars and was a true student of his craft.

In addition to the exactitude he required of himself, J.T. mentored a number of apprentice horseshoers. His high standards were passed along to the younger fellows, as was his ongoing support. J.T. was well aware injury and prolonged recovery could spell the end of a horseshoer's career. Disability and unemployment are as close as one powerful kick from a fractious horse. He had a plan for that.

Whenever one of the local horseshoers was sidelined with injuries, J.T. would rally the others to take up the slack by shoeing horses for their laid-up colleague so the injured fellow wouldn't lose clients and income. Grasping for every dollar, even if it meant battening on the misfortune of others, seemed increasingly to be the mentality in America business. But, that wasn't J.T.'s style. He was confident there was enough work to go around and his own personal excellence would always attract and hold clients.

Indeed, I was a devoted customer. I looked forward to seeing J.T.'s truck pull into the driveway every six weeks. Looked forward to seeing his burly form emerge from the cab, extract his tools and leather apron from the back of the truck, and head into the barn.

J.T. was six feet tall with the Popeye forearms typical of horseshoers. His bow-legged, rolling gait bespoke many years of riding, roping, and barrel racing. His foxy red hair, closely shaven to his head, indicated both his Scottish ancestry and his roguish sense of humor.

Where horses were concerned, J.T. was an equal opportunity horseshoer. He made little distinction between aged horses living out their years in the pasture and the paragons of the showring. All of them got quality workmanship. But, shoeing high dollar horses for shows and competitions was a regular feature of J.T.'s professional activities. He was used to rising stars and their hopeful owners. Even so, J.T. seemed to have a soft spot for Speedy. I kept him and Dr. Penny informed of all the news in Speedy's show career.

That spring, J.T. had Speedy's hooves in excellent condition. Speedy had not yet been shod and the matter of what type and weight shoes should be applied to his hooves would be left to Tyler Wragge, who would know the horseshoe specifications IAHA required. But, the correct angulations of Speedy's hooves had been scrupulously maintained by J.T. and the bottoms of the hooves were almost perfectly round. Whenever I used the hoof pick to clean out Speedy's hooves, I admired their smooth circular shape.

To save time for Tyler Wragge, I covered the training basics. I accustomed Speedy to carrying a bit in his mouth. I *sacked* him out and exercised him with the saddle on his back. I ground drove Speedy with long lines. He was *tied off* with a rein from the bit to the saddle to teach him to respond to the mouthpiece and to turn. I employed a neighbor, who was an excellent and featherweight rider, to come to our farm and ride Speedy several times.

Speedy's introduction to the saddle and bridle and a rider, one of the primary rites of passage in a horse's life, was accomplished without causing trauma or fear in the young horse. Speedy responded beautifully. He was curious, compliant, caught on quickly, and didn't fuss or resist anything he was asked to do. Throughout the new experiences, he demonstrated the trainability that was one of the most desirable attributes of Imperial V's offspring.

In preparing Speedy to go back to Tyler Wragge Elite Horses, I observed the rule I had laid down to Tyler: Speedy was to be trained, not for the next show, but for the rest of his life. Even though our aim was a title at the 2002 U. S. Nationals, I was opposed to any shortcuts or aggressive training methods, which might affect Speedy's life and longevity.

As one saying goes, "Trainers chase the ribbons. Horsemen chase the dream."

Tyler had already expressed he was in agreement with my philosophy. Where Speedy was concerned, we were both chasing the dream. We were entering the third year of what had been a satisfying partnership.

On March 2, 2002, I loaded Speedy into our old horse trailer and hauled him to Tyler's facility at his parents' farm. We entered the barn, and Tyler put Speedy in the cross-ties while I went over a few agenda items.

Speedy's weight was what I thought appropriate for a still-growing young horse. I didn't like the practice of packing weight onto Western Pleasure Arabians to make them look like stout Quarter Horses and told Tyler so. In my opinion, Arabians, like Saddlebreds and Thoroughbreds, are by Nature sleek and lean-bodied and that's what I wanted for my horse. Speedy wasn't to be bulked up to conform to the dictates of the Arabian Western Pleasure look.

As to conditioning, I'd been moderately exercising Speedy. I subscribe to the philosophy of a friend who says, "Only condition for the level of work the horse is to do. An endurance horse will need more conditioning than a Sunday showhorse. The more you condition unnecessarily, the greater the risk of injury."

I concluded my instructions to Tyler as I had before: I was to be informed of any and all matters pertaining to Speedy.

Tyler led Speedy to a stall freshly bedded with sawdust and furnished with a manger of hay and a bucket of clean water. T&T Stables and Tyler's business were housed in an older barn, and the box stalls were smaller than are recommended nowadays, but, the facility was always spotless, with every item of tack and grooming supplies in place. Every indicator of good professional horse care was present.

Speedy was placed in the stall and his halter removed. I drank in the sight of him. I married late in life and never had children, so my horses were very dear to me. I took a last look at my golden boy with his sweeping flaxen mane and tail, his lovely head with the wide white band down his face. I was going to miss the daily rituals of caring for him and enjoying his good humor and mischievous ways.

In the next seven months, Speedy would be trained for the 2002 U.S. Nationals where he would likely attract a buyer and pass out of my life. *Remember, he's for sale*, Mike told me in the beginning. I had tried to respect that, tried to keep an emotional distance. But, it was impossible to be around Speedy without being captivated by his beauty and intelligence.

I planned to visit Speedy at least once a month during his training, but, the plan didn't go smoothly. On a number of occasions, Tyler cancelled our appointments. He suggested medical tests he was undergoing were the reasons for the interruptions. There was no point in going to visit Speedy and view his progress if Tyler was at the doctor and unavailable to ride my horse, so, we rescheduled. After several cancellations, I said, "Is there anything about your health that you can share with me?"

Without specifically saying so, Tyler alluded to cancer. Naturally, my sympathy and concern were aroused. How awful that a young man, who was struggling to succeed in his career, was also dealing with the frightening specter of cancer.

Despite the disruptions to my own plans, I never complained about Tyler's cancellations. How could I? It might be cancer, for heaven's sake. And, given the fearsomeness of the disease, surely, no one would tempt *karma* by making false claims of cancer.

In between the cancelled appointments, Tyler did phone frequently, often saying he was riding Speedy as we spoke. He reported my horse was training beautifully, and he believed Speedy to be a serious contender for a national title. At one point, he even mentioned a horse he thought might be Speedy's most serious competition, a Half Arabian named Broadway Bey Bee. Tyler said that horse, which had recently sold for $22,500, was not as beautiful as Speedy, but had the advantage of more showring experience.

On the occasions when I did see Speedy, everything seemed to be on track. Once I noticed Speedy had small *raspberries*, round red abrasions, at the corners of his mouth, but that didn't seem unusual when a horse is first carrying the bit. And, as a Junior Horse, Speedy would be shown for a couple years in a hackamore and bosal, a bridle with a rawhide noseband instead of a bit.

Between my visits and Tyler's frequent cell phone calls, I felt I was comfortably in the information loop. In addition to reporting on Speedy's training, Tyler phoned to ask permission for various procedures and additional expenses. Speedy's teeth had to be *floated*, a process of rasping off the sharp edges of new teeth, which is routine for young horses. I approved the expense.

Then, Tyler asked permission for Speedy to be given a Panacur Power Pac. What is that? I asked. A vitamin treatment, replied Tyler. I approved the expense.

Later, I learned a Panacur Power Pac is a multi-dose worming treatment. Why did Tyler tell me it was a vitamin? The Power Pac didn't appear on my monthly bill from Tyler as other procedures did, but came as a separate invoice from "L. Weed."

I sent a check to L. Weed.

Thus, it seemed the seven months following my delivery of Speedy to Tyler Wragge Elite Horses and the training, which was to lead to the U.S. Nationals, were going along according to plan.

Chapter 6

Since McKenna's impassioned outburst in the fall of 2000, our relationship had gone dormant. Yet, Tyler's animosity was still alive. He claimed McKenna was conducting an unfair vendetta against him. She was smearing him to other people by spreading false tales, he said, and once she tried to sabotage him by spooking his mount awhile he was riding in a horseshow class.

When she'd been his client, Tyler said, McKenna was a nosey nuisance, who went into the stall of each and every horse at T&T Stables to snoop around, a charge, if true, that went beyond nosey to inappropriate and dangerous behavior. Tyler seemed to have a continuous supply of McKenna gossip.

Years ago, I came across a saying, which intrigued me: "Gossip is the beginning of moral inquiry."

The observation seemed to explain some of the appeal of gossip. Our reactions to the gossip we hear about the conduct of others would seem to define where we are on the ethical spectrum. We can be outraged at shocking behavior. We can make excuses for it. We may not understand what all the fuss is about. Or, we may recognize our own behavior and implement changes.

Naively, I failed to consider someone may act outraged at gossip to appear as though they have standards of goodness they really don't. That's the difference between con artists and their marks.

Tyler's gossip was not confined to McKenna. He gossiped about the dark side of the Arabian horse industry and trainers, who abused horses with drugs and harsh training methods. Some of the top trainers, he said, had so many clients and horses, that, if they fried the minds of young horses by terrorizing them or rushing their training, they just tossed the damaged horses aside and went on to the next one.

Often, the clients didn't even know what happened to their horses, Tyler said. He didn't hesitate to be specific in his accusations, claiming two famous trainers by name as culprits, who abused and ruined horses.

Those character digs by Tyler served two purposes: There was the guilty pleasure of having the inside scoop that appealed to human nature, but, also to my instincts as a writer. And, the gossip also suggested moral inquiry. By condemning the bad actions of others, Tyler put himself on the side of the good guys. He was that horse-loving young trainer, who wasn't getting ahead because he refused to engage in detrimental practices.

Tyler's insinuations about McKenna managed to keep warm the embers of my disappointment with her. Thus, another incident was sufficient to cause one more flashpoint. And, it erupted from that which first brought McKenna and me together—Imperial V.

McKenna was not just an admirer of Imperial V, she was a good friend of the stallion's owner, Gordon Meriwether. So, she was as stunned as his other friends when Meriwether suddenly disappeared, taking Imperial V with him, but leaving behind his broodmares, his business, and bewildered clients. Friends stepped in to care for the horses while rumors circulated about Meriwether and Imperial V's whereabouts.

Eventually, it was learned Meriwether ran away with a person he met online. He liquidated his business and cut off all ties with his past. The fate of Imperial V was uncertain for quite some time. Mike and I wanted to re-breed Queenie to Imperial V, but, no one knew where the stallion was.

Finally, Imperial V was put up for sale. McKenna and her husband were interested in acquiring Imperial V, but, the stallion was sold to Cody and Natasha Smoak.

Cody was a cowboy type with a squat chunky build and a dour personality, who bred and raised Quarter Horses. He expressed disdain for Arabians until he met Natasha, a perky blonde with a pink and porcelain complexion whose lovely face glowed like a sunbeam. She was an Arabian horse enthusiast, who shot down Cody's rudeness when they first met, but later fell in love with and married him.

McKenna and Natasha were longtime friends from the Arabian horseshow world. The interest McKenna had in Imperial V when the stallion was owned by Meriwether, was transferred to the new owners, the Smoaks. McKenna, after all, owned two of Imperial V's successful offspring, had avidly promoted and secured breedings for the stallion before, and would continue to do so for her friend.

I also felt a connection to Imperial V. Not surprisingly, a vested interest develops among clients, who use the same stallion as the basis of their breeding programs. If they succeed, it reflects well on the stallion, and if the stallion succeeds, it reflects well on the clients' investment. Therefore, we were all bound together in a web of financial involvement, hopes and dreams, high expectations, and individual egos—which could be a volatile mix.

When Imperial V was finally settled in with Cody and Natasha, Mike and I brought Queenie and another mare to SmoakNShow Horses, for breeding. Our agreement with Cody was the same as we'd had with Gordon Meriwether. We'd make payments on the breeding fees as we could, but, the foals would be paid for by the time of their births. Those terms were agreeable to the Smoaks, who were trying to reconnect with Meriwether's clients, attract new mare owners, and get Imperial V back on the career path as a desirable stud.

The Smoaks never disclosed what they paid for Imperial V, but, even in the distress sale that might have resulted from Gordon Meriwether's abrupt exit from the breeding business, it's not unreasonable to guess Imperial V could have commanded a price tag of $100,000. Thus, the Smoaks had a considerable investment to recoup, and the horse business is fraught with the unexpected, as they unfortunately discovered when one breeding season was side-lined because Imperial V had to be rushed to Ohio State University veterinary college for emergency colic surgery.

Colic is a disease of the bowel, which can be progressive. It may begin as abdominal distress or a small obstruction. If not successfully resolved in the early stages, colic can advance to devastatingly painful contortions of the digestive organs—and death. When colic surgery is successful, it leaves a huge incision on the belly, and, in the case of a stallion, prohibits breeding activity until healed.

After Imperial V recovered from colic surgery, his breeding career suffered another setback. That one came from the human side and from one of his admirers.

In 2001, McKenna learned her horse Imperial Echo+ had Cushing's Disease. A disorder of the endocrine system that produces pituitary tumors, Cushing's Disease had long been associated with aged horses. Its appearance in young horses was still considered rare. Imperial Echo+ was only eight years old when he was diagnosed with Cushing's. Given that a horse's working life can extend to the age of twenty-plus and many senior horses can still be competitive, McKenna could rightly have anticipated many more years of success in the showring and of companionship with an animal she adored.

McKenna was determined to fight for the life and longevity of Imperial Echo+. Her horse was placed on daily treatments of Cyproheptadine which, along with Pergolide, are the two medications used to manage the disease. McKenna also monitored her horse closely, as Cushing Disease predisposes its victims to colic and laminitis.

McKenna researched as much information as she could to battle the disease. She sought to share the information with others, including the fact that Huckleberry Bey++, one of the illustrious stallions in the pedigree of Imperial Echo+, developed Cushing's Disease and was euthanized (although at the age of sixteen.)

Her observations to other people about Huckleberry Bey++ and Cushing's had unintended consequences. McKenna's comment traveled through the Arabian horse community in our area and morphed into a rumor Cushing's Disease was genetically transmitted, and Imperial V was a carrier.

It was the kind of innuendo, which can sweep through the larger Arabian community like wildfire and ruin the reputations of people and horses.

When the rumor reached me, I phoned Natasha Smoak to express my alarm. Natasha assured me Cushing's as a genetic transmission had no basis in fact, but she, too, was upset with McKenna. As the rumor was making the rounds, Natasha said twelve breedings for Imperial V, about half his bookings, had cancelled. As the Smoaks' breeding business took a hit, I imagined the market for my horses disappearing.

I contacted McKenna to express my displeasure. Our discussion was heated and bitter and ended with a mutual agreement that we didn't need to ever speak again.

I related the matter to Tyler Wragge around May of 2002, not to spread gossip about McKenna, but to make a very strong point about Speedy. If there was even a remote chance Speedy might have a predisposition to Cushing's Disease, it was all the more important my horse be drug free. I emphatically repeated my prohibition against steroids and all other unnecessary drugs.

At that time, I had only vague notions drugs were used in the horse-show world. Tyler had mentioned trainers, who drugged for performance purposes. Massively built halter horses in the Quarter Horse breed suggested anabolic steroids were being used.

One year, my horseshoer, J.T. Laney, came back from the All-American Quarter Horse Congress held in Columbus, Ohio, and related a competitor, who was also a veterinarian, was selling a concoction of his own formulation, which he called *Slow Lope*.

The vet was arrested at the Congress show and taken away by federal agents of Alcohol, Tobacco, and Firearms. The problem for officialdom was not that the vet was openly drugging horses and encouraging others to do so, but that his brew contained alcohol.

My generalized concerns about drugs arose from the encroachment of performance-enhancing substances into all kinds of sports. Barry Bonds was closing in on the all-time home run record amid allegations of steroid use. The Tour de France, despite efforts of the organizers to monitor and clean up its reputation, was continually plagued with problems related to performance-enhancing drugs. The monstrous physiques of professional wrestlers and football players spoke to the use of steroids and human growth hormone. Sadly, the conduct of professional athletes was filtering down to the high school level where performance drug use was proliferating among teenagers seeking a competitive edge.

What happens after the short-term dividend of steroids expires? My answer to that was always Lyle Alzado. Near the end of his life, the former NFL defensive end made the rounds of TV shows to warn against steroid use. Alzado's once massive physique was cadaverous, and he attributed his longtime use of anabolic steroids to the brain cancer that was killing him. Medical professionals disputed steroids were the cause of his disease, but, Alzado, who died at the age of forty-three, was firm in his belief.

Besides the rising tide of steroids in sports, I'd had my own memorable experience with a steroid. In my early thirties, I had an accident, which badly bruised the rotator in my left shoulder. My left arm was completely without feeling or mobility. My left hand couldn't grasp or hold anything.

The prospect of a permanent disability loomed while my doctor tried numerous therapies to restore movement. I had hydrotherapy, ultrasound, and physical therapy, all without success. Finally, the doctor told me there was only one remaining option, cortisone injections into the shoulder joint. He warned me the injection of the steroid was a one-time only treatment, and I would experience an excruciating *cortisone burn* for a period of time.

With no other alternatives, I had the injections and, thankfully, recovered full use of my arm. Afterwards, the word cortisone was always associated in my mind with a powerful, last-resort healing instrument and with a high level of temporary pain.

Between the dustup with McKenna about Cushing's Disease and my own experience with the cortisone, I had ample reasons to repeat my prohibition against steroids to Tyler. I speculated to Tyler that increased drug use on horses might account for the appearance of Cushing's Disease among younger horses.

Tyler Wragge was in complete agreement with me. He endorsed my concerns about Cushing's Disease and the advisability of avoiding any and all drugs, which might affect Speedy's, indeed any horse's, natural hormone balance.

On August 31, 2002, Tyler was again taking Speedy to the Jubilee Arabian Show. At that time, IAHA rules required a horse had to place first or second in a class at a major show in order to qualify for the Nationals, and Speedy had not yet shown in 2002.

I invited Gigi Greiko to attend the Jubilee with me. Knowing there was bad blood between us, Gigi split her time shuttling between Speedy and me at Tyler's stalls and McKenna, who was showing Imperial Echo+ that weekend. But, Gigi and I were together when I caught sight of Speedy for the first time in a month or so. I gasped at the change in my horse.

Speedy was visibly taller and nearly obese. His skin seemed to be stretched over slabs of fat, and he was just what I did not want, an Arabian that looked like a corpulent Quarter Horse.

I confronted Tyler and demanded to know, "Have you given Speedy steroids?"

Tyler calmly brushed aside the question and said, "No, of course not. He's just been eating good."

"What do you mean by 'eating good'?" I asked.

"He's getting a bale and a half of second cutting alfalfa and fourteen to sixteen pounds of grain per day," said Tyler.

I was speechless. If this was Tyler's idea of basic horsemanship, it had no resemblance to my notion of the basics. Alfalfa, particularly second and third cuttings, is considered by many horsemen to be too rich for horses. A bale and a half? What does a bale weigh? Fifty pounds, maybe. Was Speedy getting seventy-five pounds of alfalfa per day?

The grain ration, as much as sixteen pounds per day, seemed excessive for a horse Tyler told me was being trained and conditioned for only twenty minutes each day. A horse with nothing to do for most of the day would certainly eat continuously, but, I had a disturbing image of Speedy being force-fed like a Strasbourg goose.

Tyler dismissed my concerns about my horse's diet by saying, "Don't worry. Speedy's used to it."

I looked around. I was in a world I didn't know. I'd hired an expert to guide me. He was doing so at a reduced rate to make the adventure affordable. It seemed presumptuous and ungrateful to second-guess him. So, I refrained from complaint and tamped down my anxieties. And, continued to tamp them down throughout the day.

Speedy had not been in a big show setting since he was a yearling. Tyler, who had numerous clients that weekend, mentioned he'd been too busy to practice-ride Speedy in the Main Ring. Tyler said, "I'll ride him during the lunch break."

Gigi and I sat in the bleachers throughout the lunch break, but, Tyler and Speedy didn't appear. I was irritated such an important part of Speedy's training—exposing him to what was essentially his workplace—had been ignored.

Several classes after the lunch break, Tyler appeared with Speedy in a *limit* class, that is, a class for horses, which have yet to post a win. There was only one other horse in the class, a lovely Half-Arabian buckskin, a rare and highly-prized color.

An old horsemen's saying goes like this: "A good horse is never a bad color." And, color is not supposed to figure into the judging process. Yet, there's no denying unusual and eye-catching colors garner attention. The palette of horse colors among purebred Arabians had been reduced by the popularity of certain bay and gray stallions, whose genetic ability to pass on their traits included their colors.

But, there were many more colors among Half Arabians. As a flaxen chestnut, Speedy's color was somewhat unusual and therefore a plus. But, Gigi and I agreed, chestnut was not going to trump buckskin.

Therefore, Speedy had to perform well and demonstrate his graceful movement in order to win. Tyler had regaled me with how successfully Speedy was training and my horse's movement, I knew, was special.

So, I watched the class with increasing dismay as Speedy lumbered tentatively around the arena as though his legs were hobbled. Speedy kept his neck arched over in the Western Pleasure position, but, he turned his head from side to side checking things out. Given that he was in strange territory, Speedy was doing what his instincts told him to do—be on the alert for predators. But, that was not what a well-trained and properly exposed showhorse is supposed to do, and the judge undoubtedly marked Speedy down for inattention.

In the limit class and in the subsequent Western Pleasure Junior Horse class, Speedy and the buckskin were the only entries. Speedy placed second both times. Tyler had probably checked the entries, which are posted prior to the classes taking place, and he knew Speedy would qualify for Nationals on a technicality—two second-place wins.

In my mind, I made excuses for Tyler. He had his hands full with clients that weekend. And, I assumed they were all paying full price. I was the newbie, who was paying cut rate. I didn't know how things worked in the show world and was inhibited about speaking up, much less complaining.

The Jubilee Show of 2000 when Speedy made his yearling debut was an exhilarating experience. The Jubilee Show of 2002 felt messy and dissatisfying.

But, we were headed for Louisville.

After Speedy's less-than-stellar appearance at the 2002 Jubilee, I expected two things in the forty-one days, which remained until the U.S. Nationals, that Tyler would concentrate on Speedy's training and that the intervening time would be uneventful. I couldn't have been more wrong.

Shortly after the Jubilee Show, Tyler called with news that knocked the ground out from under me. He had a buyer for Speedy. I had anticipated going to the Nationals as Speedy's owner and offering my horse for sale there. It simply hadn't occurred to me a buyer might appear beforehand. My thoughts were a jumble as I tried to process the new development.

I said, "Tyler, you already know that I'm not going to take Speedy away from you before the Nationals, so, what is this about?"

Tyler told me the interested party was already a client of his, so he would still show Speedy, only for a new owner. The client, he said, was in a hurry to acquire Speedy, so they could enjoy the glamour of attending Nationals with a serious title contender.

I'd only met a few of Tyler's clients, and I tried to imagine who among them might have the means and motivation to buy Speedy. There was Rhonda Mueller, who seemed like an accomplished amateur horsewoman, but, she had just purchased a stud named Khookaburra Bey from Tyler, and they seemingly had plans to collaborate on breeding and promoting that stallion.

Then, there was Mickey Ambrose, who, Tyler said, had recently come into a considerable inheritance, a fact he related rather gleefully, as though he planned to help her spend it. Mickey had a couple of horses at Tyler's, including a stallion named Rock Steady Baby, so neither she nor Rhonda seemed like candidates.

In any case, Tyler wouldn't reveal the name of the buyer to me when I asked. He was calling to get a price from me, and he would act as intermediary. That's what I'd anticipated from the beginning. Tyler would be my agent, take a commission on the sale, and would be knowledgeable about the current market for Arabian and Half- Arabian horses.

But, I was surprised because Tyler wouldn't give me any guidance on the asking price. He said, "That's for you to decide."

I reminded Tyler I was a newcomer to the Arabian show world and needed his assistance precisely in matters like pricing my horse. However, he was adamant. I would have to name my price.

I phoned Gigi, who had recently sold a big, bold Half-Arabian Hunter for $22,000, and asked her opinion. She put Speedy in the

$25,000-30,000 range. I also recalled Tyler's comments about Broadway Bey Bee, the horse Tyler professed would be a rival to Speedy at the Nationals. According to Tyler, Broadway Bey Bee was not Speedy's equal, but had sold for $22,500.

When I called Tyler back and put Speedy's price at $25,000, he hit the roof. He said, "Half-Arabians don't sell for that kind of money!"

That ran counter to the industry scuttlebutt I'd picked up along the way. One of the reasons for creating the Half-Arabian registry was to revitalize the marketplace. The prices for purebred Arabians were down, but Half-Arabians were selling well.

I stuck to my price. Tyler could begin shopping Speedy to the potential buyer at $25,000. I figured if my horse didn't sell that year at that price, he would sell for $25,000, or more, somewhere down the road.

Grudgingly, Tyler agreed to enter negotiations with the buyer. Acting as the go-between, Tyler called me several times. Then, on the buyer's behalf, Tyler asked if I could come down on the price. I dropped to $20,000, but still the deal didn't close.

I began to get nervous about the situation and asked Tyler to identify the purported buyer. Speedy was not going to be for sale to just anyone, certainly not to some fly-by-nighter, who was trying to lowball me on the price.

Under pressure, Tyler revealed the buyer was Rhonda Mueller. I'd observed Rhonda with her horses at T&T. And, she was one of Speedy's admirers at his yearling debut. I felt comfortable with the idea of Rhonda owning Speedy. Nevertheless, no financial arrangement was forthcoming, and the Nationals were looming. Finally, I told Tyler to break off the discussion with Rhonda. We would go to Louisville to look for a buyer.

In mid-September, Tyler called again. He wanted permission to spend money on what he called a *tune-up* for Speedy. I asked what that entailed and how much it would cost. Tyler said Speedy would be treated by a practitioner of acupuncture and equine chiropractic. The appointment would simply ensure Speedy was in optimum health going into the Nationals.

Although Mike and I were strapped for money, and I was anticipating the expense of Nationals, I approved what sounded like a holistic appointment if it could be done for no more than $100. When I again heard from Tyler, it was not about the tune-up appointment. It was something very worrisome.

On September 30, 2002, Tyler phoned to say Speedy had experienced a problem. He reported, during the morning feeding, his father, Tom Wragge, noted Speedy was standing off-kilter. Horses will assume uncharacteristic positions when they are trying to relieve pain in their hooves, legs, or back, so an unusual stance can be a tip off something is wrong.

Upon hearing this, my heart froze in my chest. But, as Tyler related the day's events, my fears were assuaged. On the chance the problem might be inflammation in the front hooves, Tyler had placed Speedy's legs in buckets of ice. He was unable to get a veterinarian to respond right away, but, Tyler said, a horseshoer had come out and inserted a product called Equilox into the front hooves in the event the problem was laminitis.

I knew a bit about laminitis, although I'd usually heard it referred to by the old horsemen's term *founder*. I'd learned early on founder and colic are the diseases most feared by horseowners.

In the case of laminitis, many of the causes have been known for years. Grain overload is one of the causes first-time horseowners are warned of. Keep the grain supply securely out of reach of horses. If they get into the grain, horses will gorge, and very likely will founder.

Lush springtime grass can also cause a horse to founder, as can obesity, improper shoeing, black walnut shavings, colic, Cushing's Disease, and prolonged or rigorous exercise on hard surfaces. That was about as much as I knew about laminitis at the time. I'd always implemented preventive measures and never had a horse founder.

However, I'd seen how horrific the final outcome of laminitis could be. A negligent horseowner had an old horse, which was put out to pasture and not inspected on a regular basis. The old-timer had grass-foundered. The hard exterior of the left front hoof completely detached and was found lying on the ground. The stumpy remainder of the foot looked like a cigarette ash. Without the protection of the hoof wall, the stump had gotten infected. The poison traveled up the leg into the shoulder, and the whole left side of the horse's forequarters was feverish and grossly swollen.

There was absolutely no hope for the old horse. Any intercession, which could have saved its life, was long past due. It was an image of suffering I'll never forget.

The process, which led to that disastrous outcome, began in the *laminae*, tubular blood-supplying structures between the hoof wall and the tissue and bones that comprise the interior of the equine foot. The laminae act as adhesive for cementing the inside of the hoof to the hard exterior wall.

When the laminae become inflamed, blood flow retreats, the adhesion begins to fail, and the interior of the hoof starts to separate from the exterior. The *coffin bone* within the hoof is what the horse stands upon. During the progression of laminar retreat, the coffin bone changes position. This is referred to as *rotation.*

The painful rotation process can escalate to the point where the coffin bone tips forward and drops through the sole of the hoof. X-rays can track the angle of the coffin bone and seriousness of rotation. But, if laminitis isn't detected and treated in a timely fashion, the horse may have to be put down.

Since laminitis tends to reoccur after an initial incidence, it becomes very problematic in a showhorse. The onset of a bout of laminitis at a show far from home or in transit compounds the seriousness of the disease, so, even a case of laminitis that is successfully treated, may be a career-ender for a showhorse.

Thus, when Tyler said the horseshoer inserted Equilox to prevent rotation, I was particularly attentive.

"How does the product work?" I asked. Tyler said Equilox was a putty, which could be packed into the hoof, hardens quickly, and manually forestalls the process of rotation.

"Has there been rotation?" I asked. Tyler assured me there hadn't been. The insertion of Equilox had just been a precaution.

"Are we dealing with laminitis?" I asked. Laminitis is progressive, therefore, rotation is not necessarily a first stage. Tyler assured me we were not dealing with laminitis.

Later in the afternoon, he said, a veterinarian had seen Speedy and my horse was much better, quite comfortable in fact.

"On a scale of one to ten, with ten being where Speedy was this morning," said Tyler, "He's about a one now."

That still left two questions: What was the problem? And, what did it portend for the Nationals, which were eleven days away?

Transient lameness issues like stone bruises, abscesses, muscle strains, and the like, are not uncommon in horses. Indeed, Tyler floated terms like *protein soreness* and *laminitis flare-up* to account for Speedy's problem.

I consulted with the Home Team, Dr. Penny and J.T., as I did about all the major events in Speedy's unfolding adventure. I related to them what I'd been told. We all agreed, if it wasn't laminitis, there was a good chance Speedy might be fully recovered and able to go to the Nationals. *Wait and see* was the consensus we reached.

After the first of October, when bills for the month of September began to arrive, I received two unexpected invoices. I was accustomed to reimbursing Tyler for all Speedy's expenses, so additional charges, arriving separately, came as a surprise. The amounts were shocking.

First, there was an invoice of $725 from someone named Dr. Lance Albright for work done September 30, the day when Tyler reported Speedy had a lameness problem. The amount seemed pretty steep, and the bill wasn't itemized, but, I was grateful a veterinarian had reduced Speedy's problem from a ten in the morning to a one in the evening, as Tyler told me.

Who was Dr. Albright? I wondered. Owing to contacts I'd made by writing for Ohio horse publications, I could usually find an acquaintance in any given area when I needed information. I phoned a contact who lived where Dr. Albright practiced, and asked for an opinion.

"Oh, he's a fine fellow," my contact reported, "His father was a vet we used until he retired, and now we patronize his son."

With the assurance I was dealing with a good guy, I phoned Dr. Albright's office, requested a payment plan of $100 per month and was accepted.

The second invoice was from a Dr. Linus Weed for $325 for services on September 23, one week prior to the emergency Dr. Albright responded to. Dr. Weed's bill had several unfamiliar notations. It read: "DEPO HOCKS, DEPO STIFLES, DEPO RF ANKLE, IB HIPS, BUTE INJECTION, ROMPUN INJECTION" as well as exam and farm call charges.

The notations were perplexing. What was the bill for? It didn't seem to have anything to do with acupuncture and chiropractic, the only procedures I had approved. The references to Bute and Rompun caused concern.

Bute is short for *phenylbutazone*, an equine pain medication comparable to human Tylenol that most horseowners usually have on hand in tablet form to treat horses for muscle soreness. Injectible Bute is a more serious matter. And, Rompun, I seemed to recall, was a drug used as part of euthanasia. What was IB HIPS? And, Depo, what was that?

I phoned Dr. Weed's office and spoke to a secretary, who identified herself as Linda. She said she wasn't familiar with Dr. Weed's notations, but speculated Depo was "something like cortisone."

Cortisone? At the mention of the powerful drug, which restored the use of my arm, I was aghast. I recalled the intense discomfort of the cortisone burn. I thought a horse, subjected to the prolonged fiery sensation, would be driven to distraction. And, why had that cortisone-like Depo been injected into so many of Speedy's joints?

I phoned Tyler in a state of fury and anxiety and demanded to know the meaning of the bill from Dr. Weed. Tyler listened calmly while I vented. He was remarkably unruffled by my diatribe and answered coolly and without hesitation. The bill was a paperwork error. Tyler said, "We did a lot of horses that day."

Tyler explained, Dr. Weed just mixed up Speedy with other horses, which had been worked on that day. Speedy hadn't been given Depo, or cortisone, or anything for that matter. Furthermore, Tyler said, it was not the first time sloppy records-keeping on the part of Dr. Weed had upset his clients. He was almost chuckling as he recalled a time when Dr. Weed had mistakenly billed one of his other clients for $1500. Tyler said he'd gotten an angry phone call that day, too.

The billing error, Tyler assured me, would be corrected before the Nationals, if time permitted. In the event he was too busy preparing Speedy and other horses for the big show, then he would correct Dr. Weed's billing as soon as he returned from the Nationals.

Shortly after that episode, Tyler reported Speedy was sound and ready to be shipped to the 2002 U.S. Nationals.

Chapter 7

"We did a lot of horses that day," Tyler said. What did that mean?

Nothing was done to Speedy, he claimed, yet Dr. Weed got my horse mixed up with someone else's and billed me by mistake. How could that be?

If Dr. Weed's record-keeping had caused Tyler problems in the past, why hadn't he switched to another veterinarian?

Why didn't I ask those questions and many more? Why didn't I add up my dissatisfactions with the Jubilee Show, and Tyler's evasiveness in handling the purported sale, and the mysterious brief lameness situation, and, then, the so-called mistaken billing? Why didn't I get suspicious?

The fact was my mind was often elsewhere. As exciting as Speedy's quest was, those events coincided with a more compelling and tragic drama, my father's losing struggle with Alzheimer's Disease.

The year Speedy was born, 1999, was the same year Dad was diagnosed with Alzheimer's. Nevertheless, he still planned to make his annual visit to Ohio. He was anxious to see the colt we were so keen on. But, Mike and I could both see the disease was already attacking my father's ability to think and to remember.

After what was to be Dad's final visit, Alzheimer's continued its relentless assault on his mind. I made several trips to Florida at times when Speedy was in training with Tyler. I felt grief and guilt that I was merely commuting to see my father, rather than helping on a daily basis. When

I was in Florida, I tried to be fully present for my Dad and to disconnect from other concerns.

Since I was only a visitor in my father's life, the burden of Dad's care was shouldered by his second wife, Doris. The two of them were touchingly devoted to each other. She was a tiny dynamo, who had lavished Dad with affection in the best of times, and the alternation of their circumstances hadn't changed that.

Eventually, Dad's physical needs were more than Doris could manage. She found a care facility for Dad near their home where she could visit him twice a day. But, it was possible Dad, who was still having lucid periods, could live for many more years.

Mike and I considered selling the farm in Ohio and moving to Florida. In addition to Dad's situation, my mother, who also lived in Florida, was nearing eighty years old and would soon need help. On one of my southern trips, I investigated the price of horse property and feed costs in the area where my parents lived. They were prohibitive. If Mike and I moved, we would have to sell our horses.

While Mike and I contemplated what we should do, we tried to carry on with our dreams for Speedy. The time was fast approaching when our emotional and financial investment in him could pay off. What happened with Speedy at the Nationals could change everything.

The morning of October 11, 2002, I was up early and packed the truck with my overnight bag for the trip to Louisville, Kentucky. The 36th Annual U.S. Nationals Arabian and Half-Arabian Championship Horse Show officially began that day and would run through October19th. Tyler had phoned a few days earlier to say he was leaving his facility at T&T Stables for Louisville, he had outfitted Speedy's stall in the horse trailer with extra stall mats to guarantee a cushy, comfortable ride, and Speedy was in excellent shape.

Fortunately for my peace of mind, Mike and I had houseguests, who were experienced horse people. I could relax knowing our other horses and the farm were in good hands while I was gone. I wouldn't be away long in any case. Speedy's class on October 12th would be one of two qualifying classes that day, which chose horses to advance to the finals for the Half-Arabian Western Pleasure Futurity on October 15th. If our luck went that way, I would come home for a couple of days and return for the finals.

The site for the Nationals was the Kentucky Fair and Exposition Center, which occupied an area of Louisville that included the airport and Churchill Downs, the home of the Kentucky Derby. The Exposition Center, like its Ohio counterpart, was a featureless concrete monolith surrounded by parking lots. I drove around until I found the entrance to Freedom Hall, the indoor stadium, which served as the Main Ring for the horse show.

Once inside, I searched among rows and rows of portable horse stalls trying to locate Tyler and Speedy. The ornamentation of stalls and the glitz and ballyhoo I'd seen at The Buckeye were more extravagant at the Nationals. Everywhere were gorgeous, impeccably groomed horses, kids in tailor-made riding outfits, adults turned out in equine finery, costly saddles and bridles, lavishly decorated lounges where the elite could seek repose, and vendors offering all manner of horse-related goods and services.

The atmosphere fairly screamed wealth, opulence, excess, and an abundance of discretionary income. Because I knew McKenna and some of her friends, I understood not everyone, who competed at Class A, was super rich. There were participants, who had to work and budget to support their hobby. But, the outward impression generated by the stabling area of the U.S. Nationals, one year after 9/11, was that the gravy boat was full to the brim and couldn't be tipped over.

Finally, I spotted the stall drapes of Tyler Wragge Elite Horses and entered the curtains. There was Speedy. He'd been body clipped recently so his normally russet-toned coat had the subdued color of an antique gold coin. My beautiful golden boy was standing in his stall and mechanically munching on contents of a hay net. I rushed to the stall grating and called his name. I was joyful at seeing him. Surely, he'd return the greeting. But, Speedy seemed oblivious to me.

Tyler appeared, and we exchanged greetings. He said Speedy was creating a buzz at the show, and he'd had a couple purchase inquiries. If that were the case, it was all the more important my horse make a good impression in the showring. I asked, "How is Speedy doing?"

Though they had been there a couple days, Tyler said he hadn't yet worked Speedy in the Freedom Hall arena. I suppressed a rush of anger.

Dammit, Tyler, I thought, *This is what we've been working towards for three years. Speedy's class is tomorrow and you still haven't prepared him. What the hell are you thinking?*

At the Jubilee Show, I'd forgiven Tyler's failure to school Speedy in the Main Ring because he had quite a few clients. But, that didn't seem to be the case at the Nationals. He was showing a stallion for clients, and there were only a few other horses in his stabling area. (Whenever his other clients were around, they gave me the cold shoulder, something I wrote off as horseshow snootiness.)Tyler also mentioned that he was *catch-riding*, that is, making extra money by riding horses for other people.

Since my horse was supposed to be Tyler's ticket to the big time, Speedy should have been Priority One for Tyler. Why the hell was he letting things go until the last minute?

I didn't express my frustration, but, Tyler may have felt anger radiating from me. He quickly offered to demonstrate how well Speedy was doing by working him on a long *lunge* line in a nearby practice arena.

As Tyler led Speedy through the crowded aisle-ways, amid the hustle and bustle of people and horses coming and going, I marveled at how calm Speedy was. His experience was limited, but, he seemed like an old horseshow trooper.

The practice arena was being used by quite a few riders, who were mostly doing trot and canter work on the rail. In the center, however, there seemed to be enough room to lunge a horse. Tyler took Speedy into the unused part of the arena.

Suddenly, Speedy reared on his hind legs. He didn't seem to be frightened, and I expected Tyler would reprimand Speedy and make him work. Instead, Tyler led Speedy out of the arena and mumbled, "It's too busy in there."

By that time, it was late afternoon. Tyler said he was going to practice ride Speedy in the Main Ring later. I would like to have seen that, but, I still hadn't located the motel where I'd reserved a room and wanted to do that while it was still daylight.

Speedy's qualifying class the next day would be among the classes, which followed the lunch break. I told Tyler I would see him then. I stroked Speedy's neck and said goodnight. My horse still didn't acknowledge me.

The next morning I checked out of the motel early. Since I might never be in Louisville again, I wanted to get in a quick bit of sightseeing, which would also serve to calm my nerves. I drove around downtown Louisville and checked out the Bardstown Road area. Heading back towards the Expo Center, I spotted the famous twin spires of Churchill Downs and couldn't resist a closer look at the legendary horse racing mecca. One of the buildings housed the Kentucky Derby Museum. I paid my admission and went inside.

Among the displays was a screening room where museum goers could select and view memorable Kentucky Derbys, some recent and some with the grainy sepia color of Fox MovieTone news.

The old newsreels included names and races, which will live in memory as long as there are horsemen: Sir Barton. Gallant Fox. War Admiral. Whirlaway. Count Fleet. Citation. There were races I watched as a horse-obsessed kid: Swaps. Needles. Tim Tam. Northern Dancer. And, the incomparable Secretariat.

What horse-lover could ever forget the 1973 Belmont and the astonished sports announcer yelling, "Secretariat is blazing along!...Secretariat is widening now! He is moving like a TREMENDOUS machine!..."

So great was the appeal of the 1973 Triple Crown Winner, affectionately nicknamed "Big Red," that Secretariat was well-known even to the non-horse public. The super horse was featured on the covers of Time, Newsweek, and Sports Illustrated, and ESPN listed Secretariat among the one hundred greatest athletes of the 20th century.

After his racing career, Secretariat faded from the general public's attention but remained on the radar of horsemen, who knew Secretariat was retired to stud at Claiborne Farm, where he occupied the stall of his illustrious sire, Bold Ruler.

The only other horse in the same category as Secretariat was Man o' War whose racing career followed World War I. Man o' War lived to the ripe old age of thirty. Thus, it was sad to learn in 1980, Secretariat, at the age of nineteen, had to be euthanized owing to incurable laminitis. It speaks to the potential seriousness of laminitis that the most famous horse of the modern era could not be saved.

As I left the Kentucky Derby Museum, it was late morning. I headed for the Expo Center where I expected Speedy would begin to make his mark in the show world. I checked in with Tyler, then, went to watch a few classes, and to check out the offerings in the vendors' area. There was no point in hanging around Tyler's stalls. I would just be in the way, and it seemed clear I wasn't going to make any new friends among Tyler's aloof clients.

About 1 p.m., when the afternoon session was to get underway, I returned to Tyler's area. He and a lovely blonde teenager were grooming Speedy. Tyler introduced us, "Judy this is Shannon."

She gave me a chilly nod and continued with her work. Tyler stepped into the conversational gap by taking a blue object off a shelf and showing it to me. He said, "This is the Equilox that was put into Speedy's hoof the day he had that flare-up."

I assumed Tyler brought the object along as a curio, which might interest me. With the first section of the Western Pleasure Futurity so close at hand, I gave no thought to the blue object. Tyler and Shannon began saddling Speedy.

The equipment and fittings for Speedy were attractively coordinated with Tyler's clothing. A gilded black saddle was placed on a tan and black striped saddle blanket. The hackamore, woven rawhide bosal, and reins were black and tan as were Tyler's clothing choices. The ensemble was attractive and tastefully selected to highlight Speedy's coloring without detracting. I could hardly wait to see how it looked in motion.

I left Tyler and Shannon to finish their preparations and headed to Freedom Hall.

A Western Pleasure show class takes its inspiration from the traditions of cowboys and the American West. Riders wear Stetson-style hats and leather chaps. The horse carries a Western saddle that has a horn, which was and is used for roping and working with cattle. A rope or hobbles, also tools of a working cowboy, are optional and acceptable on the show saddle.

In the real West, all those items are likely to bear the patina of wear and work and the dirt and dust of ranch landscape. In the horseshow world, the West is highly stylized, and at the national championships level, the gear costs a fortune. A show saddle alone, made of hand-tooled leather and encrusted with silver mountings, may run to many thousands of dollars. It's kept spotlessly clean and is only put on the horse at show time.

The gaits called for in a Western Pleasure class are walk, jog, and lope. Those are slowed down versions of horses' natural gaits, walk, trot, and canter. The slower gaits come more naturally to the Quarter Horse, a breed developed for the cattle industry of the American West. The pokey constraints of Western Pleasure classes don't seem like a good fit for the natural movement and exuberance of Arabian horses, but, WP attracts many participants at the Arabian Class A level.

As I settled into a bleacher seat in Freedom Hall, I heard snippets of conversation from three people sitting in the row behind me. They sounded quite knowledgeable, and I was interested in some of their observations. But, my eyes were focused on the in-gate to the Main Ring.

As the Western Pleasure Futurity was announced, I expected Tyler to be among the first to enter the ring. He once told me he thought it gave a psychological edge to enter early, that doing so projected a sense of confidence. However, horse after horse entered the ring, but not mine. Tyler told me later he was delayed at the warm-up arena by people admiring Speedy.

The class announcer reported there were seventeen horses in the class. As they came slow jogging through the gate, there were a number of flashy paints, some dark bays, and finally, finally, a flaxen chestnut—Speedy. As the horses jogged around the ring, I saw Tyler had resolved the inattention and hesitancy in Speedy, which had marred my horse's performance at the Jubilee Show.

Speedy was completely on task. His neck was curved like a drawn bow, his head was firmly in place, his gaits were smooth and cadenced. And, he was so graceful. Speedy flowed across the ground. Unlike a number of horses in the ring, Speedy's hind legs reached well under himself and propelled him fluidly forward. His flaxen mane and tail, shimmering like corn silk, rippled with each stride.

I was transfixed by the moment I'd awaited for so long.

One of the people in the threesome behind me made a remark that caught my attention. She said, "Now that taffy horse is something special."

Taffy horse? Quickly I checked the color of all the horses in the ring. Taffy could only be Speedy. Something special, she said. I thought my heart would burst with excitement and pride.

The class took forever and yet mere moments. I tried to drag my eyes off Speedy and assess the other horses. But I kept coming back to Speedy. Tyler was riding beautifully. At times, he'd take the rail, then, he'd look for a place to ride through the other contestants and present Speedy to the best advantage for the three judges.

How I envied Tyler his place on Speedy's back. I could see how comfortable my horse was to ride. While his legs worked beneath his body, Speedy's back was level and still. I imagined the thrill when Speedy came home after Nationals, and I could ride him for the first time myself.

The ring announcer called for the lineup. The riders brought their mounts to a walk and stood abreast forming a long line down the middle of the arena. The judges walked down the line, asked the riders to back their horses, gave the entries a final look, and retired to the booth in center ring to mark their cards.

The horses, which would advance, were called according to the number pinned to their rider's back, from lowest to highest number. I had forgotten to note Tyler's number, and he was facing forward in the lineup. The ring announcer said eight of the seventeen horses would be advancing. As number after number was called, I kept thinking, "Maybe they will get to Tyler's number now."

Horse after horse was announced, till it got to six, seven, eight, but not Tyler and Speedy. While the eight qualifiers jogged a victory lap, the others exited the arena. Tyler must have slipped away quickly. I didn't even see him leave.

My mind whirled with confusion. How was it possible we had not even gotten to first base? Had Tyler and I been mistaken about Speedy's quality? Had Speedy's gaits been too fast? Had I missed something? As a newcomer, that was certainly possible, but, the trio behind me had noted Speedy's charisma. I hadn't imagined that.

I hurriedly made my way to Tyler's stalls. Speedy had already been untacked and was back in his stall. I said to Tyler, "What happened?"

Tyler told me Speedy made a hard transition from the lope down to the jog at the end of the class, re-instigated soreness in his right front hoof, and stumbled. The judges had caught the lameness. For a moment, Tyler expressed frustration at Speedy. He said, "You'd think he could have sucked it up for one class."

After that flash of bitterness, Tyler got his emotions in check. He looked at the ground for awhile. Then, wistfully, he said, "He's the best horse I've ever ridden."

I was already in a state of shock. As usual, I couldn't corral the stampede of my thoughts and render coherent questions. I listened mutely as Tyler began a litany of explanations, which seemed to come from outer space.

He said horses sired by Imperial V were proving to have faulty hooves, and the same was true of horses sired by a stallion named Instigator V, who was a full brother of Imperial V.

Tyler said Ronnie Borland, one of the top Western Pleasure trainers, who was riding Stage Right, a stallion sired by Imperial V, had complained to him during the Nationals about Stage Right, saying the stud had weak hooves that couldn't hold up under the work required of a showhorse.

I knew Stage Right was a product of Gordon Meriwether's breeding operation. I also knew Stage Right was standing at stud at Borland's training facility. Was Tyler suggesting Borland was knowingly standing a stallion Borland believed had a serious genetic flaw? That didn't sound right.

Tyler then outlined problems Speedy was having, which he hadn't mentioned to me earlier. He pointed out Speedy's sheath, the fleshy channel where the equine penis is retracted, was swollen. Tyler said Speedy had been peeing frequently and doing so inside his sheath, causing irritation.

Was this an indication of a kidney problem, I asked. Had the drugs given to Speedy during the mysterious lameness episode caused urinary problems?

Tyler didn't know, but promised he would have Speedy fully checked out by the official show vet, who he called "Dr. Sam."

He then proceeded to argue in favor of Speedy returning to his parents' T&T Stables for rest and rehabilitation. Tyler claimed to be particularly good at overcoming lameness issues, and he invoked a familiar name, Kiss Me Kate.

It was Tyler's success with Speedy's half-sister, Kiss Me Kate, when the mare was owned by McKenna Jamison, which first drew my attention to Tyler. When I brought Speedy as a yearling to Tyler, Kate had been sold by McKenna but was still in Tyler's barn. At that time, Tyler anticipated having both Speedy and Kate in his show string, a one-two punch that would surely propel him to the big time, he thought.

However, Kate's new owner suddenly took the mare out of Tyler's care. When I asked why Kate was gone, Tyler told me the new owner was a know-it-all woman, who had unfounded grievances against him, a charge, which echoed his characterization of McKenna.

As part of his argument for rehabbing Speedy at T&T, Tyler said Kate's owner was sending the mare back to him. According to Tyler, an apprentice for a big name trainer had mishandled Kate so badly, the once push-button showhorse needed to be retrained. Kate's owner finally realized his value. He said smugly, "They all come back to Uncle Tyler."

Tyler's remarks tended to revive the idea he'd already implanted; bad trainers were out there causing harm and he was still holding out against those practices. However, the more compelling argument for letting Tyler keep custody of Speedy was forming in my own mind. Winter was not far off. I didn't have facilities, which would allow me to properly rehab Speedy, even with the help of the Home Team of J.T. and Dr. Penny.

Speedy had a large comfortable stall in the barn, but, my outdoor arena, where careful exercise and observation of Speedy's progress would have to occur, was often covered over with a sheet of ice. Indeed, one winter an apron of glare ice formed all the way around the barn. For fear of a horse slipping and breaking a leg, I'd kept all the horses inside for ten days until a thaw relieved the situation.

I agreed to allow Speedy to return to Tyler's for the winter months. Before leaving for the long drive home, I made it clear to Tyler Speedy was to be examined by a vet, I must be informed of the results immediately, and, I must be kept up-to-date on his condition despite whatever other duties Tyler had for the remainder of the Nationals.

Those were all perfectly reasonable expectations, and Tyler agreed. Once again, I was leaving valuable property in his care, property that now required special attention, so, of course, he would phone soon and often, Tyler said.

Chapter 8

The phone didn't ring. Days went by and I heard nothing. Our houseguests, who were undergoing frequent delays in the construction of a new home, were often on the phone. A welter of notepaper with phone numbers and jotted information from their contractor lay next to the phone. But, none of the incoming calls was from Tyler.

I was frantic with worry. I had inquired about Tyler's cell phone number before I left Louisville, but, he claimed it wasn't working. I cursed the lack of communication. I considered hooking up our horse trailer and driving to Kentucky to pick up Speedy. However, the trailer's lights weren't operating properly, and I feared creating a scene. I consoled myself some of the best veterinarians in the world must be in Kentucky, and surely Tyler was attending to Speedy, even if he wasn't calling.

Finally, I remembered the program for U.S. Nationals listed a phone number for the show office. I called the number and explained to an office staffer I wanted to have a message delivered to Tyler Wragge, saying I really needed to talk to him.

Instead of relaying a handwritten note with my phone number, a message went over the PA system that Tyler Wragge had an emergency back at the farm. Or so Tyler said when he called me in a furious mood. He ranted the message had embarrassed him and made him look bad.

My mental response was: *You irresponsible jerk! If you were doing what you are supposed to, I wouldn't have to be chasing you down in whatever way I can.*

As usual, civility triumphed over candor. There was no point in confronting Tyler with the exasperation I was finally allowing myself to feel. He had my horse, and, if biting my tongue ensured good care for Speedy, then, I certainly needed to do that.

However, good care for Speedy did not seem to be a high priority for Tyler. I asked what the veterinary exam had revealed regarding kidney problems. Tyler said Dr. Sam had cleaned Speedy's sheath.

That was it?

I was seething about the lack of medical follow-up. From the tone of the phone call, I believed Tyler felt Speedy had let him down and he had no further use or regard for my horse. My brain was reeling with frustration, and my heart longed for Speedy.

I tried to talk myself through the jumble of emotions. *Be sensible,* I told myself. *If I go racing down to Louisville and try to remove Speedy, what might happen? What if Tyler raised an objection and refused to release Speedy to me? If I could collect my horse, would I be able to load Speedy into the trailer by myself and safely transport him home?*

Perhaps Tyler and I were both overheated by disappointment. Perhaps things would look better when we cooled down. Perhaps decisions should be postponed. Perhaps, for now, it was best to stick to the plan that Tyler rehab Speedy at T&T Stables.

Before concluding our phone call, Tyler raised another issue. He claimed a couple potential buyers had approached him about purchasing Speedy. What price, he asked, would I accept now?

For a moment, the vague misgivings, which had passed through my mind at various times, came close to forming a clear thought and that was: *I'm being lied to.*

No horse person I'd ever encountered shopped for their next purchase among lame horses. True, Tyler was still maintaining Speedy's health and lameness issues were not serious, but, it just didn't sound right that a horse, who had limped out of the Main Ring, would still be sought after—unless it was for a bargain basement price.

I told Tyler, "I would never knowingly sell a sick or lame horse to anyone. Until Speedy is fully recovered and I can sell him in good conscience, I won't consider selling him."

After the unsatisfactory conversation with Tyler, I phoned J.T. and Dr. Penny yet again. I had already notified the Home Team about the sad outcome of the Western Pleasure class.

J. T., who'd handled Speedy's feet every six weeks for three years, said he'd never had reason to think the hooves were weak, or incapable of performing reasonable work. While the quality of hooves varies among horses, said J.T., the job of a good horseshoer is to mitigate deficiencies. He wasn't aware of a genetic link for hooves so grave the horses couldn't be used.

Following the input from J.T., I contacted Natasha Smoak and queried her about Tyler's claim of faulty hooves. She angrily denied the charge. I located the owner of Instigator V, the full brother to Imperial V, who likewise denied the offspring of his stallion were having hoof problems.

Dr. Penny shared my disappointment at the outcome of the Nationals, but, mainly she was perplexed about the on-again-off-again lameness issue. The symptoms seemed to suggest laminitis. But, Tyler had two vets examine Speedy in late September, and, apparently, they didn't diagnose laminitis or Tyler surely would have relayed that to me. And, if Tyler suspected laminitis, he certainly wouldn't have taken Speedy to the Nationals, would he? That would be like taking a race car with flat tires to the Daytona 500.

Circumspect by nature, and a cautious medical professional, Dr. Penny may have had suspicions she didn't share with me. She opined Speedy might be *tying-up*, the only condition apart from laminitis, which might account for the symptoms, but, her tone sounded dubious. When I told her about Tyler's claim of purported buyers at the Nationals, who were interested in Speedy, she said, "There's something fishy about all this."

The Nationals ended October 19th. Allowing for a couple of days to transport horses and equipment back to Ohio, I phoned T&T Stables and made an appointment to see Tyler and Speedy soon after their arrival. I went on October 23, 2002.

My horse was in his stall and looked fabulous. Even better, he acknowledged me and welcomed my affection. Tyler reported Speedy was still sore on his right hoof but was already recovering. With a period of stall rest and a few tablets of Bute, the usual treatment for moderate soreness, Tyler said Speedy would soon be "right as rain."

That I would not be Speedy's only visitor that day was something Tyler didn't mention. Nor was Kiss Me Kate back in Tyler's care as he had claimed at the Nationals.

When the first week of November came, so did another invoice from Dr. Linus Weed. Tyler did say he would get the erroneous billing corrected before the Nationals if time allowed or afterwards when his schedule was less hectic. I assumed the latter was the case and set the bill aside.

Additionally, Tyler's invoice for the month of October arrived, including his charges for the Nationals. Among the items were two charges for horseshoeing totaling $275 with dates that seemed odd. There was also a billing from "Sam Hawkins, DVM" for $350. If all Dr. Sam did was clean Speedy's sheath, that charge was way out of line.

Before I could begin sorting through the paperwork, Doris called. My father had suffered another medical setback, which further empowered the Alzheimer's. Doris believed Dad was at a point where he would soon lose the ability to recognize any of us even for short periods. Come home, she said.

I quickly arranged for our houseguests to feed and water the horses. My brother, who lived in British Columbia, booked a flight to Florida. And, Doris's three grown children, who had adopted my father as their own, also gathered.

We all took turns visiting the nursing home and spending time with Dad. For the most part, he was happily unaware of us. Happily may seem an inappropriate description, but, Dad had a sunny disposition that was so much a part of him, the disease, which can render its victims angry and difficult to manage, could not conquer his essence.

Now and again Dad's habitual cordiality would drain away, and he would recognize someone in the family fleetingly. I saw his eyes alight when he turned to me. During my visits, we had a few brief moments of connection, of recognition and reunion, and, then, his mind resumed its retreat.

A fragment from the writings of J. Frank Dobie drummed through my head continuously. Dobie was a Texan, an English professor, and writer on Southwestern history and folklore. In a few sentences, Dobie described the stage in a horseowner's life when Time is taking its toll, when friends and loved ones are passing away, and one is pondering what remains to remember and cherish.

He wrote that a man, who knows what it is to have ridden a good horse, remembers it as "a certitude amid the flickering vanishments."

The flickering vanishments. I thought I'd never read anything so perfectly coined, so complete, so sad. My father was flickering out of my life. Some of my childhood friends were dead. Doris and my mother were aging senior citizens. Mike's health was being diminished by the relentless demands of his job. And, I had begun to calculate my own life expectancy in terms of what I still needed to do in the time that was left.

The part of me that was tuned into the life of my country, also felt a flickering out of the American way of life as my parents and my generation had known it.

In mid-November, I returned from Florida. I phoned T&T Stables to set up an appointment to see Speedy. Tina Wragge answered the call. She informed me her son Tyler was away on business. Then she cheerily offered that Speedy was doing fine, and, she and Tom were administering his meds and injections.

Meds and injections? I thought Speedy was on stall rest and Bute. I asked Tina for clarification and she began to waffle. She was just following Tyler's instructions, she said nervously, just doing what she was told. I'd have to take matters up with Tyler when he returned.

That call was unsettling but the next phone call relating to Speedy was devastating.

On Friday, November 29th , the phone rang late in the evening. Mike usually called from the road about 11 p.m. to say good night. This call was earlier than Mike's usual call, but rather late for a social call. Our houseguests had already gone to bed, and I felt alarm as I picked up the receiver.

The caller identified himself as Dr. Linus Weed. He wanted to know why I hadn't paid his bill. I explained Tyler said a mix-up had occurred, that Speedy had not received the Depo injections I was being billed for, and that Tyler was supposed to have cleared up the mistake.

Dr. Weed said he would check his computer records, if I would hold. When he came back on the line, he said his bill was not in error. The charges for injections into five of Speedy's joints represented the work he'd performed on September 23, 2002.

I was immobile with disbelief. I could scarcely breathe, let alone speak. As Dr. Weed's assurances sank in, wave after wave of outrage, betrayal, and fear swept over me. Tyler had blatantly lied to me time and time again about the injections. *What else? What else had he lied about?*

I tried to call upon my experience in the newspaper business to get me through the call. I groped about for pen and paper to make notes. I'd never been a great interviewer, but, I'd learned silence on my part often prompted the interview subject to fill the gaps with their own comments. I hoped that might be the case because I was practically gagging with shock.

Dr. Weed responded to the silence. He said, "Maybe Tyler meant to pay for the injections."

He went on to say Speedy "had a little rotation early on, about one or two degrees" but, he'd examined Speedy two days ago, on Wednesday, and Speedy was "ready to go back to work."

Rotation? ROTATION!

"My God," I prayed frantically, "Don't let me faint."

Rotation was *de facto* laminitis. And what was "early on"? Was rotation what happened on September 30th? What Tyler called a laminitis flare-up or protein soreness? What Tyler denied repeatedly?

As best I could, I kept my emotions in check. I didn't know what role Dr. Weed had played. He had not obtained my permission to treat my horse. He just alluded to the possibility Tyler meant to pay for the injections. Shouldn't that have tipped him off Tyler might be exceeding his authority?

Had the two of them made a side deal? And, what was the nature of Depo? I only had the sense from Dr. Weed's secretary, Linda, Depo was like cortisone.

To buy some time while I scribbled notes, I asked Dr. Weed to talk about causes of laminitis. He identified high blood sugar levels as the primary reason, in his opinion, for founder. In a laboratory situation, he said, experimentally-induced founder could be brought on by high sugar.

I related to Dr. Weed the daily feeding schedule Tyler described to me at the Jubilee Show, which was fourteen to sixteen pounds of grain and a bale and a half of second cutting alfalfa. Dr. Weed said, "Feed correlates with sugar in the blood. [The diet fed by Tyler] may be a predisposing factor."

Dr. Weed concluded his comments on the causes of laminitis without referencing any other possible causes, and returned to the subject of his unpaid bill. I told him I wouldn't consider payment until I understood how Speedy came to be treated without my knowledge or permission. Perhaps he should follow up on his own suggestion at the outset of his call, if Tyler Wragge meant to pay for the injections, he could phone Tyler about payment, I said.

After hanging up, I sat by the phone and felt whole chunks of my sanity were crumbling. I ran my memories backwards trying to find the places where I should have seen something, should have known, should have trusted my gut feelings.

McKenna Jamison's passionate attempt to warn me about Tyler reared up. I cringed with shame and regret.

When so many lies had been told, what was the truth? What was Speedy's real condition? I clung to Dr. Weed's assertion Speedy was ready to go back to work. *Maybe, just maybe, Speedy was okay. Maybe there had been a small problem that was now cured. After all, a doctor of veterinary medicine had just said so.*

I rechecked notes I made during the call and added several more. I put the sheets of notepaper in a shoebox where I stashed paperwork, receipts, show programs, and memorabilia related to Speedy.

When my horse had performed so brilliantly as a yearling at the Jubilee Show, my writer's instincts were stirred. I thought Speedy's destiny and my time with him might have the makings of a nice publishable Cinderella story, so I saved everything. As I placed my notes in the shoebox, I had a sinking feeling I had believed for too long in fairy tales.

The phone rang again. It was Mike calling to say goodnight. I told him, "Something is terribly wrong. We have to go get Speedy as soon as possible."

I outlined what I'd learned from Dr. Weed's call, that Speedy had received injections for something and had rotation at some point. And, Tyler withheld all that from me. Mike's rage was quick and intense.

"I'll beat that sonofabitch to a pulp," he said.

I had no doubt he meant it. In the world Mike inhabited most of the week, the gritty dangerous world of hard-bitten truck drivers hauling heavy loads up and down the interstates, frontier justice still prevailed.

At that moment, Speedy was my main concern, not Tyler. A brawl might just complicate everything. I told Mike, "We have got to get Speedy out of there right away. We can't accomplish that if you get hauled off to jail."

We agreed to notify Tyler we were coming for Speedy and to act as though nothing was out of the ordinary. It was the end of the month, so Tyler might conclude we had just decided to cut corners financially by bringing our horse home.

I was concerned Tyler might not release Speedy. I owed him $1,845.00 for board and expenses from the Nationals. I had two credit cards with small lines of credit I held in reserve to cover emergencies. I would have to charge the outstanding amount to one of the cards. If Tyler demanded cash, we were sunk.

Mike drove all night to get home and arrived looking haggard and hair-triggered. I cautioned him again to stay cool. We hooked up the pickup and horse trailer and made the trip to T&T Stables in fretful silence.

Tyler had gotten my phone message and greeted us with creepy composure. He didn't ask why we were unexpectedly retrieving our property. He didn't ask what our future plans were for Speedy or ask whether he'd be a part of those plans. He was emotionally flat and unflustered.

Had Dr. Weed relayed my position to Tyler? That I wasn't going to pay his bill without an explanation. That if Tyler had approved procedures without my consent, then Tyler could damn well pay the bill. Tyler's icy composure gave me no hints.

Tyler and Mike walked back to Speedy's stall. Tyler put a halter on Speedy and led him down the aisle-way. He showed Mike Speedy could walk a straight line without showing lameness, but, if asked to turn right or left, Speedy would limp.

That was a horse Dr. Weed had examined a few days earlier and declared in his phone call was ready to go back to work. *Ready to go back to work as what? A lamp post?*

While Mike loaded Speedy in the trailer, Tyler and I settled the account in his office. To my relief, he accepted the credit card. Then, Tyler gave me two sheets of paper. One of the documents was a hand-drawn calendar from November 12th through the 30th, divided into A.M. and P.M..

In the morning sections were four and sometimes five abbreviations representing various medications with an X through each med to indicate it had been given. In the evening sections were two and sometimes three medications Xed through.

On the Wednesday (November 27th) that Dr. Weed referred to in his phone call as his last examination of Speedy, when my horse was supposedly ready to go back to work, Speedy was still receiving six daily medications.

The other sheet of paper spelled out what the abbreviations for the medications on the calendar stood for. Some of them were unfamiliar: Thyrozine, Isoxuprine, and Pergolide. Some of them I recognized: Bute and Banamine.

Bute I had in my own supplies. It's what's called a non-steroidal anti-inflammatory or NSAID. I used it occasionally on my horses for muscle soreness. But, I knew Bute used for prolonged periods could cause intestinal distress just as long-term use of aspirin and Tylenol can in humans. According to Tyler's calendar, Speedy was on Bute twice a day for two weeks.

Intravenous or intramuscular shots of Banamine may be used as a muscle relaxant to give relief to colicky horses. The use of Bute and Banamine together, which is referred to as stacking, has been implicated as a cause of gastric ulcers.

Speedy had been on Banamine, along with Bute, for two weeks.

One final notation on Tyler's medication schedule referenced Acepromazine, a horse tranquilizer. The entry gave me a chill. It read:

"2cc Ace—once a day if real sore"

On November 30th, when Speedy was home and back in his old stall, I immediately phoned Dr. Penny. She listened to Tyler's list of medications and used the word *overkill* to describe the treatment, if indeed the word treatment even applied. She said, "It sounds like they were shotgunning, just firing drugs at Speedy in an attempt to hit something."

Dr. Penny advised I begin weaning Speedy off the drugs. We set up an appointment for December 4th for an examination of Speedy. In the meantime, Dr. Penny said, tell the vets, who have treated Speedy, to send their medical records. Those would include x-rays, medications, lab results, and lameness exams.

She particularly wanted to review the lameness exams. Those are veterinarians' diagnostic notes on a horse's condition, steps taken to arrive at a diagnosis, rationale for treatment, and follow-up.

I was entitled by law to that information, Dr. Penny said. Under the *continuation of care* statute, complete medical records must be supplied to a veterinarian, who assumes care of an animal, the same as with a physician, who takes over care of a human patient. In order to evaluate

Speedy properly and to begin sorting through all the lies and misinformation, Dr. Penny needed as complete a picture as possible.

I'd already set up a payment plan with Dr. Lance Albright for the $725 work he'd done on September 30, 2002, the day of the mysterious lameness issue. When I requested his medical records for Speedy, Dr. Albright was again accommodating. By phone, he said he had considered the possibility of Cushing's Disease, rare though it was in three-year-old horses, and had drawn blood from Speedy for lab analysis. He'd also taken x-rays both lateral and dorsal views.

Usually, lateral x-rays, which give a side view of the hoof, suffice to establish whether or not rotation has occurred. But, a dorsal view, which is an x-ray shot downward that shows the interior of the hoof and the horseshoe, can also be informative.

Dr. Albright also said he'd been relieved, without prior notice or explanation, as Speedy's veterinarian. After his initial visit on September 30th, Dr. Albright had scheduled a follow-up visit for October 2nd. But, when he arrived at T&T Stables on that date, Tyler dismissed him, saying Dr. Weed was taking over Speedy's case.

Within days of my request, I received Dr. Albright's records, which included an itemized bill for services showing all the medications he prescribed, the laboratory analysis of blood work, and his x-rays, four laterals and two dorsals.

Dr. Linus Weed was less forthcoming. I phoned his office three times. On December 3rd, I finally received a fax, which itemized the dates of Dr. Weed's visits and his charges for medications. There was the September 23rd appointment with charges for Depo and a $50 charge for something noted as "IB hips."

And, indeed, Dr. Weed had seen Speedy on October 2nd, after Dr. Albright was dismissed, and had taken x-rays, $80 worth.

The day of my post-Nationals' visit to Speedy at T&T Stables was October 23rd, when Tyler said my horse was doing fine on stall rest and Bute. He didn't mention Dr. Weed also visited that day—and injected Speedy with Bute and Banamine.

According to Dr. Weed's fax, there were also appointments on November 2nd, when more x-rays were taken, November 7th, and November 22nd. His final appointment was Wednesday, November 27th, when five veterinary appointments in one month culminated in Dr. Weed's evaluation that Speedy was *ready to go back to work.*

However, the itemized bill was all Dr. Weed sent. The x-rays he took on October 2nd and November 2nd were not included. Nor was there a lameness exam, which explained Dr. Weed's diagnosis and treatment of Speedy.

On December 4, 2002, when Dr. Penny arrived to examine Speedy, I had Dr. Albright's medical records and the single sheet of fax paper from Dr. Weed ready for her inspection. She reviewed Dr. Albright's lab results and concurred he was testing for Cushing's Disease.

Then, carefully, so as not to scratch them, Penny withdrew Dr. Albright's x-rays from a manila envelope and held them up to a lamp in the tack room.

The exposures were clear, concise, and correctly identified. A metal slug bearing Dr. Albright's name, patient's name, client's name, and date, had been placed on the radiographic plates at the time of exposure and appeared on the x-ray film as proper medical practice and law require. Permanent identification ensures x-rays can be read by anyone and mix-ups can't occur.

The lateral views showed the coffin bone properly aligned with the hoof wall. The laminae, the blood supplying adhesive between the hoof wall and the coffin bone, was not visibly disrupted.

The dorsal views, however, showed something different. Enclosed within the round shape of Speedy's horseshoes, were the coffin bones. Their outer edges were not sharply delineated but frayed.

In Dr. Penny's opinion, the fraying represented the early stages of rotation, when the tip of the coffin bone is just beginning to pull away from the laminae. When founder advances, the tip of the coffin bone gets pulled into an irreversible banana shape, which permanently identifies a previous occurrence of laminitis. The early-stage fraying, Dr. Penny felt, was significant.

After reviewing the information sent by Dr. Albright, Dr. Penny turned to Dr. Weed's scant offering. Depo, she informed me, was Depo-Medrol™, a synthetic corticosteroid, which is injected into joints to reduce inflammation.

Synthetic corticosteroids duplicate natural corticosteroids, which are present in all mammals and have a wide range of important functions.The delicate balance of those miraculous regulators of the body's physiology, should not be gratuitously altered. That was Dr. Penny's philosophy.

She used synthetic corticosteroids sparingly and only for medical purposes, to treat highly-resistant inflammation, for example. But, she wouldn't give them solely for performance purposes, even for an insistent client, because of the potential for harm vets call *systemic effects.* One of those systemic effects is laminitis.

Dr. Penny again consulted Dr. Weed's paperwork with its notations of Depo-Medrol™. She reviewed Dr. Albright's x-rays one more time. She paused for a few moments, seemed to weigh her words carefully, then said, "I think Speedy was foundered with steroids."

Chapter 9

On January 1, 2003, International Arabian Horse Association entered a joint operating agreement with Arabian Horse Registry of America that resulted in an official merger four months later. The new entity, called Arabian Horse Association, was to be located at what had been IAHA's headquarters in Aurora, Colorado.

As with all such reconstitutions, there was talk of a new era. In a press release, AHA promised to be a "full service organization to serve the needs of Arabian, Half-Arabian and Anglo-Arabian horse owners throughout the United States and Canada."

In recent years, the number of members reported by AHA fluctuated by thousands, but, the press release put the number at 40,000 members, who were to be provided with "all the services expected of a top quality equine breed association."

Those services included: administering more than $4 million in annual prize money, recognizing some 400 Arabian horseshows, distance rides, and other breed-promoting activities, and maintaining a comprehensive database for 265 affiliated clubs in eighteen regions across North America.

However, the new incarnation was still the repository of all the old problems. Of course, there were no press releases, which said AHA would be addressing the long-standing grievances held by many AHA members.

Such as the deeply-imbedded problems of drugging and animal abuse.

Such as the stranglehold of big name trainers on the way halter horses were shown.

Such as the reckless use and health risks of harmful performance-enhancing drugs.

Such as conflict of interest, cronyism, and corruption, within a judging system that was staffed, not by impartial judges, but by favor-swapping trainers taking turns as judges.

No, the Arabian industry's dirty horseshow secrets weren't going to be officially aired in public. But, thanks to the Internet, secrets are much harder to keep than in bygone days.

One person, who saw the electronic potential for prying open AHA's dark secrets and disinfecting with cyberspace sunshine, was Thomas Zaffer, a longtime Arabian horse breeder from Elyria, Ohio.

As a poster to another Arabian horse website, Zaffer grew tired of the censorship and nanny-ish quashing of discussion by that site's webmaster whenever Arabian horseowners chatted too close to the truth. So, Zaffer created his own website called *ablackhorse.com* and known to its members as ABH.

Using the screen name *Geseppi*, Zaffer was opinionated, quarrelsome, and audacious. His comments on AHA were often shocking. He pulled no punches when commenting on well-known figures in the Arabian horseshow world. And, he could even be brutal in responding to apologists, milquetoasts, and the misinformed, who frequented his own website. He didn't expect courage from everyone else, but, he challenged posters and visitors to ABH to come to the aid of the Arabian breed and to its beleaguered showhorses.

The ABH membership seemed to contain enough firebrands, who might join with Zaffer in assaulting the status quo—but sadly, their blazing rhetoric was mostly confined to the safety of chat rooms. And, the flames were quickly and routinely extinguished.

Typically, a report of yet another offense against Arabians would enrage the ABH membership. Comments in the Hot Topics' forum would fly heatedly for a couple days. However, the indignation usually turned into the online version of a food fight, where one-upmanship, motive-questioning, and personal attacks prevailed instead of any judicious discussion, which might lead to beneficial changes for Arabians horses.

Nor was that likely to occur.The grassroots community of Arabian horse-lovers, owners, small-scale breeders, amateur showmen, and hobbyists, saw what happened to Michael Brown when he tried to grapple with just one of AHA's problems.With the Boggs/Brown debacle still fresh in their minds, the majority of Arabian horse enthusiasts were paralyzed by fear of litigation.

It was a worry that was also immobilizing the entire country, crushing our freedom of speech, and crumbling our collective morality. Any Average Joe, who couldn't see how the erosion of freedom of speech in America hampered regular citizens and their activities, had only to look to the hostage situation at AHA.

Were all the Arabian horse-lovers at AHA petrified of lawsuits? What about those in leadership positions? How many simply could not let go of the unteachable 1980s mindset? And, how many more were just reluctant to surrender the perks and power they had accrued or the little sphere of influence they had carved out?

We've come a long way since the Founding Fathers kicked off a revolution by signing a Declaration of Independence wherein they pledged their lives, their fortunes, and their sacred honor. What were influential members of AHA willing to pledge? A revolution can't arise among people whose biggest worry is losing their pass to the Patrons' Lounge.

The official birthday of AHA came and went without much attention from me. In January and the following months of a bitter cold Ohio winter, I was focused on Speedy's deteriorating condition. When Dr. Penny saw Speedy on December 4, 2002, the presence of drugs in his system didn't allow for a true evaluation, and she had instructed me to scale them back.

As detox began to take effect, Speedy became increasingly difficult to handle. Even when Speedy was a rambunctious youngster and still a stallion, I'd never been fearful of him. During withdrawal, Speedy was dangerous and unpredictable. He exhibited more and more pain in his hooves. He was unwilling to be exercised on a lunge line, then unwilling to be led anywhere, and finally unwillingly to leave his stall.

On December 26, 2002, I phoned Dr. Penny and reported Speedy's distress. She arrived quickly and x-rayed his front feet. We were dealing with full-blown laminitis. The coffin bones in the left and right front hooves had rotated away from the hoof walls, and abscesses had formed within the gaps. The amount of rotation was serious, seven degrees in the left and nine in the right. Before treatment for laminitis could begin, the abscesses had to be drained.

Dr. Penny relayed instructions for John Travis Laney, who rearranged his schedule so as to care for Speedy the following day. J.T. removed round horseshoes and leather pads that had been applied to Speedy while at Tyler's.

Then, J.T. trimmed Speedy's hooves and changed the angles to try to make Speedy more comfortable and to facilitate drainage. Per Dr. Penny's instructions, I began soaking Speedy's feet twice a day in a solution of warm Epsom Salts. Speedy was often uncooperative and would send the soak buckets flying. Then, I'd have to trek back to the house to mix a fresh batch. In passing, I'd note the temperature on the barn thermometer, twelve degrees, ten degrees, eight degrees.

In addition to the soaks, J.T. and I wanted to use magnets on Speedy. We both used Nikken™ magnetic insoles in our own shoes and boots and believed they staved off sore feet. Dr. Penny, though skeptical, didn't object.

After Speedy's twice daily soaks, I'd dry his feet, wrap strips of magnetic material around each hoof, and secure it with a layer of Vetwrap. Then, I'd apply a layer of Duct Tape™. Ripping off his shiny silver slippers became a game for Speedy.

I knew the Home Team of Dr. Penny and J.T. were as committed to Speedy as they had been when we all shared the dream of a national champion. I had to do my part despite the sub-zero discomfort and annoyances. If Speedy could not be made more comfortable on his front hooves, he might begin shifting his weight backwards and initiate laminitis in his hind feet. If that were to happen, there'd be no chance of saving him.

For two months, buckets of Epsom Salts solution were overturned, hoof wrappings were ripped, and freezing temperatures went on, until the abscesses finally drained. Then, Dr. Penny x-rayed Speedy and said we were ready for the next stage of treatment, corrective shoeing.

J.T., who regularly attended laminitis symposiums to stay current with the latest technology, had a new light aluminum horseshoe and a frog support pad he was anxious to try. The new shoes and pads were set and reset for the next couple of months.

Every time J.T. trimmed and reshod, he reported the rate of Speedy's hoof growth was promising. The damaged laminae was growing out and being replaced by healthy new hoof wall. He predicted, as did Dr. Penny, Speedy would recover and be rideable again by late spring.

I believed I knew what rideable meant, undemanding exercise in the riding arena and leisurely hacks around the pasture. Strenuous work would have to be avoided. Speedy's diet would have to be carefully monitored. He could no longer have free access to grass and the sociability of other horses as they grazed in our pasture. The Home Team and I all recognized Speedy's career as a showhorse was over.

When I wasn't tending Speedy, I pursued information. *How had my horse come to be in such a state? What did Tyler know and when? Why had Speedy been shot-gunned with drugs? Why had so many corticosteroid injections been given? Why was I kept out of the loop?*

Dr. Weed's lameness exam might have contained much of this information, but, he hadn't sent those records in December as I requested, and, he continued to ignore my requests. Frequent phone calls on my part and unresponsiveness on Dr. Weed's part raised my suspicions—and my blood pressure.

In January 2003, Dr. Weed's secretary, Linda, phoned to say my account was being referred to collections. I repeated what I'd said before; I would not pay until I understood who had authorized injections for my horse and why. And, my vet and I must be able to review Dr. Weed's complete medical records for Speedy. No records were sent.

On February 3, 2003, Dr. Weed himself called saying, "I want to clear my books. So, where do we stand?"

You want to clear your books? Well, guess what! I want to clear my life. I want a healthy horse again. I want things the way they were before you and Tyler meddled with my property.

That's what I thought. What I said was, "Since Tyler apparently authorized the steroid injections, then Tyler can pay for them."

Dr. Weed said, "I'm caught in the middle of this thing."

He whined several times, saying, "I was only doing what I was told."

The latter remark was infuriating. Dr.Weed was a medical professional with a doctorate from a prestigious university. That his justification for his actions was to say he was taking directions from a high-school-educated twenty-five-year-old, was stupefying. I didn't trust myself to respond to his whiny excuse-making. I hung up.

On February 24th, Dr. Weed's secretary, Linda, called to say Tyler had paid for the steroid injections, which reduced my outstanding balance from $1,425 to $1,140. When could Dr. Weed expect payment?

"When can I expect the medical records?" I asked. "And who is going to reimburse me for the loss of $25,000 on my horse?"

Still, no records were sent.

After Mike and I picked up Speedy on the last day of November at T&T Stables, Tyler didn't call to ask how his formerly favorite horse was doing. So, it was something of a surprise to hear his voice on the phone on February 28, 2003. He was calling on Dr. Weed's behalf, he said, to inquire about the money I owed the vet and to ask what the problem might be.

I didn't let on Linda had phoned four days earlier and reported Tyler's payment of the steroid portion of the bill. But, for the first time I could question Tyler when Speedy was not in his possession. I didn't have to curb my tongue for fear of Speedy's safety. But, Tyler seemed to be in the grip of a massive amnesia attack.

Tyler disavowed any knowledge of the charges on Dr. Weed's bill. Disavowed Speedy received steroid injections on September 23rd. Disavowed any responsibility at all. Disavowed even when he contradicted himself. He said, "We did a bunch of horses that day. You can't expect me to keep track of all of them. I just do what Dr. Weed tells me to do."

My indignation boiled up, and I yelled, "How dare you call yourself a professional! People have entrusted you with their property and it's your job to know what's going on! I have seven horses in my barn and my vet and I know what's been done to each and every one of them."

Even while trying to maintain Speedy had not been injected, Tyler said, "Those injections have to be done on showhorses. That was implicit in our agreement."

There was nothing implicit in our agreement. I had clearly stated over and over: NO STEROIDS. Nothing vague, nothing ambiguous, nothing implicit. No steroids. But, no matter how many times I reminded Tyler of our conversations on that topic, he simply couldn't remember.

I was so angry, I yelled, "Damn you, Speedy's a mess and you're trying to tell me you have no idea how he got that way!"

An innocent person, a misjudged person, a person of integrity, I believed, wouldn't stand for such verbal abuse. But, Tyler remained unruffled throughout the conversation, denying, disremembering, and diverting the blame to Dr. Weed. He had only done what Dr. Weed recommended.

At the conclusion of the phone call, Tyler said, "I've never had a problem with a horse or client in my barn before. You're the first one."

Oh really? Apparently, Tyler had forgotten his claim McKenna Jamison was conducting a vendetta against him. And, Kiss Me Kate's owner was a know-it-all, who removed her horse. Those certainly bespoke client problems, which pre-dated me. And, I'd also spoken to a few other disgruntled former clients and would discover more, about twelve altogether, but, I kept that to myself for the time being.

Since Tyler's phone call failed to produce payment of the bill, Dr. Weed resumed his efforts. My formula was still the same, no medical records, no payment. On March 5, 2003, I spoke to Linda at Dr. Weed's office and insisted he call me back. He phoned from Florida where he was working, and promised to send Speedy's records when he returned.

On a hunch, I decided to try checking on Dr. Weed's license status in Florida. His license had expired May 31, 2002, but, in what sounded like bureaucratic double-speak, his license was classified as *delinquent—but still active.*

On March 18th, when the records still hadn't been sent, I was again on the phone to Dr. Weed's office and spoke to the vet's wife, who was staffing the office in Linda's absence. She said the records were on her husband's desk, ready to be sent, but would have to be handled by him personally when he returned from Virginia.

Virginia, eh? I phoned the licensing board in that state. If Dr. Weed was working there, it was without the benefit of a Virginia veterinary license.

From January to March 2002, my phone records, stashed in the shoebox with Speedy memorabilia, indicated I made nine phone calls to Dr. Weed's office. My notes of our conversations indicated I talked directly to Dr. Weed twice and Tyler once. That would seem to be ample communication, however, the medical records were not sent.

Besides the information I believed Dr. Weed possessed, there was another person, who could shed light on Speedy's condition—Dr. Samuel Hawkins, the official show veterinarian of the U.S. Nationals. The same show program, which yielded a listing for the Nationals' show office, also had a cell phone number for Dr. Hawkins and the state where he lived, Florida.

In December 2002, I phoned Dr. Hawkins and explained I had received a non-itemized bill for his services from Tyler Wragge and I would like a breakdown of the charges.

Dr. Hawkins promptly complied and faxed a document on December 13, 2002. The contents were shocking.

He had performed two lameness exams on Speedy, the first on the day of my horse's arrival in Louisville, and another on the following day. On the second day, Dr. Hawkins injected Speedy with ACTH.

I had to get educated on ACTH. The letters are shorthand for *adrenocorticotropic hormone.* It is the *uber*-steroid, which regulates all the other corticosteroids in the equine body. The synthetic form of ACTH, I was to learn, is a powerful substance that's a staple of trainers, who use drugs for performance-enhancing purposes. ACTH depresses the heart rate, achieves the slow jog by artificial means, and can have serious health effects.

In addition, Dr. Hawkins injected Speedy with calcium on the day of the Western Pleasure class. Calcium is naturally present in the equine body. But, calcium injections are also used by trainers for performance-enhancing purposes, even though calcium injections have the potential to cause death or blindness.

Dr. Hawkins's final charges were for x-rays of Speedy's front feet and for sheath cleaning. The last item was the only procedure Tyler told me about.

When I related the contents of Dr. Hawkins' fax with the notations of calcium and ACTH to Dr. Penny, she recommended I call her former colleague at the Drugs and Medications sector of the United States Equestrian Federation (USEF).

The governing body for American equestrian events had undergone a series of name changes in recent years. At one time, it was American Show Horse Association (ASHA), then USAEquestrian, and then USEF, with perhaps a few other nomenclature changes in between. The *nom du jour* phase is still a source of amusement among horse people.

Before invoking Dr. Penny's name to a high-ranking official, I decided to check out USEF's position on drugs. I sent for a copy of

USEF's Drugs and Medications rules and regulations, which were printed in a dark blue pamphlet.

On paper, USEF was on the side of horses. There were prohibitions against the use of foreign substances on horses for performance purposes; prohibitions against the use of therapeutic substances for non-therapeutic outcomes; prohibitions against stimulants, depressants, tranquilizers, excessive NSAIDs, corticosteroids to enhance performance; and on and on, in what seemed like ethical protections for equine athletes. That was heartening.

The USEF pamphlet also included a full-page list of forbidden substances, which included awful-to-contemplate substances used on horses, such as arsenic, cocaine, LSD, nitroglycerin, methadone, strychnine, and many other unrecognizable chemical concoctions dreamed up by disreputable trainers and veterinarians. The list of forbidden substances was incomplete, the pamphlet noted, as there were thousands more forbidden substances.

The suggestion the list was open to additions, was reassuring given a rumor in Arabian horse chat rooms about the newest substance in the trainers' bag of tricks for slowing down the jog: cobra venom.

Dr. Penny's acquaintance at USEF was Dr. Paul Shepherd. The two met early in Dr. Penny's career when she did drug testing for ASHA. She held Dr. Shepherd in high esteem and told me, "Paul has spent his professional career trying to protect showhorses from being abused with drugs."

Dr. Shepherd returned Dr. Penny's regard. He took my call and complimented Dr. Penny's skill and devotion to the veterinary profession. He listened patiently to my story. As I ran down the drugs that were given to Speedy, he said, "What was done to this horse is deplorable. They've tampered with its physiology."

Inwardly, I felt a chill at that remark since it echoed something Dr. Penny had said. While I was still fretting about founder, Dr. Penny said, "I'm more concerned in the long run about the number and amount of drugs they gave Speedy."

Dr. Shepherd outlined the dark side of veterinary medicine. He said, there are gypsy vets, who follow the hunter-jumper circuit and frequent the horse racing tracks, and, they will provide whatever drugs and injections the trainers ask for.

He confirmed what my research was indicating. Calcium lactinate, an electrolyte, was used as a calmative. ACTH, he said, "is a backdoor way of getting a horse to look trained. It should never be used in a healthy horse."

Calcium and ACTH, because they occur naturally in the equine body, can't be traced in a drug screen, and so, are used to alter performance. In describing the kind of veterinarians, who resort to such tactics, Dr. Shepherd's word choice was quite succinct: "Prostitutes!"

My experience with Dr. Shepherd was positive. He invited me to call him for help, which I did on several occasions. Much later, I had an encounter with USEF that was less satisfying.

The lameness exams noted on Dr. Hawkins' bill seemed to indicate what I already suspected, Tyler knew Speedy was lame and incapable of competing, but took my horse to the Nationals anyway. After all, Speedy had been lame and under a vet's care from September 23rd when the steroid injections were given (though for what, I still didn't know) through the time he was at Tyler's prior to the Nationals, and then again when Speedy returned to T&T Stables afterward.

To prove Tyler shipped a lame horse to Nationals, I needed Dr. Hawkins' lameness exams, diagnosis, and x-rays. I phoned him again and requested those items. I also asked him for the medical justification of injecting Speedy with ACTH and calcium.

Dr. Hawkins was under the same obligation to provide medical records as any other veterinarian. He didn't see it that way and became uncooperative. We reached the point where only our phone message machines were talking to each other. In one message he said, "In all my years of practice, working on million dollar horses, I've never been so insulted by a client."

Million dollar horses? I took that to mean my measly $25,000 horse was not deserving of his attention. Insulted? I had not been rude, merely persistent.

I continued to press for Speedy's medical records. Dr. Hawkins furiously messaged back he was due to undergo major surgery and would send the records later. No records were sent.

By March 22, 2003, I'd had enough. I was sick of being treated like a non-entity, who, along with my crippled horse, had been kicked to the curb, unworthy of an explanation, but still being badgered for payment and threatened with collections.

In point of fact, I was a non-entity, a small fry, a person with no power. I was no longer in a position to do what Editor Burgin used to say: "Comfort the afflicted and afflict the comfortable."

I felt the powerlessness many Americans feel.

But, I could still write and I was going to fight back with the only skill I had. So, on Saturday, March 22nd, I wrote a letter to Dr. Weed and said:

"...I've requested more times than I can count, that you or your staff send me the medical records and x-rays for my horse Imperial Marquis. You are required by law to provide this information. You have repeatedly ignored my requests. On Monday, March 24, 2003, I will be initiating complaints with the Ohio Veterinary Medical Licensing Board, the Better Business Bureau, and the Attorney General of the State of Ohio..."

Chapter 10

In response to my letter that complaints were forthcoming, Dr. Weed finally replied. He would send copies of his x-rays of Speedy—if I would pay for them. There were ten x-rays, and, he would charge $10 each, plus shipping. Or, Dr. Penny could travel to his office to view the originals.

The proposals were irksome. Dr. Albright had supplied his original x-rays of Speedy without charge. When I had Dr. Albright's x-rays copied at a nearby animal hospital, so I could return his originals, the charge was only $3 per copy.

And, Dr. Weed was pompous in suggesting Dr. Penny take time off from her busy practice to travel to his office and meet with him in order to get information he was under legal and ethical obligations to send. Nevertheless, I cut a check for $110 and mailed it immediately. While I awaited the x-rays, something interesting happened.

On March 28, 2003, Dr. Penny received a phone call from Dr. Weed. Unlike me, she was not rattled by the unexpected communication. With her usual levelheaded professionalism, she was able to get additional facts that were helpful.

First, she asked Dr. Weed about his use of Depo-Medrol™. The synthetic corticosteroid was available in different concentrations. She ascertained Dr. Weed used the 40 mg/cc formulation. Dr. Penny then asked about the amount used on each joint. From amounts Dr. Weed related, it was possible to calculate Speedy received a total body dose of 460 mg of Depo-Medrol™.

In medical literature, recommended amounts for a total body dose of Depo-Medrol™ ranged from 200 to 400 mg.The use of 460 mg by Dr. Weed would seem to indicate a horse with extreme lameness issues. If that were the case, a detailed lameness exam, which could include the use of diagnostic methods like hoof testers, flexion tests, x-rays, nerve blocks, venograms, MRI, ultrasound, thermography, and such, should have been performed.

Nothing in the materials we received so far from Dr. Weed indicated any diagnostic methods at all were used or that any diagnosis was arrived at before the injections were given.

A diagnosis for lameness may be anything from a stone bruise to tendon or ligament injuries to bone spurs to ringbone to navicular disease, to myriad causes, right up to a broken leg. To give treatment without determining what was being treated and recording the findings was medically unacceptable.

So, during the phone call from Dr. Weed, Dr. Penny inquired about the most basic diagnostic measure, a flexion test. In that simple test, the suspect joint is flexed and held, then the horse is asked to trot away, what vets call *jogging off*, and the resultant movement is observed. She asked Dr. Weed if Speedy had been flexed and jogged off.

He said no.

With no other diagnostic tests charged on his bill, and not so much as a flexion test done, that left open the staggering possibility Speedy was given an excessive amount of Depo-Medrol™ without any acceptable medical justification.

Shortly after hanging up, Dr. Weed called back to tell Dr. Penny he had "watched the horse travel," which was to say, yes, he had observed Speedy jog off, the most basic diagnostic testing.

Additionally, Dr. Penny learned the meaning of the cryptic "IB" noted on Dr. Weed's itemized bill. It stood for *internal blister*, a process of injecting a caustic agent at an injury site to create an inflammation that supposedly induces faster healing.

Dr. Weed had performed internal blisters on both of Speedy's hips, again for no stated medical purpose. Dr. Penny did not use blistering in her practice.

The large manila envelope containing Dr. Weed's x-rays of Speedy's front hooves, which finally arrived at Dr. Penny's office, was postmarked April 1, 2003. Given the contents of the envelope mailed on April Fools' Day, we had reasons to believe the postmark was a bad joke. For openers, the x-rays looked as though they'd been stored between concrete blocks. They were scratched and appeared old. Secondly, they were dark, poorly exposed, hard to read, and were unmarked with the requisite doctor/patient/client identification.

According to Dr. Weed's itemized bill, he took x-rays of Speedy on October 2 and November 2, 2002. Those dates did not appear on any of the ten x-rays, so there was no way of determining which were which.

Additionally, the lateral and dorsal views were suspect. In Dr. Weed's late night phone call to me on November 29th, a call he was later to deny ever occurred, he told me Speedy had rotated. However, Dr. Weed's lateral views showed no rotation. And, the dorsal views did not correspond with what Dr. Penny had observed in Dr. Albright's x-rays that were taken on September 30, 2002, and which served as a baseline for assessing later x-rays.

In my haste to meet Dr. Penny at her home office and to view Dr. Weed's long-sought x-rays, I had dashed out of my house and forgotten to bring along Dr. Albright's x-rays for side-by-side comparisons.

But, Dr. Penny recalled the conspicuous feature of Dr. Albright's dorsal view x-rays, the fraying of the tips of the coffin bones that would indicate the early stages of rotation, an alteration, which is irreversible. In the dorsal views submitted by Dr. Weed, the coffin bones were not frayed.

In light of the condition of the x-rays and the discrepancies of Dr. Weed's x-rays, Dr. Penny and I contemplated what seemed almost inconceivable—Dr. Weed had sent bogus x-rays. Such a move by a medical professional, if provable, was unethical, fraudulent, and clearly malpractice. Why would Dr. Weed do such a thing? If he had faked x-rays as part of a cover-up, what was he covering up?

The filing of official complaints I'd referenced in my letter to coerce Speedy's medical records from Dr. Weed, now became an imperative. He hadn't provided continuation of care to assist Dr. Penny in treating Speedy. What little information he sent had to be forced out of him. The x-rays were unmarked and highly questionable. And, Dr. Weed still hadn't sent a diagnosis of Speedy's problems on September 23rd, which justified all those steroid injections.

For openers, a complaint to the Ohio Veterinary Medical Licensing Board seemed appropriate. I consulted OVMLB's website, where I read the following statement:

"The Ohio Veterinary Medical Licensing Board was established for the purpose of licensing veterinarians and registering veterinary technicians...Its mission is to insure that the citizens of Ohio are served by professional, trustworthy and competent veterinarians and veterinary technicians..."

The description sounded encouraging. Surely, an agency, which sought to provide trustworthy and competent veterinary medicine for the citizens of Ohio, would conclude Dr. Weed deserved, at the very least, a serious reprimand. Dr. Penny was doubtful. She told me, "Don't expect much. You'll be dealing with a Good Old Boys' Network."

While I respected Dr. Penny's opinions, I thought she might be unduly cynical. After all, OVMLB was taxpayer-funded state agency, and I'd be asking it to investigate flagrant violations of acceptable standards of care.

In any case, I couldn't let the actions of Tyler Wragge and Drs. Weed and Hawkins go unchallenged. The three of them together represented a confluence of Arabian horseshow abuses that had swept through my life and wrecked my finances and dreams. Their potential to damage other horses and their owners, I believed, would continue.

I had only to go out to the barn and look at Speedy to be reminded of their villainy. By spring 2003, Speedy had recovered from the attack of laminitis. X-rays showed Dr. Penny and J.T. had done a remarkable job of pulling him through the crisis and restoring the coffin bones to normal positions.

On radiographic film of his hooves, Speedy was fine. Friends of mine and fans of Speedy rejoiced and encouraged me to leave the past behind and to forget the miscreants, who had caused such pain and misery. Move on and get over it, they said, just get on your horse and ride him.

The problem with moving on and getting over the damage to Speedy, the problem with the advice to just ride my horse off into the sunset, was Speedy couldn't be ridden.

The moment I dreamed of when I watched Tyler ride Speedy at the Nationals, the dream of riding my own horse, was a nightmare. Oh, I had the experience of stepping in the stirrup, throwing a leg over the saddle, lifting the reins, watching the beautiful curve of Speedy's neck with its long flow of silken mane, looking between his forward pricked ears, and, then, feeling my darling boy stumble and misstep as he tried to carry me.

Dr. Penny tried to determine the source of Speedy's chronic lameness. Absent any information from Dr. Weed on Speedy's original lameness issues, she was working in the dark. With her portable x-ray unit, she radiographed Speedy's hocks and performed various other tests.

She suspected a problem in the left stifle, but wasn't able to x-ray that area with precision owing to the limitations of her portable unit.

In order to get a complete picture of Speedy's condition, Dr. Penny said I could take Speedy to Ohio State University veterinary college for nuclear scintigraphy, a medical imaging process, which might isolate the problem area. I phoned OSU, but, the procedure was beyond my means. I couldn't justify spending more and more money on Speedy.

Mike and I were in debt already owing to my misplaced trust in Tyler Wragge. If I believed Speedy could be restored to his former self, we both would have sacrificed even more to make it so. But, I knew innately Speedy would never be right again and, moreover, that worse things were to come.

I wasn't used to living with pessimism. I was like my father, sunny and upbeat by nature. I tried to combat the feeling I was being stalked by dark fortune, by concentrating on whatever was left to celebrate. After all, I could still enjoy Speedy without riding him.

True, his life was very circumscribed. I monitored his food carefully. Since laminitis is often recurrent, I eliminated sugar and carbohydrate-rich foods from Speedy's diet to avoid triggering another episode. He ate low-protein hay and was not allowed to graze freely.

His weight and condition reflected the restrictions. Speedy lost the corpulence I had objected to and became slim. His muscle tone declined. Speedy didn't look like the gleaming substantial showhorse he had been, but, his altered physique and simple diet were more likely to protect him from laminitis.

My affection for Speedy no longer had to be restrained. Chronically lame, unable to be even a trail horse or child's mount, he was of no use to anyone. He would never be sold. A new owner would never enfold him with love, never thrill to his beauty, never rejoice in his victories. There was only me to love him. He was completely mine.

I could scarcely wait to see Speedy each morning. His eyes would be watching for me to come through the barn door. He would call out a greeting and rumble appreciatively as I pitched a flake of hay into his stall. My eyes would quickly scan Speedy's stall to ascertain he'd passed manure during the night. An absence of droppings is an early warning sign of intestinal blockage and colic.

After his breakfast, I groomed Speedy, picked his hooves and checked them for heat, ran a comb through the long silken strands of his blond mane and tail. Then, I'd try to devise a change of routine or something fun for him. *Should we take a walk together? How about a few slices of carrot? Would you like a little exercise on the lunge line? How about a few bites of grass on the lawn?* Then, he would spend several hours in his paddock where he particularly enjoyed head-sparring across the fence with the other horses, who liked to visit and play with him.

Speedy's physical constraints fostered more and more mental activity. He became hilariously mischievous. His big brown eyes seemed to dance with merriment, and he was always cooking up new tricks. Every lead rope, glove, riding crop, grooming tool, sponge, or towel he could grab in his teeth, was turned into games of Keep Away or Fetch. His grain pan, when he finished eating his half scoop of oats, came whizzing out of his stall like a Frisbee. He liked to head-fake when I was putting on his halter and swoop down to bite the toe of my boot.

All horses have distinct personalities, and I thought of our horses in human terms. One was like Gary Cooper—a no-nonsense, humorless, workmanlike horse. Another was like Paris Hilton—a glamorous diva, who had to be the center of attention. Speedy was Jim Carrey.

Elsewhere another relationship was changing. McKenna and I, encouraged by Gigi, were moving toward repairing our relationship. At the

Jubilee Arabian Show where Speedy qualified for Nationals, McKenna competed with Imperial Echo+.

Gigi and I were sitting ringside for McKenna's class. Despite the differences we'd had, the sight of McKenna, looking slim and beautiful, and riding her beloved horse, made me smile with pleasure. She happened to look directly at me, and smiled back. That's how the mending began.

Later, when I brought Speedy home and began to learn what Tyler had done to my horse, Gigi arranged a meeting between McKenna and me. I tearfully admitted to McKenna that her assessment of Tyler had been entirely correct. Had I heeded her warning, Speedy would still be safe and sound.

McKenna kindly replied that despite all her many years of experience with trainers in the show world, she had also been deceived. She, too, had friends try to discourage her from employing Tyler, but, she trusted her own evaluation and bought his hard-luck story.

In addition, McKenna saw distressing incidents, which should have warned her. While visiting Imperial Echo+ at T&T Stables, she saw a horse hidden behind a plywood partition with blood pouring out of its mouth. She immediately confronted Tyler about the injured animal. He blamed the damage on a stable hand. McKenna demanded the stable hand was never to touch Imperial Echo+.

At a later date, McKenna and Tyler were showing Imperial Echo+ at The Buckeye. She again saw a horse in Tyler's care with a bloody mouth. The stable hand was not present at the show.

The specifics of what happened to McKenna's horses, which prompted her first nearly hysterical phone call to me, were finally spelled out.

When McKenna first sent Kiss Me Kate to Tyler, the mare was already trained. He was to show and promote Kate for the purpose of finding a buyer. McKenna was very clear on two points, her price was

$15,000, and, she must approve the buyer. Later, McKenna herself located a buyer, who satisfied her own conditions, and arranged for the buyer to travel to Ohio to assess Kate.

As the potential buyer was flying in, Tyler took Kate to an out-of-state horse show, without McKenna's permission. At the show, Tyler sold the horse for $12,500 to a buyer not vetted by McKenna. She got less than Kate was worth, had to pay Tyler's commission on the reduced amount, and felt the need to reimburse her thwarted buyer for a plane ticket.

The situation with Imperial Echo+ involved further violations of McKenna's stated conditions. Imperial Echo+ was not only a seasoned and winning showhorse when McKenna placed him with Tyler, he was a treasured partner in McKenna's dream. He was not, McKenna emphasized, to be abused or given drugs. She was to be apprised of everything having to do with her horse. Tyler agreed.

Then, McKenna received a large bill from a veterinarian she didn't know—Dr. Linus Weed. She learned Dr. Weed performed a two-day dexamethasone suppression test (for Cushing's Disease) on her horse on June 14-15, 2000.

She also learned Tyler had been giving Imperial Echo+ a powerful drug called Thyro-L. Her permission had not been obtained for any of the procedures nor had she approved the expenses.

Alarmed at the use of drugs on her horse, McKenna removed Imperial Echo+ from Tyler's facility in June 2000. She called Dr. Penny for advice and was told to gradually wean the horse off the Thyro-L. Despite attempts to minimize the effects of withdrawals, Imperial Echo+ endured weeks of discomfort.

When McKenna demanded an explanation of the Thyro-L from Tyler, he said trainers use the drug to achieve a slow jog.

McKenna also raised a fuss with Dr. Weed's office about Tyler's high-handed behavior, and she was given a reduction in the bill.

McKenna was unwilling to correlate the administration of Thyro-L to the onset of Cushing's Disease, which was diagnosed in her horse early in 2001, but I did. The pituitary (site of tumors that cause Cushing's Disease) and thyroid gland release numerous hormones, which regulate all kinds of body functions. Even a layperson might safely bet that dumping a bunch of unnecessary steroids, hormones, or drugs, into the complex endocrine system of horses is a bad idea.

Two years after the Cushing's diagnosis, McKenna was anticipating the show season with Imperial Echo+. The daily doses of Cyproheptadine and her scrupulous maintenance program seemed to be working just fine. The bay horse was as beautiful as ever.

Then—tragedy.

On July 19, 2003, Gigi phoned with the awful news. The previous evening, Imperial Echo+ had a sudden catastrophic colic. A veterinarian had responded within twenty minutes. Injections of painkillers had no effect. From the onset of symptoms to euthanasia to end the horse's dreadful suffering was a mere ninety minutes. McKenna stayed next to the body all through the night.

Several months after the submission of my complaint about Dr. Linus Weed to Ohio Veterinary Medical Licensing Board, about the vet's failure to provide medical records, continuation of care, and his unmarked x-rays, I received an answer.

OVMLB found no fault with Dr. Weed.

Chapter 11

Long after I should have done so, I placed a call to Arabian Horse Association to ask what professional criteria are required of horse trainers to participate in the Arabian horseshow industry. Shockingly, the answer was NONE. Trainers were not required to provide credentials of any kind—not resumes, not licenses, not letters of recommendation, not proof of equine education, and not liability insurance.

Indeed, AHA didn't even demand a fee or dues from trainers to allow them to operate in the high-stakes world of Class A horseshows. A representative of AHA told me all a trainer had to do was to contact AHA and ask to be put on the trainers' list.

Once signed up, the guidelines for trainer conduct were indistinct, perhaps even nonexistent. The Code of Ethics in the AHA handbook spoke loftily of the Golden Rule and repeatedly invoked good sportsmanship. One entry read:

"That the noble Arabian Horse, most ancient of all breeds, a creature of beauty and an athlete of renown, has earned and deserves the company of true sportsmen."

Deserves the company of true sportsmen? Was that jolly-good-pip-pip-old-chap lingo supposed to ward off grifters, predators, and animal abusers? In an age when the Golden Rule has been subverted to "Do unto others before they do unto you," and sportsmanship is compromised by a win-at-any-cost mentality, perhaps the Arabian horse would be better served by a long list of specifics under the caption Will Not Be Tolerated, followed by the phrase "Don't let the screen door hit you in the backside."

So, if a not-so-true sportsman was undeterred by the lofty language in the Code of Ethics, screwed up monumentally, and was discovered, what recourse was available?

The aggrieved party would have to file a complaint, convince witnesses to give testimony, compile evidence, and the matter would be placed before the Probable Cause Panel. If the complaint survived PCP scrutiny, a hearing by an Ethical Practice Review Board would be scheduled at AHA headquarters in Colorado.

While the rest of American business struggled under the increasing weight of regulations and restrictions, trainers for AHA enjoyed a professional environment where there were no explicit rules and virtually no mechanisms in place for dealing with those, who carry out animal abuse, fraud, and malfeasance. And, it seemed, there was no determination to do any self-policing. The Boggs/Brown situation had dampened any rectitude, which might have existed.

Given the *laissez-faire* attitude of AHA, the conduct of some trainers was often egregious and occasionally produced scandals, which breached the code of silence. Thus, I heard about a stallion that went berserk at a major show and could scarcely be contained by multiple handlers. To ensure the stallion moved with the requisite slowness in a Western Pleasure class, the trainer had cinched a leather strap around its testicles. After the class, the testicles were so raw, inflamed, and swollen, the strap couldn't be removed. The horse was wild with pain and violently uncontrollable.

An apprentice trainer, who was appalled by the incident, reported the reason for the horse's behavior—and was fired. The trainer, whose bag of tricks included the use of leather straps, was still training.

The whistle-blower showed uncommon valor and probably anticipated the damage his integrity would do to his prospects, since the customary career path for young wannabes in the Arabian horseshow industry is to apprentice with a *big name trainer*, referred to in the industry as a BNT.

Whatever methods the BNT employed were passed along to students, and there was an institutional belief the constraints of time and money made a certain level of brutality necessary. And, so, abusive training methods were perpetuated to the next generation.

Furthermore, BNTs and large training facilities often required employees and apprentices to sign confidentiality agreements, ostensibly to protect their *valuable* training methods, but also to send a strong message to youngsters, who sought a career with horses: There's no future for you in this business unless you keep your mouth shut.

Keeping mouths shut had become routine. The ability to honestly express *something* occasionally resided with a newcomer. A lovely young woman, who pursued her passion for Arabian horses despite very limited means, saved up enough money to realize a longtime dream, to travel to Arizona in 2007 for the prestigious Scottsdale Arabian Horse Show held annually in February. She came away with an indelible memory.

"Do you know what hanging is?" she asked me. Unfortunately, I did, owing to a confidence that was shared with me.

A fellow whose business took him to a large Arabian breeding and training facility, said after hours he regularly saw many horses with their halter ropes winched over the barn rafters so their front feet barely touched the ground. The strain of being suspended weakened muscles of the neck and encouraged Western Pleasure horses to plod around the arena with their heads in the unnatural but highly desirable lowered position.

The young woman, who visited the Scottsdale show for the first time, had no problem discerning *hanging* was going on. But, somehow show stewards and officials at most major shows seem incapable of observing bad behavior.

When hanging, or a related abuse, taping a horse's mouth around a block of wood to weaken neck muscles, was reported to show officials, the burden of proof fell on the complainant. They were required to provide properly time-dated videotape, write up a report, and pursue the matter with AHA.

Thus, a well-meaning informant, who simply wanted show officials to check out the abuse while the show was going on, was often unwilling to undertake a lengthy procedure on behalf of someone else's property—particularly when the owner of the victimized horse might not back them up.

The lethargy in the Arabian horse community persists despite routine outrages to the breed. When a young up-and-coming trainer drew outrage from spectators at the 2007 Nationals for his brutal shanking of a stallion in the Main Ring, was he shunned? After the booing faded away, was there any lasting fallout? No. Not even close.

Instead, he was rewarded with a fancy new training facility. Moreover, he was only emulating his mentor and other BNTs, who were also shanking excessively at the same show.

The unabashed public shanking of even very young horses was a fairly regular feature of Arabian horseshows, and always begged the question, "If that's what's done out in the open, what is done to the horses in private?"

One of the abuses, which take place in private, is the *hot shot.* Variations on this method of teaching the hard stand-up to halter horses include standing the horse in a pool of water or strapping it into a wet blanket—and applying an electrical shock. Alternatively, the tender tissue in the horse's nostrils is dampened with mineral oil and water, then, zapped with a pig prod.

The administration of a hot shot causes the horse to recoil, tense up, and become extremely attentive, the look, which forms the basis for the hard stand-up.

Then, in the showring, the buzzing sound of the electric shock or zapping pig prod is imitated by the trainer. The Pavlovian response of the horse is to strike the desired pose in expectation of pain.

In one instance, a mare being shown at halter was so traumatized by the anticipated pain when the trainer buzzed at her, that she trembled violently, collapsed in the ring, and wouldn't get up. She had to be hoisted into the back of an open box truck and transported home. She still refused to get up for quite awhile and was never able to show again. The person, who related the story, noted the reaction in the Arabian clubhouse: "Everyone clucked and looked the other way."

Clucking and looking the other way enabled Arabian horse trainers to be Teflon polecats in shirking responsibility and coming up with another life after trashing a previous one. Abandonment of one barn for another without regard to the investors' interests. Public displays of brutality in the Main Ring. Destruction of valuable horses. Damaging horses with drugs. Inflicting mind-altering trauma on horses. Reneging on agreements to exhibit horses if something better comes along—without refunding money. Requiring clients to purchase expensive horse blankets and cooler sheets bearing the trainer's logo. Performing unauthorized procedures. Charging for services never rendered. Inflating prices for services, which are rendered.

No accountability was demanded of the Teflon polecats. No penalty was paid. And, no one made much of an issue of it. Unlike Woody Allen's observation that he wouldn't join a club, which would have him as a member, the desire to be part of the Class A Arabian horse club seems so intense, its members appear willing to overlook a multitude of sins just to be involved. And, to provide a multitude of excuses for the status quo.

One of the most absurd excuses made for abusive trainers is to blame the victim. Insiders would say, rather haughtily, newcomers to the Arabian show world are responsible for their property and should thoroughly investigate trainers before entrusting them with their horses. Oh, really. How would newcomers begin investigating trainers? What resources are out there?

Can they read up on it? In general, horse industry print media is solely geared to selling stuff and to endlessly rehashing the same old topics. No discouraging word or breath of scandal or unpleasant reality about horse abuse is allowed to divert readers' attention from photo-shopped horse pictures, articles on oft-repeated topics, glossy ads, and page after page of relentless sales pitches.

The magazine published by AHA did list trainers under suspension, most often for not paying membership dues, but certainly didn't deviate from the industry-wide media pretense that everything is just fine in Horsey World.

Can newcomers investigate trainers by doing research on the Internet? They may encounter fearful stories there, but, authors of unflattering commentary generally retreat from naming names for fear of litigation.

So, in the *omerta*-driven horseshow world where honest information is scant, secrets are harbored, and unimaginable horrors lurk, newcomers may have to learn hard lessons—and find little in the way of remedy. Thus, when novices have a bad experience, veterans of the horseshow world sagely advise them to "Vote with their wallet."

Spending one's money elsewhere does nothing to solve the problem. It just endangers the next person's wallet.

And, the smug blame-the-victim attitude exists in an industry, which badly needs newcomers to survive, since AHA membership and the number of Arabian horses being bred each year, are both declining.

Only a few in AHA are wise enough to understand that telling newcomers "You're on your own," is hardly a welcome mat.

Often the excuse for subjecting horses to abuse is to achieve an elusive gold standard: What the Judges Want.

Pandering to the supposed desires of judges is rampant in the Western Pleasure classes. It is said judges want to see WP horses moving very slowly. If leather straps, drugs, blood-letting, and lungeing to the point of exhaustion, are used to accomplish that, well, the trainer is only trying to satisfy the judges.

It is said judges want to see WP horses moving in a certain *frame*. If tie downs, draw reins, and hock hobbles attached by straps to hurtful bits, are used to accomplish the desired posture, well, the trainer is only trying to satisfy the judges.

Ironically, attempts to satisfy What the Judges Want exist with constant complaints from competitors that "The judge didn't like my horse," and "I don't know what the judges are looking for."

Adding to the tortuous pursuit of What the Judges Want is the fact judges very often are trainers. So, if the trainers, who are judges, and the judges, who are trainers, don't know What the Judges Want—well, who the hell does?

Other factors, which contribute to the enabling of trainers, come from The Eighty Percent. The statistic is often invoked to describe the vast majority of participants in equine activities—females. Women and girls comprise 80% of horse enthusiasts. Does that number translate to clout in the industry? Do women have influence proportionate to their passion? In my opinion, no. And, here's why:

For starters, our society has grown accustomed to majority rule being superseded by minority agendas. Additionally, many women have forgotten or turned their backs on the positive contributions of feminism—both of which allow for a let-the-guys-run-things attitude.

Consider the imbalance between male versus female trainers. Of course, there are successful women trainers, but, their numbers don't reflect the demographics of equine sport. And, there seems to be a client gender bias in favor of male trainers.

In recent years, the supply of trainers for Class A hasn't met the demand. Was the industry answer for more women to be groomed to take positions in the top tier? Or, was it for BNTs to fill the gaps by importing young men from South America, some from cultures where bull-fighting and ritual torture of animals still occur? (If those green card trainers brought with them rough horse-handling practices, which put them at odds with American preferences, well, it would be politically incorrect to notice.)

Advancement for women in the Arabian horseshow world may be complicated by another factor that harkens back to my friend's teasing remark about women, horses, and Dr. Freud. The sexual charge generated by proximity to horses, as Freud alluded, operates on the unconscious level but may prompt powerful biological responses and conjure up primordial images:

The chest-thumping, testosterone-pumped primitive male dominates and subdues the wild beast. Today's version of that archetype, the high-profile horse trainer, is clad in sexy riding apparel, which enhances the Alpha male stereotype: Tight riding breeches. Knee-high boots. Riding crops.The codpiece effect of leather chaps strapped over jeans.

The ancillary archetype, the cave women, who stokes the cookfire and awaits the arrival of the male provider, has a modern incarnation in the kind of females who are giddy, gushing, horse-trainer groupies.

In the hormonal soup of the horseshow world, with its sexual tension, suppressed desires, unacknowledged competition, romanticizing, and mooning about, such women find ways to enable bad trainers with a bevy of reality-bending, protecting-my-man excuses like these:

"The owner made him show a rank stallion, so, he had to shank it."

"The cost of maintaining a barn and equipment puts so much pressure on him, he has to get results."

"I'm not sure that shanking, spurring, and whipping are actually abuse."

"My trainer has gotten my horse to a whole different level, but, I just know he would never do anything abusive."

What role do men play in an industry where trainers wield inordinate power and the preponderance of participants are women? It appears men write the checks. Of course, there are many individual women, who pay their horse expenses out of their own pockets. But, in the grand scheme of things, men seem to foot the bills.

Big breeding farms are generally owned and operated by husband and wife teams, but, financing often comes from hubbie's outside business interests. The youth division of Class A, here again a preponderance of female competitors, is generally funded out of Daddy bank accounts.

Men, who can finance costly enterprises like dazzling horse breeding operations, are men who are accustomed to getting a return for their investment. Do they apply a rigorous bottom line policy even when the commodity is living creatures?

Trainers make that claim. The most common excuse for abuse of horses by trainers is: The owner is making me do it.

The pressure placed on them by demanding clients, who want, expect, insist upon, blue ribbons and prizes, forces them to take extreme measures with horseowners' property, so say the trainers.

Certainly fortunes are paid for showhorses whose bloodlines, beauty, or talent suggest they can be winners. Having paid a fortune for a potential champion, are businessmen willing to destroy their investment to win, as excuse-making trainers suggest? Are there indeed instances where a client harangues a trainer about winning at any cost? Let's imagine the scene:

"Listen here, Trainer," says the horseowner, "I'm paying you big bucks and this damn nag better win. I don't care what you have to shoot into its bloodstream—calcium, ACTH, cobra venom—whatever it takes, even if it kills my horse. I want that ribbon!"

Or possibly this version of a client pressuring a trainer:

To maximize a young stallion's appearance for the showring, so as to attract breeding fees, the horseowner tells the trainer to give the youngster anabolic steroids. Then, when the stallion has to perform its function, that is, breeding mares and making money for the owner, guess what? The steroids have rendered the stallion infertile. Shooting blanks, can't make babies...

The inability of some stallions that sold for astronomical sums, to put babies on the ground is the subject of behind-the-hands snickering among Arabian horse industry insiders. But steroid-induced infertility and the consequent loss of valuable bloodlines is no laughing matter. And, the claim by trainers they must physically and chemically mistreat innocent animals to satisfy the business demands of clients suggests the perilous position occupied by Arabian showhorses—caught between the aggressive expectations of their owners and the cowardly submission of trainers.

If, indeed, the business of Arabian horses has set such high standards of perfection and performance that drugs and abuse are required to attain them, perhaps it's fair to ask how well the administrators of the business have done.

Now, there's nothing inherently wrong with making money by breeding, showing, and selling horses. Profit is a good thing. It's what allows non-essential activities like showing horses to exist. Competition is also a good thing. It's one of the engines of capitalism. Breeding quality Arabian horses is a long-term enterprise with high costs, which is very competitive. And, there were breeders, particularly in the glory days of the 1980s, that were extremely successful.

Unfortunately, Arabian business practices from those days left a stink on the industry, which has yet to dissipate. Horse people have long memories, and, there's still a lingering sense the business model from thirty years ago was to fleece a bunch of suckers, to breed out the brains and breed in conformational faults by chasing the living art aesthetic, and to ruin the reputation of the paragon of horses. And, when the high-flying Arabian horse entrepreneurs found they could not sell the product—sent it to slaughterhouses.

A business disaster of such epic proportions should have been addressed with a comprehensive, coordinated business plan for restoring, not just perceptions about the Arabian horse industry, but the well-being and vitality of the breed itself. That doesn't appear to have happened.

Instead, three decades later, I see the Arabian gene pool has been reduced by chasing trendy stallions rather than having a well thought out breeding program to preserve bloodlines and the Arabian's once legendary athleticism. I see genetic diseases have not been rooted out. I see the industry show contempt for Arabians by allowing the horses to be physically and chemically abused and preyed upon by hucksters. And, I see some exhibitors, amateur and professional, preening in expensive finery, riding Arabians that are robotically programmed with drugs and abuse, in a ludicrous parody of horsemanship.

I see an industry where ineptitude on the human side is excused and tolerated, but perfection and flawless performance are demanded only of the horses.

Am I too harsh? Is the industry stuck in the 1980s and wedded to thirty-year-old practices, as I believe? Or is there a sensible new business plan that I just haven't observed yet?

Reminder to self: Keep an eye out for the new and improved Arabian horse industry plan.

The old business plan of Class A Arabian horseshows was well-established by the time Tyler Wragge turned pro. Since his parents were professional horse trainers, Tyler grew up in that anomalous world, watching and learning from his earliest days. Those observations were his strongest influence, not formal schooling. Tyler told me he'd been an unremarkable student, couldn't wait to get out of high school, and never wanted to be anything but a trainer.

I envied him in a way. I appreciate what I experienced and learned in my years prior to owning horses. But, as I got older and could never get enough of horses, I sometimes wished my life had been front-loaded with horses.

When I saw a photograph of Tyler, at about ten years of age, completely outfitted with English riding gear, jodhpurs, boots, jacket, shirt, cravat, and velvet helmet, I thought, "You lucky little twerp."

As I spent more time around horseshows, I began to wonder if youngsters, who are born into horse-showing families, were as fortunate as I assumed.

The horse obsession, when it takes hold, or the demands of being a horse professional, can be so consuming as to exclude or detract from other relationships.

My husband joked about the amount of time I spent in the barn, but, he was an adult and could relate to my fervor. But, how would a kid emotionally handle the situation when parental love and attention were so divided and sometimes inequitably doled out?

Perhaps something like a cross-species sibling rivalry develops.

Perhaps a child, who is part of a family of horse professionals, subconsciously harbors resentment against horses and clients, which steal away the parental attention the child craves. Should that be the case, would the horses become the unconscious targets of anger? Would the clients be included in the displaced sibling rivalry?

If so, it might explain how some professional trainers, who profess to love horses, can harm the animals and victimize clients.

In the years following Speedy's ruination, I considered many possibilities as I tried to fathom what I thought to be Tyler's pathological behavior. He professed to understand what the people expected in terms of righteous behavior. He mimicked that over and over. Yet, he consistently chose to do the opposite.

When good is understood, but bad is chosen, there's a word for that—Evil. The word is seldom used in modern times. Other words, other concepts, and psychological terms, are offered to help us accept there are monsters living among us.

However, I wasn't pondering Tyler's grubby motivations in the early months of 2003. My thoughts were clear. My horse, I knew intuitively, was harmed beyond repair. The harm occurred on Tyler's watch, was initiated by his disregard of my clearly-stated instructions about Speedy, and was covered up to the further detriment of my horse's well-being.

I had sufficient documentation to support my beliefs. I could show Speedy was lame prior to the Nationals and immediately after. I still wanted proof positive Speedy was lame during the Nationals. That would irrefutably demonstrate Tyler's duplicity. But Dr. Samuel Hawkins held the key, and he continued to withhold information.

Nevertheless, I felt I had sufficient grievances and evidence against Wragge and Hawkins to take action against them with IAHA. In April 2003, I filed a complaint with IAHA (during the transition period to AHA) naming Tyler Wragge and Dr. Samuel Hawkins and enumerated their actions in a ten-page statement.

I was required to pay a filing fee of $100 to IAHA, an organization that required nothing in the way of payment or credentials from trainers.

Chapter 12

Dr. Samuel Hawkins was the third member of the trio, who could provide answers about Speedy, but, he continued to shrug off my attempts to build a complete picture. After sending the initial information, which noted x-rays were taken and injections of calcium and ACTH were given, and after the exchange of several phone messages, Dr. Hawkins simply faded away.

Nevertheless, I was determined to get some answers from him. Though I was disappointed with OVMLB's failure to find fault with Dr. Weed, I felt sure there was an agency or official that would see Dr. Hawkins' actions as problematic and would pressure him into sending Speedy's medical records.

As I had done with Dr. Weed, I checked on the status of Dr. Hawkins' licenses in the states where I knew he practiced. In New Mexico, the bi-annual site for the Nationals, Hawkins had been licensed since 2001, seemingly from the time he began providing vet service for the Albuquerque site of the Nationals.

In Kentucky, the alternative site for the Nationals, Dr. Hawkins was issued a license in 1984 and kept it current. As the international epicenter of the Thoroughbred breeding industry, Kentucky has some of the premiere equine veterinary facilities in the world. However, the state's racing industry has been criticized for its liberal use of Lasix, drugs, hormones, and steroids.

Despite the state's ambiguous stance on horse welfare, I filed a complaint with Kentucky Board of Veterinary Examiners citing Dr. Hawkins' lack of compliance with continuation of care, his failure to provide Speedy's x-rays, and his use of calcium and ACTH for, what appeared to be, performance-enhancing reasons. The Board notified Dr. Hawkins of my complaint, solicited his records, gave the matter due consideration—and found no fault with Dr. Hawkins' conduct.

My license research continued. I checked with the Florida licensing board. Dr. Hawkins was currently licensed there. A licensing board representative assured me Dr. Hawkins, despite his residency in Florida, still had an obligation to provide continuation of care information and to send Speedy's medical records to me.

How about Dr. Hawkins' standing in Ohio? He was the onsite vet contracted by the organizers for the annual Buckeye Arabian show. What was his license status? Well, he wasn't licensed in Ohio and never had been.

As the 2003 Buckeye approached, I brought that professional oversight to the attention of the Ohio Veterinary Medical Licensing Board. I figured OVMLB might be offended by Hawkins' carpetbagger mentality. He was operating without a license and taking work away from licensed Ohio veterinarians. Apparently, OVMLB was not offended by carpetbagging.

In response to my complaint, OVMLB quickly granted Dr. Hawkins a license "via reciprocity with Pennsylvania," meaning, a license he held in Pennsylvania was translated into an Ohio license. The problem with that, in my mind, was Hawkins' Pennsylvania license had expired in 1984.

Frustrated at what I felt was the leniency of the veterinary licensing boards, I engaged the services of a local lawyer to write a letter to Dr. Hawkins requesting Speedy's medical records. The lawyer advised me the letter was probably a waste of time. Dr. Hawkins was beyond the jurisdiction of the Ohio court system, his actions had taken place in

Kentucky, and he could safely ignore the request. I asked the lawyer to try anyway.

Since veterinary medical licensing boards had proved so worthless, I sought other avenues for dealing with my belief that drugging at horse-shows in Ohio might be a serious problem. The impression was deepening as more insiders began speaking to me. It was frustrating so many accepted chemical warfare as an established and unchangeable fact of life in the show world. I wasn't willing to accept it.

Surely, some other agency or official would also be troubled if systematic drugging of horses was going on. I searched the Internet for humane societies and animal protection groups in Ohio, and contacted by phone or email every one I found, asking them to investigate. Not one agency ever got back to me.

I attempted to contact officials in the Federal Drug Administration and Ohio Department of Agriculture. I even called the FBI to see if drugging horses at shows might fall under RICO, the Racketeer Influenced and Corrupt Organizations Act. The FBI agent was polite, but not helpful. If he thought I was nuts, he kept it to himself.

Occasionally, I would get through to a real person at an animal protection agency, who allotted a smidgeon of time to my concerns. But, they seemed to feel they had done a good day's work if they gave me the phone number of someone else, who might be helpful.

At one point, I talked to the Ohio state veterinarian, who listened patiently. He said he and his family were involved in showing cattle and had just returned from a big cattle show where he had seen evidence of drugging.

Okey dokey, I thought. Here's a guy, who can do something. He has a title and a position paid for by Ohio taxpayers. And, Ohio Revised Code 901.76, which prohibits tampering or sabotage of livestock at exhibitions might be something he could use. Strictly speaking, the definition of livestock doesn't include horses. But, where there's a will, there seems to be a way. Unfortunately, there was no will.

The state vet suggested I contact my state representative to lobby for new legislation. Yes, that's what we need all right, more rules and regulations—which will not be enforced.

I exhausted every alternative to legal action I could think of. No agency, tax-supported or non-profit, federal or state, showed the slightest interest in pursuing an investigation into the drugging activities I believed were taking place at horseshows. Besides bureaucratic inertia, I figured there was another explanation. Since the days of Watergate, the explanation for the inexplicable has been "Follow the money."

Ohio is an important center of Arabian horses. Breeders and trainers are established in the state. Arabian horse activities generate considerable revenue for many businesses. If there were to be a crackdown on abuses in the Arabian horseshow industry in Ohio, participants and the money might well relocate to a more accommodating state. A certain level of corruption, if it protects the flow of funds into the coffers, is probably considered tolerable.

As the one-year anniversary of Speedy's foundering at Tyler Wragge's facility approached, I felt panicky. I figured statutes of limitation were in play and the opportunity to do something was winding down. Officialdom was not going to help. I'd have to consider legal action. The prospect was extremely distressing.

Why should it come to that? Why were there no protections or accountability available by other means? Has the legal establishment painted all of us into a corner by wielding the threat of litigation over the whole country and rendering all other authorities impotent? Why did it seem that rules, which I believed in and tried to live by, only worked to the advantage of rule-breakers?

Besides, I'd already had one creepy encounter with a lawyer.

Mike's one-man trucking business was buffeted by the difficulties of the freight industry. Fuel costs were on the rise. Rates were on the decline. Repairs and maintenance for equipment were enormously expensive. And, a fair amount of Mike's working capital had been diverted to promote and show Speedy.

That money and the return on our investment through the sale of Speedy were irretrievably lost. Vet and horseshoeing bills to save Speedy's life had eaten up more of our scant resources. So, when another trucker gave Mike the name of a bankruptcy attorney, it seemed we had no choice but to consult with him.

Ainsley Killbuck's office was in a gloomy older building in the downtown area of Denton, Ohio. The building's exterior was ornamented with timeworn Art Deco motifs, and its faded glory bespoke the moribund condition of many American cities. Mike and I rode the hesitating elevator up several floors, opened the door with Killbuck's name on it, and entered an office that was airless and musty.

An elderly woman, who was Killbuck's wife, was crocheting at a round table. She put down her needles, rose arthritically from her chair, and showed us into the attorney's chambers. I struggled to keep my composure at what I saw. Sitting behind a vast desk was a figure so old and emaciated, I thought I was looking at the mummy of an Egyptian pharaoh.

His skin, lax and liver-spotted, lay in weary wrinkles on his folded hands and clung to the bones of his skull. In the middle of Killbuck's scrawny neck was an open tracheotomy hole that was covered by a small crocheted curtain, apparently the work of Mrs. Killbuck. When Attorney Killbuck talked, by holding a speaker device to his throat, the tiny curtain, which was attached to a string around his neck, fluttered with each vented breath.

As I sat in a worn overstuffed leather chair, watching the tiny wafting square on the neck of what seemed to be a reanimated corpse, a realization slowly enfolded me and grew in clarity: *I am a character in a story.*

Killbuck's voice, raspingly interpreted by the speaker, droned on about our financial situation while I grappled with the insight. I looked back at the twisting path and other characters whose actions had brought me to that bizarre moment.

I am a character in a story.

The thought took greater hold on me as I reviewed the story: The happenstance acquisition of Queenie. The unlikely gift of a superb foal. Speedy's derailed Cinderella story. The false facade of the horseshow industry. My horse's duplicitous caretakers.The flickering out of courage and virtue across the land.The diminishing fortitude of the citizenry. The plot twists went on and on.

I was being spoken to in a language I could understand—as one writer to another. And, if the story I was living seemed extravagantly drawn, overwrought with drama and improbable characters, that, too, made sense.

An outrageous plot line was needed just to get my attention. I had lived my life without plan or resolve, unconscious of a higher power, heedless of my spiritual life, and oblivious to any earthly purpose. If the course of my life were to change, The Author, who was composing the plot, had to penetrate my encompassing self-absorption with a story I could not dismiss.

The Author had done so.

While the epiphany was unrolling in my brain, Ainsley Killbuck was shuffling through our bills, tapping the keys of a calculator with a long bony finger, and assessing our financial situation. He was ready to announce the results. He placed the speaker to his throat, the tiny curtain fluttered several times, and he said, "You're too broke to file bankruptcy."

Too broke to file bankruptcy? What did that mean? We probably should have asked for a fuller explanation, but, I could scarcely wait to flee that place with its oppressive smells of entrapped air, moth-eaten carpets, psoriasis ointments, senior citizen fustiness, and moldering humanity.

It wasn't the ancient attorney's disability, which spooked me, rather, it was the overall freakiness of the scene: Hoary old Killbuck, long past the age of retirement, still suckling on the law like a freeze-dried vampire in that sepulcher office, with his antique spouse sitting in the ante-chamber, clicking her crochet needles and turning out those diaphanous tracheotomy covers.

Only years later did I understand The Author had sent me an extravagant image as a means of indicating that the voice of the Law is broken and does not speak truly.

Since we were deemed too broke to file bankruptcy, Mike and I returned to our fruitless routines. He spent days on the road trying to amass enough miles and haulage fees to pull us back from the financial brink. I continued to care for Speedy and the other horses, to shore up our sagging fences and crumbling barn with whatever I could scavenge, to maintain our household, and to mow and chop the vegetation, which sought to take over the farm during the lush summer of 2003. But I did so with a writer's intuition that I was, as a character in a story, only midway through the plot.

In spite of the weird interlude with Ainsley Killbuck, I began to search for a lawyer. One piece of the puzzle still eluded me, that being, proof Tyler knowingly shipped Speedy lame to the Nationals. But, I believed I'd assembled enough documentary evidence for an attorney to launch a lawsuit. With their legal resources and the discovery process, it seemed the rest of the case could be built.

Given how litigious our society has become and how often the phrase "Get a lawyer" is heard, I was surprised at the difficulty of retaining a lawyer. Countless times I left messages on answering machines and with secretaries and never had the courtesy of a call back.

On several occasions, I got past secretaries and spoke to attorneys, who expressed interest in my case, asked that I send the particulars and documentation, and then just left me hanging. They couldn't be bothered to decline the case with a phone call.

I couldn't conceive of another business, profession, or enterprise, which could operate successfully with such haughty disregard for public relations.

One lawyer I spoke to was quite forthright about the difficulties I was encountering. He said, "If an attorney doesn't think your case is worth a million dollars, he's not interested."

Million dollar lawsuits probably didn't abound in our rural area, so I kept trying. Eventually, I was put in touch with a local female attorney, who was also a horseowner.

During our consultation, she *tsk tsk*-ed sympathetically about what had been done to Speedy, accepted my case—and shelved it for three months. When she wouldn't answer my phone calls, I notified her office staff I would be picking up my documents.

Later, I learned the horseowning lawyer was lobbying for the job of Village Solicitor in a nearby town. She eventually secured the job. I imagined my case and probably others were accepted as a fallback position in case the political appointment didn't materialize. The lawyer seemed to give no thought to putting clients' lives on hold, and perhaps damaging their cases by allowing statutes of limitations to expire, while she pursued her personal career ambitions.

I had lost valuable time. My distaste for lawyers had grown exponentially. And I seemed to have no choice but to file a complaint, myself, in Gordon County Small Claims Court. If I were successful, the maximum award would be $3,000, only a sliver of what Tyler's misconduct had cost us, but, Mike and I could use it.

Then something unexpected happened.

The local attorney, who sent a letter to Dr. Samuel Hawkins and told me not to expect anything, called to say there was a reply. I hurried to his office and opened the envelope. It was Hawkins' notes on his four examinations of Speedy at the Nationals.

On October 9, 2002, the day I calculated that Speedy arrived at the Nationals, Hawkins noted:

"increased pulse both front feet
turns sore both ways
take off shoes + take off medicines
+ evaluate in the morning"

Take off shoes. I recalled Tyler had included $275 in horseshoeing charges on his invoice for the month of October 2002. I reviewed his invoice, which had arrived in November, and saw Tyler assigned October 17th and October 22nd as the dates when a horsehoer performed work, dates that were apparently fabricated to cover when Speedy's shoes were actually removed and reapplied during the U.S. Nationals.

Take off medicines, Hawkins' records said. After the lameness scare, Tyler told me a vet for his facility pronounced Speedy sound, recovered, and ready to go to the Nationals. In my mind, that meant sound, recovered, ready—and functioning without medications. But, Hawkins' notes suggested otherwise.

I pulled out Dr. Weed's bill to see what meds Speedy was getting prior to Tyler's departure for the Nationals. On October 2nd, a week prior to the Nationals, Dr. Weed prescribed Isoxuprine, Banamine, and Ketofen—medications associated with laminitis.

Take off medicines. In a perfect world, and the Arabian horseshow industry was far from that, Dr. Hawkins would have called a show steward on October 9, 2002, and reported he'd just performed an examination, which demonstrated Tyler Wragge was attempting to exhibit an incapacitated animal and was seeking his medical assistance in doing so, something that was ethically offensive to him as a veterinarian.

Apparently, that didn't happen since Dr. Hawkins' notes showed he examined Speedy the following day, October 10, 2002. He noted:

"much improved—better than yesterday ACTH"

How the mere removal of Speedy's shoes and the discontinuation of medicines could account for improvement were not explained and *better than yesterday*, what did that mean? Better is not a quantifiable assessment. And, ACTH, the *uber*-hormone of the endocrine system, was not a medication.

On October 12, 2002, the day of Speedy's Western Pleasure class, Dr. Hawkins' notes read: *"CA I "*

The cryptic notation indicated a calcium injection.

On October 15th, three days after Speedy's class, Hawkins' notes read:

"X-ray R+ LF 2 laterals only
acepromazine
exam + clean sheath"

Dr. Hawkins again acknowledged taking x-rays, but, he still withheld Speedy's x-rays. *Why? Why?* I wondered so often. *If they showed no abnormalities, why wouldn't Dr. Hawkins send them? If they showed rotation, well, that was a different story. Was it possible, he charged for x-rays but didn't actually take any?*

Following receipt of Dr. Hawkins' medical notes at the lawyer's office, I wrote him another letter requesting his x-rays and included a check to cover the cost of copies and shipping. The x-rays were never sent.

But, Dr. Hawkins' notes provided the missing link I'd sought, proof Tyler shipped Speedy lame to the Nationals and withheld that from me when I arrived.

I thought back over the small incidents at the Nationals, which had no significance at the time. Tyler not practice riding Speedy in the Main Ring. Tyler offering to demonstrate Speedy's fitness by lungeing him in the warm-up ring. Speedy unaccountably rearing. Tyler claiming the area was too crowded and taking Speedy back to his stall. The presence of the blue object that was inserted into Speedy's hoof to prevent rotation, which I assumed was no longer in use.

The information in Dr. Hawkins' notes revealed Speedy must have been in pain. My horse had been taken off medications, which offered some relief, while Tyler attempted to bluff his way through the horseshow. His plan, when Speedy failed to respond to treatment prior to the Nationals, must have been to dope Speedy to disguise his true condition, to prey upon the ignorance of Speedy's distracted owner, to collect his money, and to dump my horse and move on as soon as he could.

I recalled Tyler's snotty remark after Speedy limped out of the Main Ring. He said, "You'd think he could have sucked it up for one class."

The remark infuriated me when I thought of the suffering Speedy was subjected to by Tyler's attempts to cover his mistakes. *Yes, Tyler, why couldn't an animal in pain have been more helpful to you?*

The one-year-anniversary of the U.S. Nationals was near. I had worked hard in the past twelve months to quell the rage and sense of betrayal that overwhelmed me when Dr. Weed's phone call revealed Tyler's duplicity. I had divested myself of the most scalding emotions, settling instead into a routine of dreary determination I hoped would produce justice for Speedy. However, the confirmation of Tyler's outrageous behavior, coupled with the sad state of Speedy's health, again caused a flare of anger. I resolved to try once more to find a lawyer.

Chapter 13

The human mind is intolerant of mysteries. When confronted with an unresolved story, even regular folks pursue the questions that guide journalists: Who, what, where, when, why, and how? As a regular person, who had passed through journalism, I was particularly compelled to know more when the outline of Tyler's conduct began taking shape.

I could track the paper trail myself using the tools of journalism, but, I needed entry into the secretive world of Arabian horseshows. McKenna was willing to help. By tapping into her network, McKenna supplied names and leads. I planned to use the contacts as I would if investigating a news story, asking questions and gathering information while revealing as little as possible of my own situation.

The first contact I phoned was Rick Sims, a wealthy contractor, who had sued Tyler Wragge and his parents, Tom and Tina. When I reached Sims, I was poised to take notes of his comments, but, I could scarcely keep up with the flow of his fiery complaints. Saying he'd had several horses with Tyler at various times, he claimed his grievances included unauthorized veterinary visits, false billings for medical services, fraudulent dealings, botched sales of horses, lying, and steroids.

Tyler's response to Sims' claims had been to accuse Sims of not paying his board and training bills. In lieu of the purported unpaid bills, Tyler confiscated one of Sims' horses.

To get back his horse, Sims filed a Complaint in Replevin, an action to recover personal property, which has been claimed unlawfully. Sims had to post a bond as a guarantor. Sims' lawsuit was filed in April 2000, several months before Speedy's first introduction to Tyler's facility.

I'd heard from other sources about a callous practice in the industry whereby trainers deliberately run up large bills clients are unable to pay, as means of acquiring quality horses at a fraction of their value. Did Sims think that was the case? He was unwilling to speculate.

As I probed for more information, Sims began tamping down his heated remarks.

Did he file a complaint with Arabian Horse Association? Sims claimed he had, but called the process "a joke." By that time, his enthusiasm for the subject of Tyler Wragge had cooled. He said, "If you want more details, call my lawyer."

I returned to the other leads generated by McKenna—all women. They included:

A young woman whose stallion flipped over in a stall at Tyler Wragge Elite Horses while wearing a *bitting rig*. As it thrashed and struggled, the stallion drove a nail or wood splinter into its chin. Allegedly, Tyler did not report the injury to the owner, in order to retain the horse for the show season.

Infection at the injury site became a chronic problem that required repeated medical attention to the stallion's chin. Tyler was making payments to the owner on damages of $5,000 to the horse.

A woman trainer recalled an incident with Tyler, which she said revealed his mean-spirited side. Both of them had youth riders in a class. Tyler observed her young client had not removed a tiny rubber band from a braid in her horse's mane. He reported her oversight to the judge, who was obliged to disqualify the youngster.

Then, I heard about Priscilla Cosgrove who, according to rumor, also had a horse founder while at Tyler's. I thought I might have a good lead, but as soon as Priscilla answered my phone call, my hopes began to wilt. She was one of the most annoying types of horseowner: the Horse Mentalist.

Now, horses have unique mental abilities, which animal behaviorists have outlined. But, Horse Mentalists assign complex emotions, intellectual abilities, and cognitive skills, to horses that, uh, just don't seem to exist. Except in their horses.

The dictionary definition for that folderol is *anthropomorphism*, attributing human characteristics to animals. Considering the woeful state of human affairs, I thought it rather insulting to horses to imbue them with human attributes.

I entertained those thoughts while Priscilla Cosgrove talked incessantly. Apparently, the woman could breathe through her ears, as she never paused once. My query about her foundered horse launched a blabby dissertation about laminitis, insulin resistance, and her horse, Skippy, who was over-flowing with mental activity, always ready to comfort and to mind-meld with her. Skippy was oh so special because he was her best friend, confidante, and soul mate.

And, yes, she was a former client of Tyler Wragge, who was also oh so special, because he understood her oh so special connection with Skippy.

And, yes, Skippy did founder at Tyler Wragge Elite Horses, but Skippy kept the onset of laminitis to himself for some time, and her horse had a reason for that. Yes, Skippy, she said, refrained from showing signs of founder (painful though it is) "Until Skippy knew he could trust Tyler."

Until Skippy knew…what?? (Cue the Twilight Zone tune.)

Clearly, Priscilla was still a Tyler supporter, as were a few other former clients I spoke to. When that was the case, I said nothing to try to dissuade them.

To her credit, Priscilla applied her ardor for Skippy to his recovery. She emailed me several times to report on Skippy's progress as she pursued the goal of healing him and returning to the showring with her beloved horse. And she did.

Sadly, Skippy had a severe recurrence of laminitis several years later and had to be humanely destroyed.

When none of McKenna's leads proved useful, I wracked my brain for anyone I might have met or overlooked, who could provide information. My visits to Tyler Wragge Elite Horses were always brief and focused on Speedy. I rarely even saw other clients. Who might know something? Finally, two names came to me: Mickey Ambrose and Rhonda Mueller.

Would they talk to me?

Mickey was the heiress whose financial windfall Tyler anticipated dipping into. She was hesitant to talk, but related she had two or three horses with Tyler at various times, including her stallion, Rock Steady Baby. In preparation for a regional championship, Mickey, who lived in another state, arranged to meet Tyler, who was hauling Rock Steady Baby with other clients' horses from Ohio, at the showgrounds.

When she arrived, Mickey discovered her stallion was incapable of carrying a saddle and competing because Tyler had opened numerous painful wounds in the horse's sides with spurs. A veterinarian was called, who documented sixty gashes on the animal. By way of explanation, Tyler claimed Rock Steady Baby was "uncontrollable."

Mickey arranged for Rock Steady Baby to be hauled to her home by another horse trainer and removed her other horses from Tyler's facility.

Afterwards, Mickey, who was a petite woman, showed the *uncontrollable* stallion herself.

Rhonda Mueller, according to Tyler, was the person, who wanted to purchase Speedy prior to the 2002 U.S. Nationals. When I spoke to her by phone, she was antagonistic and unwilling to talk. Had she been burned by Tyler, too? Or was she yet another woman, who bought Tyler's guff about enemies that were out to get him?

I couldn't tell. It was all I could do to keep her on the phone long enough to answer one question: "Did Tyler ever act as your agent for the purchase of my horse Speedy?"

No, she replied, never. She had just purchased the stallion Khookaburra Bey from Tyler, and she wasn't in the market for another horse at that time.

As one woman after another declined to join me in taking a stand, I often thought fancifully of the legendary Arabian mares known as Al Khamsa. According to ancient Bedouin tradition, mares were more highly prized than stallions. The "Daughters of the Wind" were the preferred mounts for battle and much revered for their courage.

An old story claims the Prophet Mohammed devised a test of his mares' stamina and character by withholding food and water for three days. When the mares were turned loose to quench their thirst at an oasis spring, they galloped toward the water. The Prophet blew a note on the battle horn and five of the hundreds of mares ignored their thirst to turn back and answer the summons.

In recognition of their valor and faithfulness, the Prophet named the mares Al Khamsa (The Five) and used their bloodlines as the foundation for the Bedouin horses.

Those bloodlines, nurtured by a few purist horse breeders, exist to this day.

I wished I could find four other women to make my own Al Khamsa, women, who understood justice for Speedy was also about raising awareness for other Arabian showhorses whose seemingly pampered lives might be masking ugly realities.

Five seemed such a small number. Five out of The Eighty Percent. All I needed was a small band of sisters, who would be willing to go to battle against horseshow abuses—why couldn't I find them?

I was fortunate to have the assistance of Dr. Penelope Kean, but, she wasn't a candidate for my imaginary Al Khamsa. Dr. Penny was a steadfast professional for the cause of good veterinary medicine, and that's where I needed her. I thought my Al Khamsa should come from courageous Arabian horse devotees, who could no longer tolerate the abuses.

McKenna could probably be counted on to play a role, but, she was not likely to be one of my Al Khamsa. I felt she was too steeped in her longtime dream of a national championship to allow herself to fully acknowledge what I believed was the pervasive corruption of the horseshow world.

But I'd come to the end of McKenna's list of disgruntled Tyler clients. I'd found no one who seemed willing to support justice for Speed, if the need arose in the future. A couple weeks passed. I was discouraged. Then, McKenna came through again. She heard about a woman named Samantha Barlow whose daughter had a bad experience with Tyler. They agreed to talk to me.

The green-draped stalls of Go 'n' Win Farm were located at the back of the stabling area for the 2004 Buckeye Arabian Show. The Barlows and I decided to split the traveling distance between our homes by meeting at the show and the stalls of the training barn they were affiliated with after ending their relationship with Tyler. As I'd done before, I walked the concrete floors of the Expo Center, up and down aisle-ways and rows of decorated stalls, and past people involved in horseshow preparations.

But, I was no longer the clueless newcomer I'd been at my first Buckeye visit. On the second visit, I knew about the sharps containers, knew The Buckeye show managers repeatedly hired the same vet, who injected Speedy at the Nationals, and knew that somewhere on the show grounds Tyler was showing horses for a new round of clients.

What I once took at face value was distorted by new knowledge, that turned the supposedly prestigious show into a carnival midway where there was a lot of razzle dazzle, but, the hall of mirrors reflected unreliable images.

Who was trustworthy? The famous trainer with his gaggle of admirers following lemming-like in his wake as he led that season's celebrity stallion to the Main Ring—who was he really? The kind patient person he projected or a sadistic punk?

What was real? The grandiose show barn inviting prospective buyers with leather sofas sitting amid mauve-tinted shavings and potted mums—what kind of horses was it offering? Abused horses with the equine equivalent of post-traumatic stress disorder that could have a dangerous meltdown? High dollar horses with drug-induced health problems? How many culls from its breeding program had been sent to the meat auctions?

Was my revised view of the horseshow world just a personal grudge, a painful experience I inflated to unfairly condemn a whole industry?

Ah, you're just a sore loser! That would be said about me. *You're just a person, who thought your horse was better than it was, and you're bitter.* That, too, would be said about me. *You're letting an encounter with one rotten apple (or two or three) spoil the whole barrel.*

Really? Is that who I was? Is that what was going on? Or was the whole barrel rotten? Were the good apples in the barrel under the impression they could avoid infection by ignoring the few rotten apples?

I don't think it works that way. It's not enough to be a good I'm-minding-my-own-business-don't-bother-me-I'm-having-fun-apple during times of creeping rot.

Or, to put it in the more elegant phrasing of Edmund Burke: Nothing more is needed for Evil to triumph than for good people to do nothing.

When I located Go 'n' Win, Samantha Barlow was there to meet me. I was immediately struck by her air of timidity. She seemed like a person, who goes through life jumping at every noise and shying away from the slightest breeze. That was worrisome. Horses, which are timid, can be reactive and unreliable. Why not people?

Mrs. Barlow escorted me into Go 'n' Win's client lounge and tottered off with hesitant little steps to find her daughter. If the daughter were as irresolute as Mrs. Barlow seemed to be, I'd wasted a trip.

I sat down at a table where sales and training literature were laid out and looked around. The green of the stall drapes was carried out in a fabric-wrapped interior. Comfortable furniture sat upon thick carpets. Ribbons and trophies were displayed around the walls. A faux ceiling had been created with pleated fabric to block out the overhead view of the Expo Center's steel rafters. The lounge had an intimate, almost tent-like, coziness.

A pretty young woman about eighteen-years-old came into the lounge and introduced herself. She had blonde hair worn in the long straight style all young blonde women favored. Her teeth were perfect, her skin flawless. If I had even a vague notion I'd seen her before, I wrote it off to my age. All pretty blonde horseshow divas looked alike to me.

Young Ms. Barlow recounted a misadventure at the 2003 Youth Nationals in Albuquerque, which had led her family, after several years as clients of Tyler Wragge, to terminate its relationship with him. At the show, and without permission, Tyler put charcoal into the mouth of Sultan, her beloved purebred Arabian gelding.

Charcoal? Why?

Sultan was a seasoned campaigner, who knew his job. Nevertheless, Tyler thought the horse should close its mouth more firmly on the bit, something the drying properties of charcoal would accomplish.

Ms. Barlow and her aunt discovered the situation when they observed black discharge coming from Sultan's mouth. The tissue inside was so inflamed and sensitive, Sultan refused to eat or drink. Without water, dehydration set in. At the end of a long trailer ride from New Mexico back home to the Midwest, Sultan had pneumonia and was colicking and foundering.

A first-rate veterinary hospital was able to save him, but at great expense. Owing to the catastrophic event and the likelihood of recurrence, the Barlow's equine insurance policy on Sultan could not be renewed.

(Insurers may also cancel policies when unauthorized joint injections have been performed on horses, a fact that trainers and vets, who are needle specialists, likely don't convey to horseowners.)

The effect of charcoal on Sultan's mouth was to dry out mucus membranes, leave scar tissue, and caused his tongue to split.

Tyler denied any responsibility in the matter, blaming the stress of showing and transport for Sultan's problems. Young Ms. Barlow was deeply hurt by Tyler's attitude. She believed they'd had a close personal friendship, that Tyler was the older brother she'd never had. The hurt she felt at his irresponsibility and betrayal had turned to anger. She showed none of her mother's timidity. She felt a duty to Sultan. She would be willing to testify to Tyler's misdeeds, if I needed her.

Since the young woman had spent considerable time with Tyler, I asked, "Do you know a veterinarian named Dr. Weed?"

She replied effusively, "Oh, yes. Dr. Weed has injected some of my family's horses for soreness. And, he did a whole bunch of horses at Go 'n' Win before a big show."

Obviously, she liked him and saw no danger in corticosteroid injections. That door was closed. Her value to me, if litigation ensued, was as a witness to Tyler Wragge's pattern of behavior.

That was all I foresaw at the end of my conversation with Ms. Barlow. I couldn't know she had more to divulge. That she had been in a position to see and hear many things. That she had information about Tyler's treatment of Speedy, which would enrage and horrify me. Why didn't she fully confide in me at the 2004 Buckeye?

Two reasons, I suspect: Because Tyler, who habitually spread poison about anyone who fell out with him, had lied about me. And, because she realized I didn't recognize her.

I didn't recall a fleeting moment at the 2002 Nationals when a pretty young blonde woman, who was helping Tyler to groom Speedy, was introduced to me, not by her last name Barlow, but by her first name—Shannon.

At the same time I was seeking witnesses, I was following another track. I needed to enlarge my basic understanding of laminitis and find out more about the connection between the disease and corticosteroids. The connection wasn't hard to find. It was noted over and over on websites, in veterinary medical literature, and in official positions of equine agencies.

I was copying everything I found and soon had a stack of papers, which needed to be arranged for my own clarity and for presentation as evidence, if need be. The national organizations presiding over veterinary medicine seemed a good place to start.

The American Veterinary Medical Association (AVMA) occupies the same place in veterinary medicine as American Medical Association does on the human side, and, thus, has similar prestige and name recognition. AVMA's mission includes accrediting twenty-eight American veterinary schools, developing guidelines for proper use of drugs, participating in state and federal legislation, and publishing The Journal of AVMA, in which scientific studies from universities and other animal health institutes are published and peer reviewed.

All kinds of animals come under the purview of AVMA, and it may provide information on issues as diverse as grief counseling for pet loss, choosing a reptile pet, and guidelines for working with circus elephants.

Since AVMA covers such a wide range of species, many large animal vets belong to American Association of Equine Practitioners (AAEP). That organization was formed in 1954 to promote ethics in horse racing. The promotion of ethical conduct continues to be the primary goal of the membership according to an AAEP handbook, which enumerates lofty ideals in an ethical code called "The Principles."

One of the Principles spells out the VCPR, veterinary/client/patient relationship as a means of facilitating communication and expectations between veterinarians and horseowner clients. In the VCPR, the welfare of the equine patient is supposed to be paramount.

In its mission of advocacy for the horse, AAEP has adopted various official positions over the years. In 2002, AAEP officially documented its support of the Horse Protection Act of 1970, which sought to eliminate *soring* of Tennessee Walking Horses and other gaited breeds.

(The practice of soring involves cutting, lacerating, injecting nails, screws, and/or applying chemical or blistering agents to the limbs of horses to achieve more animated gaits.)

In 2003, AAEP's position on tail docking (amputation of part of the tail bone) was medical necessity or workplace safety for the horse, but not cosmetic purposes, were the only acceptable reasons for the practice.

Of particular interest to me was AAEP's 1991 position on corticosteroids, which read in part:

"Potential side effects of corticosteroid therapy: Some corticosteroids, when used excessively or too frequently, may have a negative effect on the body's natural immune response. Locally injected, corticosteroids may weaken support tissues such as the cartilage and ligaments of a damaged joint if used excessively or indiscriminately. The frequent systemic use of corticosteroids may suppress the ability of the adrenal gland to produce naturally occurring corticosteroids and other hormones, thus creating a hormonal imbalance. Some corticosteroids, when used excessively, have been implicated as a cause of laminitis."

The AAEP publishes *TheHorse*, a monthly magazine for veterinary professionals that's also of interest to horseowners, who wish to keep up with the latest medical advances, disease prevention and management, and equine news. In March 2003, *TheHorse* reported on a recent rule change approved by USAEquestrian (later USEF) whose aim was to reduce corticosteroid abuse in performance horses. The article included the following:

"Overuse of dexamethasone and other corticosteroids can promote immuno-suppression (reducing disease-fighting ability) and can cause laminitis."

As AAEP and USEF seemed candid in acknowledging the link between corticosteroids and laminitis, I wondered what position was held by British Equine Veterinary Association (BEVA). On its website, under causes of laminitis, BEVA noted:

"Certain drugs, including those which belong to the group of medicines known as corticosteroids, can in some cases result in laminitis."

Information from the Internet, I knew, was not admissible in Court, but, I thought an official printed document might be. So, I requested via email that BEVA send its laminitis brochure to me by postal mail.

My email arrived and languished during one of Britain's long holidays. The short, unintentional delay seemed to be construed as a gaffe on BEVA's part and aroused the famous British civility. Staffers were as cordial and helpful as text on a computer screen can convey. Moreover, a BEVA official drew my attention to a recently settled laminitis lawsuit that was causing a stir in European horse circles.

The plaintiff, Jane McGarel-Groves, sued two veterinarians, who injected her dressage mare with corticosteroids in the left hock in 1999, and in both hocks and the back, in 2001. The mare developed laminitis and had to be euthanized.

Arguing she would not have approved the procedure had she been advised of the risk of laminitis, McGarel-Groves prevailed in the lawsuit and was awarded damages of 350,000 GBP ($608,280 U.S. funds).

From official positions taken by veterinary associations that noted the corticosteroids/laminitis connection, I moved on to published research by universities, professors of equine medicine, individual researchers, and charitable institutions, where I continued to find the connection referenced in studies and in opinion pieces.

Because no comprehensive blind controlled studies of laminitis have been conducted, most medical opinion was based on studies of two kinds: *in vivo* (living creatures) and *in vitro* (laboratory or test tube)—and, on anecdotal information.

The way anecdotal information works is this: If a vet uses corticosteroids to treat a horse for another disease and the horse develops laminitis, that outcome added to other such anecdotes, accumulates to form a body of knowledge, which is an alternative to a clinical study.

In vivo, in vitro, and anecdotal evidence, in the articles that I collected, largely supported the laminitis/corticosteroids connection, sometimes with a proviso—that laminitis could be anticipated after corticosteroids treatment, if another factor like stress, obesity, infection, rich diet, or transportation, was also present.

The assurances of an extensive, all-revealing clinical study of laminitis as an alternative to anecdotal information and piecemeal studies may never be available for a couple of reasons. Because laminitis begins and develops within the hoof, a hard enclosed container, the disease is difficult to study. And, grant money for research reflects the state of the economy. In hard times, scientific inquiry, starved for funds, slows down.

How much money would it take to solve laminitis? An amount was speculated in an AAEP article occasioned by the misfortunes of a horse named Barbaro.

In 2006, Barbaro won the Kentucky Derby and was spoken of as a candidate to win the Triple Crown. However, after Barbaro broke from the gate in the Preakness, his jockey sensed an injury, and pulled up the colt.

Shortly afterwards, it was learned Barbaro had numerous fractures in his right hind leg. The media kept a worldwide fan club updated on Barbaro's progress, and hopes for recovery were high among the uninitiated. I was not one of the hopeful.

First of all, Barbaro was a three-year-old, a baby in horse terms, too young in my opinion, for the strenuous demands of Thoroughbred racing. But, racing babies to get the money machine going is part of the tradition in America. Training may begin as early as one or two years old. If baby legs are ruined before they're even mature and, if drugs and injections fail to keep them running, well, the meat truck is called, and a new bunch of babies are started.

With the bones of his right leg pinned together and in a cast, Barbaro's recovery required he carry his weight on three baby legs, setting him up for a second setback, laminitis caused by weight-shifting. Sadly, that's what happened. Barbaro developed laminitis in his left hind hoof and had to be put down. All the miracles of modern veterinary medicine could not save Barbaro from the cruel disease of laminitis.

As part of its Barbaro coverage, AAEP ran an article on its website explaining the disease in laymen's terms and calculated the cost of a comprehensive study of laminitis could be $10 million.

That sizeable amount wasn't raised in more prosperous times, so it's unlikely funds for in-depth research to produce all the answers to laminitis will be available anytime soon. For the time being, horse-lovers will have to settle for current treatment and what is presently known. Taking preventive measures, by acquainting oneself with the causes of laminitis, and trying to implement safeguards, are all that can be done now.

But, I learned a funny thing was going on about one of the causes. As events progressed, I would be following up on my research of the corticosteroids/laminitis connection by contacting veterinary associations and charities devoted to laminitis, and speaking to individual researchers, whose work I'd read or who'd been recommended as experts.

The reactions of various entities and people to my questions made me doubt my sanity: Corticosteroids causing laminitis? *Never heard of it.* Corticosteroids linked to laminitis? *Oh, I couldn't comment on that.* Time and again I encountered uncertainty, quasi-denial, and a kind fidgety official-speak, which I thought I recognized.

When I phoned AAEP about its official position on corticosteroids, I was told AAEP was thinking about revising the statement.

A representative of one charitable agency, which had raised and disbursed considerable funds for laminitis research, was utterly confounded that I was asking about laminitis and corticosteroids. Where did I get that idea?

I had to take a couple of deep breaths before I said, "Haven't you read your own website? Haven't you noticed the item on your own website under the heading CAUSES that says *'Drug induced laminitis from using corticosteroids'*?"

The reactions of individual academics, which I'll outline later, often followed a similar pattern of butt-covering, double-speak, backtracking, and indecision. If I hadn't held black and white evidence in my hands, copies of articles and official positions, I'd have thought I'd been hallucinating.

Instead, I felt I was back at the *Oakland Tribune*, running headlong into the politically correct barrier around an off-limits topic.

Chapter 14

My neighbor, Gigi Greiko, had been a one-woman welcome wagon from the moment we met. And, her catalogue of horse-related information was ongoing. So, it shouldn't have surprised me when I eventually found a lawyer by way of one of Gigi's numerous acquaintances, who supplied the name and cell phone number of an attorney that was familiar with horse issues: Mark Rinaldi.

When I called Rinaldi, I outlined my situation as I usually did, without specifically naming the involved parties. He sounded interested in my case and asked me to be specific. He acknowledged he knew Tyler. But, after what I hoped was a conversation that was going somewhere, Rinaldi said he was serving as general counsel on a big project and was unavailable for outside work.

He did, however, recommend another attorney, who was also a horseowner: FeliceDeWinter. After Attorney Rinaldi's referral, I presumed I'd never encounter him again. I was to be wrong about that.

Within a week, and very near the one-year mark of Speedy's misadventure at the U.S. Nationals, I was sitting across a desk from Felice DeWinter. She was a squarely built woman with lank dark hair cropped above shoulder length. She wore a blocky, unflattering pantsuit and spoke in a brusque manner.

Attorney DeWinter sorted through the documents I brought. She seemed impressed with the thoroughness of my preparation. She announced the statute of limitations was about to expire, and we'd have to file immediately to beat the deadline. DeWinter said I had a solid case and, if Dr. Penny would testify to her belief that Speedy was foundered with steroids, our prospects were good in bringing a suit against Dr. Linus Weed and Tyler Wragge.

Speculating Tyler probably didn't have any money, DeWinter also added Tom and Tina Wragge as defendants. Initially, I was uncomfortable with that, until I calculated their complicity.

They saw the same bloody-mouthed horses McKenna had seen. They were both named as parties, along with Tyler, in Rick Sims' lawsuit, so they knew the charges. And, they could observe Tyler's MO on a daily basis.

Despite what they witnessed, the elder Wragges continued to offer camouflage and a veneer of respectability to a son, who was a known liability.

DeWinter instructed me to tally all receipts, bills, and expenses to determine what Mike and I had invested in Speedy. I was astonished when I calculated from Speedy's birth through to our horse's treatment for laminitis, we had spent $12,500.

Where had all that money come from?

We were perpetually short of funds, but, somehow we had scrimped, belt-tightened, and lived without frills for over three years—only to lose our investment in Speedy, plus the money we might have recouped from his sale.

Based on those figures, DeWinter said we would seek $50,000 in damages. And, we'd have to get busy quickly. She'd have to dismiss the complaint I'd filed in Small Claims Court, file a new complaint in Gordon County Court of Common Pleas, and I had to come up with a $2,500 retainer.

Finding any real money seemed impossible. But, I had one credit card that could still produce a cash advance. I max-ed out the card and signed a contract with DeWinter, who took my case on contingency. If we settled during litigation, DeWinter would take 30%. If the lawsuit settled in the pre-trial stage, she would get 40%. If we went all the way to trial and were successful, she would get 50%. If we failed to prove the case, a possibility I didn't wish to entertain, I might have to pay court costs and attorney fees.

I was deeply convinced the convergence of characters and infamy, which befell Speedy, was representative of the state of the horseshow industry. That others had suffered due to Tyler's practices, I already knew. That he would continue to do damage and to enlist compliant vets, I felt certain. That unethical veterinarians were preying upon sport and showhorses, I also believed. A successful lawsuit might set an important precedent and start bringing about change.

I conveyed that motivation to Attorney DeWinter, who was also a horseowner, who claimed to be somewhat acquainted with horse industry abuses, and who professed to have previous horse-related trial experience. Yet, her enthusiasm for my vision never got much above the ho-hum level. I hoped she was one of those practical people, who take a wait-and-see attitude and, she'd become more engaged as time went on.

With the payment of DeWinter's retainer, I entered an arrangement that went against a personal conviction. Putting myself under someone else's control and having to settle for whatever they chose to do for me represented an abandonment of my own independence. Considering the arrogance I encountered while seeking a lawyer, I should have anticipated what was coming.

DeWinter became remote. Her communications were brief and dictatorial. I needed to appear (on short notice) for legal functions. Dr. Penny (without regard for her professional obligations) had to produce affidavits on demand. And, DeWinter's paperwork requirements, which always seemed to be on deadline, needed immediate attention.

Initially, I thought, by retaining a lawyer, I would get some rest. I was frazzled from the long tussle for medical records and disappointed with the apathy of officialdom.

To my surprise, Attorney DeWinter assigned me the task of finding expert witnesses. We were going to need an expert on laminitis to supplement Dr. Penny's testimony and an expert horse appraiser, she said. Get busy.

What? I thought lawyers had all that expert witness stuff at their fingertips. Surely there were databases, listings, or websites for locating expert witnesses. Why should I have to look for experts? And, how?

Fortunately, research I'd done on studies of laminitis and corticosteroids and the authors of the studies gave me a place to start. I was pleasantly surprised at the responsiveness of some of the country's renowned veterinary experts, who readily replied to my phone messages.

I was less pleasantly surprised at their waffling. Generally, I was told: *Most practicing veterinarians are cautious about using corticosteroids because they believe laminitis can result, but, that is anecdotal information. Since no large-scale controlled study has been done to establish cause and effect, I cannot scientifically make the connection.*

Hearing that over and over made me grumpy. Yes, a large-scale study had not been done and probably wouldn't be done. But, what about in vivo and in vitro studies? What about the official positions taken by equine veterinary associations? And, why was a large body of anecdotal evidence given such scant consideration?

Plus, I was already fed up with sentences that began with "A recent study shows…" followed by research on drinking coffee, eating red meat, mating habits of college students, bovine flatulence, and other waste-of-money studies.

My pre-existing irritation about studies was riled each time an academic cited the absence of a comprehensive laminitis/corticosteroids study as a reason for declining comment. It seemed to me scientific curiosity and common sense were being superseded by excessive caution.

In instances where the academics acknowledged the connection via anecdotal evidence, why the waffling and doublespeak? After all, anecdotal evidence was being submitted by medical professionals, not old-time horse quacks, who advocated pine tar as a cure for everything. I had a theory: Trial lawyers and the expert witness game.

Even the casual viewer of Court TV or courtroom dramas in film and television knows how that works. Each side in a lawsuit hires an expert witness. The experts may present diametrically opposed opinions. And, the trial lawyers try to tear them apart, going so far as to attack the expert on matters unrelated to their expertise, even their personal lives.

Given the toxic strategies of trial lawyers, expert witnesses understandably would like to cite an unimpeachable, infallible, irrefutable, comprehensive study. But, without the CYA security of that ephemeral study, what's left? How about exhibiting some fortitude? How about protecting horseowners by being candid about what anecdotal information indicates concerning the laminitis/corticosteroids connection?

Among the wafflers, there was one incident, which made me howl with exasperation. I spoke to a prominent veterinarian, who was considered a superb lameness diagnostician. He was generous with his time, but declined to make a connection between laminitis and corticosteroids. He did, however, recommend a colleague, who was affiliated with a university vet school. Call him and use my name, the vet said.

The professor was also congenial, talked at some length, declined to make the laminitis/cortosteroids connection with the standard disclaimer about the absence of a comprehensive study. Then, he returned to the subject of his buddy, the horse vet.

"Did he tell you about the award he won?" asked the professor

"No, what was it?" I replied.

"It's very unusual for someone outside of academia to receive an excellence award from this particular association," drawled the college prof, "But, one year they gave it to him."

"Oh, really," I said, "What was the award for?"

"Well, my buddy mostly worked at the racetracks in those days. And, he figured out racehorses that were getting lots of steroid injections, frequently came down with laminitis."

Whoa, whoa! Did I hear that correctly? The horse vet, who declined to make a connection between laminitis and corticosteroids, WON AN AWARD for making a connection between laminitis and corticosteroids? And, the professor, who had so much respect for him, couldn't make the connection either? Good grief!

While many academics were unwilling to support the laminitis/corticosteroids connection, a few were—and rather emphatically. One professor at a Midwest university was sympathetic to the problems I was having in finding confirmation of my belief.

He said, "There's no doubt at all steroids founder horses. I don't know why the veterinary medical community has gotten so wishy-washy on this subject in recent years. We have foundered horses at the clinic with steroids when that was the only thing, which could have caused founder."

Another renowned vet took my call while he was driving to an airport where he was flying out to a laminitis conference. Let's talk, he said, I've got plenty of time.

He, too, was quite clear on the laminitis/corticosteroids connection and related a story about a party that purchased a million dollar Thoroughbred stallion, which had received many steroid injections. It suffered an even worse fate than the old grass-foundered horse. The vet said, "One week after they bought the stud, it walked out of all four feet."

Occasionally, I spoke to an expert, who was sufficiently moved by Speedy's story and agreed to speak to Attorney DeWinter. Inevitably, the people I was contacting wondered why I, rather than my lawyer, was soliciting expert testimony. I didn't know myself.

When I finally asked DeWinter that question, she replied I had the ability to explain the issues, and it kept the costs down if I made the calls. But, if having a client make phone calls as a cost-cutting measure damaged our credibility, was that really wise?

Owing to DeWinter's penchant for secrecy and control, she never told me anything about her follow-up of the experts, who had agreed to talk to her. I don't know if she phoned any of them. If so, I didn't know if any of the experts were persuaded by talking to her to take the next step and officially join my lawsuit, or what it would cost me to enlist their expertise.

I related some of the conversations I had with academics to Dr. Penny. She knew many of the experts, either personally or by reputation, and seemed disappointed on my behalf that I was having such difficulty getting someone to step up.

Finally, Dr. Penny suggested I call a professor, who was highly regarded—Dr. Beatrice Quigley.

After hearing Speedy's situation, Dr. Quigley replied she was a surgeon and therefore wouldn't qualify as an expert witness on laminitis. Her response had the tone of a brush-off, but, in the hair-splitting legal world of who qualifies as an expert, I believed she was correct.

Later, I was to come across Dr. Quigley's name again.

A bona fide horse appraiser was the other kind of expert DeWinter said I needed. Gigi suggested Miranda Caxton an Arabian horse broker, well-known in the industry, who had handled a sale for her.

As it turned out, Caxton saw and admired Speedy at the Nationals. She confirmed my horse had generated a buzz among show attendees. From speaking with her, I believed Caxton might have been the woman in the trio that sat behind me during Speedy's class, who said, "That taffy horse is something special."

Would anything have been different, if, instead of privately savoring the compliment, I had turned around and introduced myself as the owner of the taffy horse? Would anything have changed the swift current of events that swept through my life? Would anything have changed Speedy's destiny? I'd never know.

Caxton seemed genuinely distressed to learn of Speedy's founder. She could do an appraisal based on her first-hand impression, if I would also provide bloodlines, videotape, and show records. I quickly sent the information, and Caxton promptly returned her appraisal.

She compared Speedy with two other horses Speedy competed against in the Western Pleasure class. One of the horses went Top Ten and sold for $20,000. The Reserve Champion sold for $60,000.

Caxton wrote, "That is the price range for these horses. I do feel Imperial Marquis [Speedy] would fit into that category."

However, Miranda Caxton lived in Texas. Attorney DeWinter informed me expert witnesses had to appear in court. (Defendants have the right to face their accusers.) Caxton's evaluation written on her letterhead stationery wouldn't do.

Caxton's credentials were just what I needed, but, even if she were agreeable, I couldn't afford to pay her professional fee plus travel and lodging expenses. I began to see why the expense and complexities of a trial put justice out of the reach of many people.

So, who could I get locally? Ohio had many breeders, trainers, and prominent industry figures, who might qualify as experts. But I believed many of them were part of the problem, either by actively participating in abuses or passively tolerating them.

In any case, an Arabian industry Big Shot was unlikely to go to bat for a Nobody like me. I'd already talked to horseowners, who had been victimized and wouldn't go to bat for themselves. Furthermore, I had another experience that reflected poorly on how some people in the Arabian horse industry operate.

In the spring of 2002, two of our mares delivered foals sired by Imperial V. My dreams for Speedy were to crash to earth a few months later. But, at the time the mares were bred, I still had a modest ambition to breed a few quality horses that were raised, trained, loved, and sold to people, who shared my horseownership values.

Thus, Bold Impression delivered her second foal, a filly, which was a full-sister to Speedy and almost a mirror-image of her big brother. Queenie cared for her little red-gold girl with the same tenderness she had bestowed on Speedy.

The other new mother was a big AQHA mare named Shesa Tuff Hot Shot. She was an eye-catching liver chestnut with four knee-high white stockings. Her fluid gaits and jumping ability were not characteristic of Quarter Horses, and, before we ran out of money, she was being shown and trained for dressage.

Her personality was another matter. It's an axiom among horse people that if you name a diminutive foal "Tiny," it will grow into a huge wooly mammoth. If you name a sweet foal "Sugar," it will develop the personality of a rhinoceros. Shesa Tuff Hot Shot's nickname was Sugar. She was capable of affection, but, it was pretty much reserved for Mike.

Sugar's first foal, a colt, arrived a week early and with none of the usual signs of impending birth to alert me. Instead, I entered the barn one morning to feed, heard nothing out of the ordinary, and began pitching flakes of hay through the stall doors.

When I opened the door to Sugar's stall, I found a strapping colt lying in one corner of the foaling stall. Sugar, looking stressed and bewildered, was backed into the opposite corner.

At my approach, the colt stood up. He did so without wobbling. His coat was fluffy and completely dry. I was amazed at that kind of dexterity in a newborn, but was alarmed at his dry coat. He'd been alive for a while, and a foal should nurse and ingest the colostrum of mares' milk within hours of birth. It was apparent Sugar had not allowed her colt to nurse—and wasn't about to.

Sorting that out was going to be at least a two-person job. Mike was on the road. I called his cell phone and related the situation. He was hundreds of miles away. So, I phoned Gigi, who said she'd be over immediately. Then, I called Dr. Penny, who was on rounds, but could stay in touch by phone.

"Get the mare and foal together no matter what," Dr. Penny said, "With Speedy to care for, and the new filly, there's no way you have time to bottle-feed that colt."

I agreed. I attempted to put a halter on Sugar, who would have none of it. Her panicked evasions in a small space put the colt and me in danger, so I waited for Gigi to arrive.

In the meantime, I looked over the colt and felt a wave of disappointment. He was a big dark bay, almost black in color, with ears like a mule. I anticipated Sugar's foal would have handsome white markings, what's called *chrome*, like its mother and Imperial V. But, the colt's chrome was minimal, a smudgy star on his forehead and two trifling white marks on his rear legs. As he stood in the corner, hungry and dejected, I thought, "You poor homely little bugger."

A short time later, Gigi flew through the barn door and exhibited an efficiency, which belied her ditzy blonde persona. The first order of business was to get Sugar under control. Gigi had a nifty trick for that. She opened the loop of a lariat, laid it on the stall floor, and placed a bucket of grain inside the loop. When the hungry mare lowered her head to eat, Gigi pulled up the loop over Sugar's neck.

We put a halter on Sugar and tied the lead rope to a ring mounted on the wall. The plan was to milk the mare, bottle-feed the colt to give it colostrum and to relieve its hunger, and, then, to work on getting the estranged mother and son together.

The first part of the plan got off to a rocky start. Sugar was uncooperative and unwilling to have her distended and painful udder touched. But, Gigi persevered, and I caught the milk in a pan. As the mare began to feel relief from being milked, she relaxed and let down more milk.

We loaded up a baby bottle and set about feeding the disconsolate colt. Since his instinctual efforts to nurse had been rebuffed by his dam, he was suspicious of the latex nipple we were trying to insert into his mouth. Finally, he gave it a try, then, began to suck enthusiastically. The problem henceforth was the colt associated comfort and sustenance with the bottle, and, Sugar, who wanted relief for her milk-swollen bag, didn't associate that relief with her foal.

Over and over, Gigi and I wrestled the tall colt to its mother's side. He simply couldn't figure out he needed an S-bend in his neck to reach under her belly to latch on to her teats. And, Sugar continued to resist the match-up.

I had discovered the colt at 7:30 in the morning. Gigi arrived soon after. By 1:30 that afternoon, we still hadn't gotten the pair together. We were exhausted and glad to see Mike arrive. My husband, though tired from a week on the road, bustled into the barn, confident he could sort things out. Two hours later, he was exhausted, too.

The three of us stared wearily at Sugar and her colt standing at opposite ends of the stall. Then Gigi, who was a devout Christian, said, "There's something we haven't done."

She asked that we join hands, close our eyes, and pray with her.

"Father God, we have done all we can. We are so tired. Please help us. Amen."

Mike and I added "Amen," and opened our eyes.

The colt took a couple steps toward Sugar. She didn't push him away. He lowered his head, curved his neck under his mother's belly, and nursed.

Gigi's squeaky voiced screamed, "It's a miracle! It's an absolute miracle!"

After eight hours of struggle, it certainly felt like a miracle.

Mike interjected a wisecrack, saying, with more wisdom than he intended, "Why didn't you ask for God's help hours ago?"

The two foals born in 2002 were the results of breedings to Imperial V after Cody and Natasha Smoak bought the stallion from Gordon Meriwether. The couple was trying to rebuild a clientele for their stallion and offered me a package deal on breeding two mares.

I told the Smoaks the financial terms would have to be the same as I'd had with Meriwether, payments in whatever amount I could scrape together and whenever I could make them, with the balance paid off by the time the foals were born. They agreed to those terms. When the two new arrivals were born, the deal had been fulfilled without problems on either side.

In 2003, Queenie was again pregnant with a foal sired by Imperial V. I had signed a breeding contract with a live foal guarantee and an option for a rebreeding as I had done three times before. The payment terms were the same.

Several months into Queenie's pregnancy, I made another trip to Florida to see my father. When I returned near the end of July, I noted Queenie seemed to be in heat. I called Dr. Penny, who examined the mare via ultrasound. The womb was empty. Queenie had lost her foal.

I called Cody Smoak to report the news and to set up a rebreeding. Cody icily refused. Then, Natasha phoned and criticized me harshly. She claimed I had only paid them $100, and I was just one of numerous people, who were trying to rip them off.

While Natasha railed at me about the $100 and the way they were being misused by their clients, I kept my mouth shut, partly from my habitual inability to think and speak coherently during moments of duress, but, also because I knew damn well that I'd sent more than $100.

In any case, if I'd only sent one dollar, I was still in compliance with our agreement, so long as I paid off the balance by the time the foal was born.

I gathered my cancelled checks and found I'd paid roughly half the amount I owed, well before Queenie's due date. I checked the re-breeding clause of the contract. It was in effect until August 15th. I still had two weeks during which to rebreed.

I was shocked at the Smoaks' attitude. I was in the process of paying for my fourth Imperial V foal. I had been more than a loyal customer. When they were desperate for clients, I supported them. When they believed McKenna's ruminations on Huckleberry Bey's Cushing's Disease had damaged Imperial V's reputation, I sided with them. When Tyler Wragge claimed Imperial V's offspring had faulty hooves, I disbelieved him and continued to patronize the Smoaks' stallion.

What accounted for their conduct? Inept bookkeeping? Something in the water? Was insanity a communicable disease transmitted by Arabian horses?

Legally, I could demand the Smoaks honor the contract. But I was done. I had been damaged by two vets, a trainer, and then ripped off by breeders in the Arabian horseshow world. The crummy circle was complete. I'd had enough.

I scraped together the balance due and sent it to the Smoaks. I paid $1,000 for a live foal the Smoaks had guaranteed by contract, but wouldn't try to deliver. I received a cheery as-if-nothing-happened thank-you-note from Natasha, acknowledging receipt of my payment.

Her ability to go from screeching money-grubber to Susie Sunshine was creepy. But, it didn't matter. I was done.

I would breed no more horses. There were already too many unwanted and neglected horses in the country. I would not try to sell the ones I had bred. The insights I had into the drugging and training practices of the Arabian horseshow industry, insights I didn't have when I bred Speedy, wouldn't allow for it. I couldn't take the chance another horse I'd bred and raised might suffer the same fate as Speedy. The red-gold filly and the dark bay colt would stay with me, safe from a world where they were considered disposable.

Chapter 15

Nearly everyone I'd met in the Arabian horseshow community appeared motivated by self-interest, greed, or cowardice. Given that pool of candidates, I thought it best to seek elsewhere for expert appraisers.

An Internet search brought up the National Association of Equine Evaluators. According to its website, NAEE offered credentials to qualified applicants, who completed home study courses or attended seminars. Once credentialed, appraisers paid annual dues to NAEE. The aim of NAEE, it seemed, was to bring some standards and legitimacy to the practice of *horse tradin'*.

The term itself, for as long as people have been selling horses to other people, has been associated with misrepresentation, scams, trickery, and hanky-panky. The more benign practices of horse tradin' were recounted in the autobiographical writings of Ben Green.

Dr. Ben Green was a veterinarian, part time horse trader, and prolific writer, who told tales on himself. In one of his many horse tradin' tricks, he used hard-boiled eggs dipped in black ink pressed against the hides of plain white horses to create attractive dappled grays. Worked great, said Doc Green, unless it rained.

Shady horse tradin' of a more serious nature is practiced at every level. A grade horse with a bad attitude is given a dose of calmative as it is run through a low-end auction. A well-bred horse represented as safe for any rider turns out to have rodeo bronc potential. A high dollar equine athlete changing hands in the world of show jumping is grossly misrepresented. And, no one is immune from the audacity of those peddling bad horses.

Such was the case when actor Tom Selleck purchased an expensive show jumper for his then twenty-year-old daughter. The horse had a broken hoof bone, a medical condition, which should have ended its use as a show jumper. However, the serious hoof condition was disguised by frequent steroid injections.

In a subsequent lawsuit, Selleck successfully proved the seller knew the horse was lame and recovered his payment and damages. One of the witnesses testified the horse's condition could have resulted in fatal injury to a rider.

Could an organization like the National Association of Equine Evaluators be useful in weeding out bad horse tradin' deals? I didn't know. But, NAEE seemed to fill the bill as an appraiser provider for my lawsuit. I contacted NAEE to see if it had a licensed appraiser in Ohio and was promptly sent the name Phoebe Fowler of Twin Maples, Ohio.

On the phone, Fowler expressed condolences about Speedy's situation and my misfortune. She said she had credentials, which would satisfy my needs. Not only was she affiliated with NAEE, but, she also owned a horse business and held judges cards for several breeds.

We settled on a fee of $200. Fowler instructed me to send Speedy's pedigree, show records, photos, and videos, to assist her in determining my horse's value prior to his lameness. And, she agreed to have her name and phone number forwarded to Attorney Felice DeWinter, who was handling my lawsuit

I assumed what seemed like a pretty straightforward arrangement with Phoebe Fowler, would proceed smoothly. However, Felice DeWinter, in one of her rare communications, advised me Fowler was not performing her task and was not responding to phone calls or faxes. Get a hold of her and tell her to get the appraisal done, said DeWinter.

Perhaps DeWinter was overstating the delay, I thought. She was demanding Dr. Penny and I jump when she said frog. Maybe Fowler was on task, but unwilling be hustled along by DeWinter. I began calling Fowler as DeWinter demanded, but, my messages went unacknowledged and unanswered.

Eventually, DeWinter said Fowler had produced an appraisal in affidavit form valuing Speedy at $25,000, so, I gave no more thought to Phoebe Fowler.

Almost a year elapsed between the filing of my lawsuit and my first contact with the defendants. That came when Attorney DeWinter took depositions at her office on September 27, 2004.

When I walked into the conference room, there were two men seated at a table, who arose when DeWinter and I entered the room. One was robust and barrel-chested with a paunch that was beginning to strain against the buttons of his suit jacket. His face bordered on handsome, but was marred by an expression, which seemed like he was suppressing a sneer.

The other man was tall and beef-jerky thin, with close-cropped gray hair, intense green eyes, and skin that had an oily sheen. I thought he looked nervous and furtive.

When introductions were made, the big man with the growing paunch was identified as Brock Hightower, who traveled to the depositions from Columbus, where he was part of a large law firm. He specialized in defending against malpractice suits.

So, the shifty-appearing character was Dr. Weed. I refrained from staring at the veterinarian, who had to be pummeled with letters, phone calls, and official complaints, before sending Speedy's x-rays, and who still withheld medical information.

After a few moments, Celinda Knott, the attorney for Tyler Wragge and his parents, joined us. She was a middle-aged woman, with long bleached blonde hair, who dressed in mini-skirts, rhinestone-studded belts, platform shoes, and other age-inappropriate gear that made her look like a post-menopausal pop star. Her clients did not attend the depositions.

I expected the depositions would be a lengthy process for all involved. In fact, it was relatively brief. Celinda Knott had little to say. Hightower asked me haughtily why I hadn't tried to mitigate my losses by selling Speedy.

I thought about my poor lame horse, his limited potential, and his diminished activities. The idea that I would or could sell such a damaged animal was ridiculous. I looked directly at Dr. Weed and said, "I wouldn't know how to market a medical mistake."

Dr. Weed's green eyes glared, and he lurched in his chair, as though he was going to leap across the table at me. Hightower blurted out an objection.

When that mini disruption subsided, Hightower played one card. He slid a document across the table towards me.

At the top of the first page was the letterhead of a college of veterinary medicine. I quickly scanned the three-page document and determined it was the statement of Dr. Weed's expert witness.

After the quick read, I went back and considered the pages more intently. The entire statement seemed to be worded with excruciating care. For example, the expert wrote, "Depo-Medrol has not been shown to cause laminitis."

Has not been shown. That Depo had not been shown to cause laminitis was, in the realm of legalistic nit-picking, miles away from stating that Depo-Medrol™ does not cause laminitis.

The expert went on to say no clinical study had been done to demonstrate a causal effect between corticosteroids and laminitis. Well, there was a refrain I'd heard before.

However, parts of the expert's statement, I believed, could be turned to good use for my case. For example, the expert noted that 400 mg doses of Depo-Medrol™ could induce systemic effects, veterinary-speak for laminitis.

I'd read studies, which suggested the total body dose of Depo-Medrol™ should not exceed even lower amounts, ranging from 200 to 400 mg.

Speedy was given 460 mg of Depo-Medrol™

So, I was not unduly rattled by what Brock Hightower must have thought would be a knockout punch. I was even less rattled after the second read-through of the statement when I again came to the expert's signature at the bottom of the last page.

It was signed by Dr. Beatrice Quigley. That was the professor Dr. Penny had urged me to phone. The same Dr. Quigley, who was a surgeon, and, who told me she couldn't offer an opinion on laminitis, since it was outside her area of expertise.

What accounted for the change in Dr. Quigley's attitude and assessment of her expertise, I wondered. *Payment of a generous expert witness fee? Doing a favor for a colleague?*

Were there other possibilities for her switcheroo? I figured veterinary medicine, like other professions, had a no-snitch code. Or did Dr. Quigley's defense of Dr. Weed just proceeded from the society-wide attitude that it was virtuous to be non-judgmental.

I knew enough about the expert witness game to know Attorney DeWinter could probably get Dr. Quigley disqualified. However, I said nothing during the deposition.

Afterwards, I told my lawyer about my previous contact with Dr. Quigley and the surgeon's self-confessed lack of expertise. The normally undemonstrative DeWinter practically squirmed with delight.

On December 8, 2004, all parties to the lawsuit were instructed to appear at law offices in Chastain, Ohio, where a three-member panel of lawyers from the area would try to arbitrate a deal that would eliminate the need for a trial. Dr. Weed and Attorney Hightower were present. And, Tyler Wragge and his parents finally put in an appearance with their counsel, Celinda Knott. All the Wragges avoided looking at me and sat next to Knott staring straight ahead.

I hadn't seen Tyler since the end of 2002. The searing anger and betrayal I felt for him then was so corrosive to my well-being I had tried to let it go. Two years later, I could look at Tyler across the conference table with a measure of detachment.

The hearing was scheduled in late afternoon, and the first order of business for the arbitrators was to announce they were only going to devote thirty minutes to the task, as they all had appointments elsewhere. That was not reassuring.

I had provided my lawyer with many documents attesting to the fraud and malpractice of the defendants. And, DeWinter should have been provided ahead of time with all the evidence and rebuttal information the defendants' counsels planned to use. Litigation is highly scripted and mapped out ahead of time, so as to avoid Perry Mason moments.

Perhaps, if the arbitrators actually studied the documentation they had been sent in advance of the hearing, well, maybe thirty minutes would be sufficient.

Thus, it was surprising to see Dr. Weed, not his lawyer, pulling papers from a folder and offering them to the arbitrators.

As Dr. Weed passed documents to the panel, Attorney Hightower raised his arms in a gesture of dismay and loudly proclaimed, "This is the first I've heard of this!"

Was it mock dismay on Hightower's part? He didn't prevent Dr. Weed from submitting the materials. And, the arbitrators, instead of disallowing documents, which clearly weren't properly entered into evidence, chose to review them.

Then, Attorney DeWinter asked to see the documents. I looked at the pages over her shoulder. One purported to be Dr. Weed's notes in his own handwriting of the calls on his answering machine for the dates September 30 and November 1, 2002.

In both instances, Tyler Wragge called Dr. Weed regarding Speedy to report "founder" and "laminitis---still lame" on the respective dates.

In another document were notes Dr. Weed claimed to have made during the phone call to Dr. Penny. He noted Dr. Penny's query about a lameness exam and wrote he only watched Speedy jog. That reflected his amended statement to Dr. Penny when he called her back.

How did Dr. Weed, and Hightower, if he did know about the contents, figure those documents were helpful? It seemed to me those pages confirmed Dr. Weed knew about the laminitis early on, as he told me in the November 29, 2002 phone call, and, he was also admitting to an inadequate lameness exam.

However, my lawyer failed to object. Then, Attorney Hightower addressed the arbitrators in a haughty I'm-a-big-deal-lawyer tone of voice. His manner combined exasperation and weariness, as though our business that day was so tedious and insignificant, and my grievances so trivial, well, it was just time for the big city lawyer to wrap up the dog and lame pony show.

Hightower said, "Counselors, Dr. Weed's medical records in this case have been reviewed and approved by the American Veterinary Medical Association."

The invocation of AVMA caused a collective physical change in the arbitrators. They sat back in their chairs and their shoulders relaxed. The supposed approval of AVMA released them from the sticky business of making a just decision.

And, they would not have to oppose Hightower. As small town lawyers, they weren't in his league, and they understood instinctively their place in the pinstripe pecking order.

And fortunately, Hightower's assertion fell within the time allowed for the arbitration hearing, so, the three panelists could stop sneaking looks at their watches.

The hearing terminated shortly after Hightower's claim, and the arbitrators quickly left the building for those appointments that were more pressing than the events, which ruined my life. I was bothered by the paper shuffle pulled by Dr. Weed, by the slap dash hearing, and by something else I figured out later. But, why wasn't anyone else bothered or paying attention?

There were six lawyers in the room when the claim was asserted that AVMA gave its blessing to Dr. Weed's treatment of Speedy. Not one of the lawyers, not even mine, asked for that supposed essential of the justice system—proof.

Attorney DeWinter and I were last to leave the conference room. As we walked through the door into the lobby of the law firm, I discovered Tyler Wragge and Dr. Linus Weed standing shoulder to shoulder, with Tyler's parents nearby, to form a gauntlet, which I had to pass through.

Both Tyler and Dr. Weed raised their arms, leaned towards me, and waggled the fingers of their hands, while they said, in the singsong cadences of schoolyard bullies, "Bye, bye, Judy. Bye bye, Judy."

It was entirely in keeping with Tyler's personality, I thought. But I had trouble accepting that a doctor, a DOCTOR for cryin' out loud, participated in the nasty display.

As my lawyer and I stood in the parking lot and watched the arbitrators sprinting towards their cars, I asked why Tyler and Dr. Weed behaved in such a way. DeWinter said, "We lost."

Was that a certainty? Had my evidence counted for nothing? The arbitrators hadn't announced their decision. How did everyone know but me? I asked DeWinter to contact me when the official announcement was made.

Tyler, Tom, and Tina Wragge walked past, swaggered actually, and made their way towards a shiny new pickup truck. Tom took the keys from his pocket and tossed them in the air, where Tyler snagged them. The gesture had the celebratory air of a high five.

What exactly were Mom and Pop Wragge celebrating? They enjoyed paying lawyers? They didn't object toTyler's actions, which, as with Rick Sims, had again ensnared them in a legal matter? They approved of Tyler's business practices? Or was their celebratory air merely an extension of the win-at-any-cost mentality of the horseshow world?

If the decision went against me, as everyone seemed to assume, I planned to appeal. I waited for my lawyer to notify me of the arbitration panel's official decision—and waited and waited. After ten days, I phoned Attorney DeWinter.

"Oh, I thought you knew," said DeWinter, "The decision was for the defendants."

"How would I know that?" I replied.

"Well, it's on the docket of the Clerk of Court's web page," she answered.

I suppressed my irritation. I had paid a retainer and signed a liberal contingency agreement, only to be given all kinds of tasks I thought were part of my lawyer's duties. She didn't respect the request I made at the beginning of our relationship, that, as an injured party, but also as a writer, I wanted communication. She didn't inform me about how the process worked or how it was going.

Then, in addition to all that, DeWinter had the nerve to suggest I was to inform myself of major developments in my lawsuit by checking an Internet website.

I told my lawyer I wanted to appeal the decision of the arbitration panel. Attorney DeWinter seemed to sputter a bit and then said, "Oh, well, uh, the deadline for filing an appeal is almost here. I'll really have to hurry to get it filed."

Again, I suppressed annoyance. Why had my lawyer allowed a critical amount of time to elapse without contacting me? She heard and saw the same things I did at the arbitration hearing, that documents suddenly appeared, and that Dr. Quigley did not meet the legal qualifications as a laminitis expert. Why had Attorney DeWinter allowed my case to lose inertia and possibly be dismissed owing to a looming deadline?

DeWinter managed to get my appeal filed just in time. The judge approved the appeal, which cost $250 to file. I imagined the two bully-boys, who stood in the law firm lobby taunting me, had an unpleasant surprise when their legal counsels notified them the lawsuit would be continuing.

After the lawsuit was allowed to proceed, there were times I had information to add to my case. But, when I felt I had to contact my lawyer or press her for progress reports, she began to say, with increasing ire, that I was asking her to break the law.

Using the tools of discovery and the power of the subpoena to gain more admissions and documents from the defendants wasn't breaking the law. It was the process of the law. I knew that from journalism, not to mention common sense. But, what was I to do with a lawyer, who unaccountably seemed to be foot-dragging?

As I tussled with DeWinter's inattention to deadlines and seeming lack of enthusiasm, I didn't know my lawsuit was nearing the end in a way I never anticipated. Following the judge's approval of the appeal, my lawyer's growing irritation quickly moved toward sustained hostility.

A trial date had been set for June 6, 2005, but, my attempts to learn about her preparations or the role I needed to get ready for, merely provoked rancorous responses from DeWinter.

In one email, she wrote, "You are the dumbest client I've ever had, and that includes the ones with no college education."

Hmmm. I had been wise enough to carry out portions of discovery and to solicit expert witnesses. But, overnight, I'd become the dumbest client she ever had. It was exasperating, weird, professionally inappropriate, and increasingly worrisome.

I asked DeWinter what became of the potential witnesses among vets in academia I had contacted, who agreed to speak to my lawyer. She replied nastily, "I don't have time to be chasing after expert witnesses."

Our phone conversations became similarly vitriolic. DeWinter informed me I needed to come up with $5,000 to hire an expert witness, or there was no point in going to trial. I was staggered at that late notice of a huge expense, mere months before trial.

In the back of my mind, I knew an expert witness, while I was making phone calls and attempting to secure one, would have to be paid. Since DeWinter never advised me an expert had been engaged, and, she didn't have time to be chasing after expert witnesses, I'd assumed we were going to go to trial, get Dr. Quigley disqualified, have Dr. Penny as our medical expert, and Phoebe Fowler as our expert of Speedy's value.

Then, out of the blue, with only months to do so, I had to come up with five grand for an expert laminitis witness, who DeWinter never mentioned before. Who was the expert witness anyway? Was there one? DeWinter didn't say. She only said we couldn't win without another expert.

I tried frantically to raise money, but couldn't. In a desperate and humiliating attempt to raise money, I even emailed people of means in the Arabian horse industry. I explained that my lawsuit, if it could go forward with their help, might be useful in addressing some of the abuses in the horseshow world.

I received only one response, a hand-written note from a well-known Arabian horse breeder, who wrote:

"Your tragic experience with Speedy has just come across my desk. It is heartbreaking to me how many similar instances I hear of. I have chosen to channel my efforts against such treatment through my support of the Arabian Horse Owners Foundation which works tirelessly in many directions and sometimes with success. You are certainly to be commended for your perseverance and willingness to pursue the outrage that was perpetuated on Speedy. The best of luck…"

While I appreciated the courtesy of a personal response, I also thought, "If you're hearing of many heartbreaking similar instances on a regular basis, then, it seems, the remedy you've chosen isn't working."

The situation with DeWinter was so perplexing. How had I become the enemy? How had the lawsuit, DeWinter told me on Day One was winnable, a lawsuit I still believed in, descended into a mire of insults, recriminations, and assertions of lost causes? The whole exercise, all the months of money, research, hard work, and traveling to appointments, seemed to have been a pointless waste of time. It was just bewildering, but, it was going nowhere. I couldn't possibly go to trial with a lawyer whose attitude was so contrary to my interests.

By February 2005, I'd had enough of DeWinter's arrogance and hostility. I notified her I would be dropping my case. I was relieved to think I would never have to speak to DeWinter again, never again have to endure her attempts to degrade my intelligence, and to break my spirit. I was wrung out by her negativity and intimidation.

While I deplored the waste of time and effort, I needed a rest. Yet, I sensed The Author was not done with me. Since I had first felt the presence of The Author in Ainsley Killbuck's office years earlier, the plot being written for me had lurched along, dragging me into more complicated experiences and uncharted territory. I hoped for time to regroup after dismissing my lawsuit. That didn't happen.

Chapter 16

In a letter, dated March 21, 2005, Dr. Linus Weed notified me he was renewing his demand for payment. His lawyer, Brock Hightower, had informed him the lawsuit was voluntarily dismissed, and Dr. Weed wanted to be paid $1,624.50.

I was not surprised to hear from Dr. Weed again. I was convinced by his refusal to provide Speedy's medical records in the months following the U.S. Nationals that he was an arrogant man with a sense of entitlement. Our face-to-face encounters during litigation confirmed my view.

Whenever we had been in the same room, Dr. Weed fairly simmered with suppressed rage. His skin would begin to ooze oil, and his green eyes took on a hard glint. He was infuriated, I believed, at being challenged by a client, particularly a woman. And, I think it was a further ordeal for Dr. Weed, who was a tall stringbean, to sit next to his large, booming-voiced lawyer with strict orders not to speak, a situation, which made him look like a gawky schoolboy in detention.

I had no sympathy for Dr. Weed. Early on, I considered he was a victim of Tyler Wragge's duplicity, as I had been. But, I quickly learned that was not the case. Time after time, he had opportunities to act like an ethical medical professional—and he hadn't. What I'd learned up to that point about his shoddy treatment of Speedy, his neglectful attitude, and careless follow-up, only condemned him further in my estimation.

Additionally, I'd formed the opinion Dr. Weed was part of a growing problem of unethical veterinarians succumbing to the lure of big money, built on shady practices, side deals with trainers, disregard for private property, and disrespect for animal life.

The lofty purpose of healing had been replaced by a money grab. I was not going to be coerced by legal threats into paying the bill. To do so, would be a counterfeit endorsement of Dr. Weed's shabby treatment of Speedy and his evasive actions after the fact.

I wrote back to Dr. Weed that I found his conduct reprehensible, from the unauthorized injections of Speedy on September 23, 2002, to his withholding of medical records, and his false statements throughout the legal proceedings. I refused to pay him and invited him to take whatever action he felt necessary.

Dr. Weed accepted my invitation. He replied he would pursue the matter via collections. That would take awhile, I figured. In the meantime, I had to get busy—very busy.

As distasteful as it was, I contacted Felice DeWinter's law office. I left word I needed my legal file, that Attorney DeWinter and her staff should organize it with all due haste, and tell me when I could pick up the file. While I waited, I prepared in other ways.

I drove to a big bookstore in nearby Denton and studied the choices in the legal section. I purchased a book, which was a primer for self-represented lawyers. It was geared for much smaller legal tasks than I would be undertaking, but gave a basic overview of the process.

I combed the Internet and downloaded the Ohio Rules of Civil Procedure and Ohio Rules of Evidence. I explored many cases of veterinary malpractice, which were archived in various Internet places. And, I also located an extensive online lexicon of legal terms.

Those resources alone were not going to be sufficient. I needed access to a law library. I was enormously relieved to learn the Parker

County Law Library in Denton was open to the public. I was even more relieved when I checked it out. The head librarian and her associates were superbly efficient and accommodating. While they made it clear they couldn't give legal advice, they were able to fulfill informational requests with impressive ease.

With those basic preparations in place, I was ready to collect my legal file from Attorney DeWinter. I assumed I would be going over much the same ground, and the first lawsuit might serve as a template for another one. And, I was looking forward to seeing what DeWinter had turned up during discovery. Though she asked me to participate in discovery, she hadn't shared the results with me.

But, there was a problem.

After some delay, my former lawyer informed me the file couldn't be found. I told DeWinter I had to have the file and pressed her to search again. After a time, she again informed me the file couldn't be found. I insisted she find it.

DeWinter replied, "What's the big deal?"

I refrained from prefacing my answer to the big deal question with the words "You clueless blockhead…".

I informed DeWinter that Dr. Weed was going to sue me, and my legal file contained everything I needed to defend myself, all the phone records, documents, invoices from Tyler Wragge, and, of particular importance, copies of the x-rays of Speedy taken by Dr. Lance Albright and Dr. Weed.

DeWinter's rejoinder was a jaw-dropper. She said, "Well, if you need Dr. Weed's x-rays, I'll just ask him to send you another copy. I'll even pay for the copies."

I could scarcely believe such a bone-headed response.

I responded emphatically, "Don't you dare contact Dr. Weed! Don't you dare let on that I don't have the x-rays he sent me!! Are you crazy? You find the damn file or else!"

Sometime later, with no further comment from Attorney DeWinter, her office staff notified me the file had been found. I made the six-hour roundtrip to pick up a hefty cardboard box, which contained a year and a half's worth of legal work. Immediately, I checked the x-rays for the tiny marks I'd used to ID them. The marks were there. I'd gotten my copies back.

At home, I cleared a large area on the dining room table and began sorting through the contents of the box, a task which took several days. My first impression was distaste for the sheer waste of paper.

Every feed bill and receipt and minutiae I'd submitted to establish our investment in Speedy had been Xerox copied and duplicated many times over. Every pleading was copied in triplicate, stapled to blue paper backings, and stacked in the box.

Reams and reams of paper had to be gone through page by page until I extracted a handful of pages, which seemed to be pertinent. There was DeWinter's original complaint. In it, she charged fraud, breach of fiduciary duty, negligence, breach of contract, malpractice, and she asked for punitive damages. Great! At the outset, my lawyer had delivered a helluva punch to the defendants. BAM, right upside of their heads!

Attorney Hightower, I could see, presented a vigorous defense of Dr. Weed in a written form that reflected his personal bombast and truculence. However, his bravado was undermined by the untruth of virtually every one of his assertions.

The file showed the defendants had nothing in the way of exhibits and no witnesses other than Dr. Beatrice Quigley. Her credentials were hyped to the max. But, all that resume inflation didn't alter the fact she was a surgeon, a well-respected surgeon, but not a laminitis expert, and could possibly be disqualified.

On my side was Dr. Penny Kean, whose affidavit outlining her beliefs was vigorously attacked by Attorney Hightower, as was an affidavit provided by another veterinarian from my area, Dr. Sophia Cortese, D.V.M, Ph.D.

Dr. Sophia's statement covered the proper medical approaches Dr. Weed had declined to follow. She wrote:

"Utilization of any intra-articular medication for the control of joint pain should be considered only after exhaustion of alternative therapies. These would include: Intramuscular injections (Adequan), IV therapy (Legend), oral supplements (Cosequin, CortaFlex, etc) or nonsteroidal anti-inflammatory drugs (phenylbutazone, Naproxen, etc)...These products combined with rest from work should always be used as a first line of defense when dealing with joint pain."

Hightower's assaults on Drs. Kean and Cortese, I thought, could have been beaten back by DeWinter, who claimed to have ample trial experience. And, I believed a jury would understand medical treatment should not begin with the most extreme solution. If a dog has a thorn in its paw, a vet should try a few remedies first before amputating the paw. But, Attorney DeWinter failed to counterpunch forcefully in the pleadings.

With Dr. Penelope Kean as an expert and other witnesses including Dr. Lance Albright, McKenna Jamison, J.T. Laney, Shannon Burke, and Phoebe Fowler, the horse appraiser, it appeared we had ample firepower to go to trial.

Therefore, it was shocking to find among the papers in my legal file that Attorney DeWinter had muddled the necessary paperwork from Phoebe Fowler. I recalled DeWinter's phone calls complaining about Phoebe Fowler's unresponsiveness, but, I assumed things had gotten back on track.

Yet, in the legal file, there was an affidavit from Phoebe Fowler appraising Speedy at $25,000, but, the affidavit had not been signed or notarized and had been stricken by Judge Barton Flint.

That meant we had no basis for ascribing damages. I stared with utter stupefaction at the botched appraisal document with Judge Flint's notation of Phoebe Fowler's invalid affidavit.

How the hell had Attorney DeWinter submitted an affidavit without signature or notarization in the first place? That should have been covered in Lawyering 101.

Later, I found a properly signed and notarized affidavit from Fowler appraising Speedy at $25,000. But, had DeWinter resubmitted it to the Court in time?

As my mind turned over those questions, I recalled DeWinter's harassment in the final phase of our association. My lawsuit was, by then, in the pre-trial stage. Discovery had closed. It was too late to add expert witnesses. And, all DeWinter's energies should have been directed towards planning and preparing for the courtroom.

Yet, my lawyer had not turned her energy in that direction. Instead, she created an untenable relationship with me and made a bogus demand for $5,000 for an expert witness.

I was sickened by what the file revealed and the unaccountable deterioration of my lawyer's commitment. From the contents of the file, I still believed the case was strong. But, my lawyer had rolled over for reasons I couldn't fathom. Later, much later, I was to learn the astonishing reasons for my lawyer's failure of resolve.

The morning of June 10, 2005, was already warm. We were in the midst of a spell of hot, humid Ohio weather, and the afternoon temperatures had been in the 90s. Instead of feeding Speedy his morning meal in his stall, I decided to turn him out and feed him in his paddock under the shade trees, then, return him to the cool of the barn for the rest of the day.

As I opened Speedy's stall door, my eyes glanced around at the sawdust bedding. There were no droppings. My chest tightened. Speedy should have passed manure during the night.

I put a halter on Speedy and led him outside to a paddock. His usually effusive personality was subdued. I walked him a bit to encourage the movement of manure through the bowels, then, I left him in the paddock with several flakes of hay. I kept checking on him visually from within the barn as I took care of other chores.

Speedy was not eating, not even picking at the hay. With his other activities so restricted, delivery of food three times a day had become the big events of Speedy's life. Yet, he was listless and disinterested in the morning meal. I felt there was a problem, but tried to stay composed.

I got a lead rope, hooked it to Speedy's halter, and took him to the riding arena where I could walk him on flat ground. I tried to remain calm as I had with other early-stage colics, but, I had to battle a feeling of panic that clutched at my throat and brought hot tears to my eyes. I was fighting back the sense of dark doom that had stalked me ever since Speedy came home with laminitis.

Be there for Speedy, I told myself. *Don't give in to unreasonable fear. You've dealt with this before. It will probably pass. Just do the right things.*

Around and around, we walked. I searched my mind for any change in Speedy's routine, which might account for the onset of colic. The random unfairness of colic is why it's so feared by horseowners, but, still there are predictors. Other than the heat and humidity, Speedy's routine was monotonously the same. And, I'd hung a large fan on the window of his stall, so the summer heat shouldn't have stressed him unduly.

After twenty minutes of walking, there was still no bowel movement. Some horseowners will walk a colicky horse until both of them are worn out. My approach was to walk awhile, then rest, repeat as necessary. I returned Speedy to his stall. He attempted to lie down. That was alarming.

If he went down and couldn't get up, extricating him from the stall might be impossible. I removed Speedy from the stall, left him in an open area of the barn, and rushed into the house to call Dr. Penny.

Triage was a regular part of Dr. Penny's practice. Routine appointments for vaccinations, castrations, and other maintenance matters often had to be rescheduled when emergencies arose. Dr. Penny said she'd move things around and come ASAP. While I awaited her arrival, I resumed walking Speedy. His head and neck were soaked with sweat. Despite the day's rising heat, the sweat was cold.

I wrapped my arms around his neck, buried my face in his mane, and attempted to suppress my fears.

"Don't go! Don't go, my darling golden boy," I pleaded. "I will love you and take care of you always. Don't go."

My arms and face were greasy from embracing the once beautiful neck, which was dank and wet with the seepage of a distressed body. I struggled to compose myself as Dr. Penny's truck pulled up to the barn.

As she had done on the day of his birth and every time since, Dr. Penny examined Speedy quickly and professionally. She looked at his gums and mucus membranes of the mouth and noted they were nearly white, an indication of shock. She listened to Speedy's heart through a stethoscope and detected a heart murmur.

A heart murmur? Speedy was sixteen days shy of his sixth birthday, still a young horse. How could his heart be damaged? I recalled what I'd learned about ACTH. That it slows the gaits of Western Pleasure horses by depressing the heart rate. Could it also have damaged Speedy's heart?

Dr. Penny drew on an arm-length vinyl glove and reached into Speedy's rectum. She removed some manure, examined it for moisture content, and dropped it on the ground. She re-inserted her gloved arm and palpated the internal organs. The large bowel was doughy in consistency and prolapsed over the spleen.

The writhing motion of the intestines in the advanced stages of colic can result in contortions of the bowel and displacement of other organs, a process that seemed to have begun.

To assist in the passage of manure, Dr. Penny prepared to *oil* Speedy. In a clean stainless steel bucket, she mixed water and mineral oil. A tube was fed through one of Speedy's nostrils, down his air passage, and into his stomach. Dr. Penny told me to put my ear against Speedy's belly and listen. She blew on the tube, and I heard a hollow gurgling sound.

The tube was where it needed to be, in the belly, not the lungs. With strokes of a hand pump, which was attached to the tubing, the lubricating mineral oil mixture was flushed into Speedy's gut.

To ease Speedy's pain, Dr. Penny administered an intravenous injection of painkillers. The amount, she said, was sufficient to make him comfortable through the night. She would be back in the morning to assess him.

Dr. Penny said, "That prolapsed bowel may come back down where it should be. If not, we'll be dealing with a surgical colic. You'll have to decide if you want to take him to Ohio State."

I thought about the ramifications of a surgical colic. The expense would be considerable. If Speedy survived the trip to Columbus in the punishing heat and, if he survived the surgery, he would have a huge incision closed with staples and a long uncertain recovery. And, a serious bout of colic was often the initiator of recurrent colicking. And colic could induce laminitis. To bring on all that expense and medical hardship for a horse, who was already dealing with chronic problems, was something I couldn't undertake.

Perhaps it won't come to that, I thought. Mentally, I pushed back against the fearful stalking darkness and prepared to do everything in my power to bring my horse through the crisis.

As Dr. Penny drove away, I resumed hand-walking Speedy and awaited the relief the injection of painkillers should have brought him. The relief did not come. Although Dr. Penny had given Speedy a sufficient dose to carry him through the night, the drugs had no effect on his expanding pain.

I recalled the words of Dr. Paul Shepherd of USEF, that the amount of drugs given to Speedy by Dr. Weed and Tyler Wragge had tampered with the horse's physiology. I remembered Dr. Penny's remark when Speedy first returned home, that the flood of drugs he'd been given was more worrisome to her than laminitis.

The mid-afternoon temperature had risen to the high 90s. I was drenched and stinking from sweat, as was Speedy. I sprayed him several times with the hose to cool him. He became less willing to walk. His hind legs began to buckle. He wanted to lie down.

That was to be avoided. A colicky horse wants to lie down and roll to ease the pain, but, rolling can increase the likelihood of bowels twisting, so allowing the horse to lie down is usually discouraged. Finally, I had no choice. Speedy's hindquarters were starting to fail. I let Speedy ease himself to the ground and rushed into the house to call Dr. Penny again.

As I reached for the phone, it rang. I heard Gigi's chirpy voice on the line. I quickly said, "I can't talk, Gigi. Speedy's colicking."

I hung up, placed a call to Dr. Penny's mobile truck phone, and rushed back to Speedy.

Moments later, Gigi came hurrying through the gate. She said, "I'm here to help. You look exhausted. Let me walk Speedy for awhile."

Shortly thereafter, another helper, alerted by Gigi, arrived. It was McKenna.

Two years earlier, she'd experienced the same ordeal, the death of her beloved Imperial Echo+, in much the same circumstances.

The three of us took turns walking Speedy with increasing futility. While he tried to cooperate with our wishes that he stay on his feet and walk, his body simply couldn't comply. He staggered on wobbly legs, sank to the ground repeatedly, and floundered to get up. I could see the physical manifestation of his longing for the cessation of pain struggling with his desire to please me one last time.

Finally, he fell on his side and stretched his neck along the ground, while his legs kicked spasmodically. I told my friends, "He's done."

Dr. Penny pulled in the driveway again and joined me as I knelt by Speedy's head watching the light flickering out of his eyes. He was bound for the far country, beyond the ability for anything in this world to call him back.Though Speedy was moments from death, I asked Dr. Penny to ease his passage with euthanizing drugs.

The four of us stood silently around the motionless body. I realized the people present at Speedy's death were the same four people who had, in various ways, brought him into being. The circle, which had shone brightly and briefly at the start, had closed in loss and anguish.

The full force of my grief would have to wait for another time. I still had a decision to make—whether to ask Dr. Penny to perform a *post mortem* exam. Once before I'd been faced with that decision and my troubled mind went back to the event.

Whistling Hills Headmaster was a huge imposing five-gaited American Saddlebred, who joined our family when Mike bought him. In addition to his five gaits, the big horse could pace, piaffe, and passage. Mike jokingly said, "That horse has more moves than a bag of snakes."

Thus, a nickname was born, Jake the Snake. The big Saddlebred eventually proved so loveable and ingratiating, I asked Mike to give him to me.

On paper, we weren't a good match, a high performance horse and a very amateur rider, but, over the years, we managed to meet in the middle. The big horse taught me so much I called him the University of Jake.

By nature and by years spent in the showring with previous owners, Jake was habitually high strung. A part of him never completely acquiesced despite the bond we shared. His head was always carried upright on a slender curved neck, a profile that reminded me of the dragonhead prow of a Viking ship.

When Jake was twenty years old, I awoke one morning to find, as was the case years later with Speedy, there was no manure in Jake's stall. Our vet at the time, a woman named Marcia, oiled Jake in late morning and arranged to return in the afternoon. She wasn't unduly concerned, but, as the morning progressed, I was.

I walked Jake and rested him. He passed no manure. I walked him more. His distress increased during the day. Then, he did something unprecedented. Jake turned his face to mine. He looked me fully in the eyes, and, then, buried his face in my chest. The proud figurehead of the Viking ship was lowered in a gesture of supplication. Jake was telling me, "Help me, please. I've had enough."

Dr. Marcia returned and prepared to oil Jake again. I told her to put him down. I read skepticism in her eyes and she asked, "Are you sure? I'll work on him however long it takes."

I told her to proceed with the euthanasia. She emptied the syringes into Jake's neck and the end was peaceful. Within moments, Jake sank to his knees and onto his side. I sensed Dr. Marcia's doubt and my own second-guessing began. I'd been so busy with Jake, I hadn't phoned Mike, who was on the road. On my own, I'd undertaken a decision to end the life of a horse we both loved.

As Dr. Marcia was packing her supplies in the truck, I said, "Can you open him up?"

Her head gave a jerk of surprise, and she replied, "Most people are so upset at this point, they don't ask. But, I'd like to know for my own reference, too."

From her toolbox, Dr. Marcia withdrew a knife of machete proportions, and my resolve faltered. The thought of beautiful Jake being carved with that knife seemed a sacrilege. I considered staying in the house and awaiting the verdict. But, I told myself that my duty to Jake was for good times and bad. And, I needed to confront the truth of my decision.

Dr. Marcia drew the machete across the width of Jake's belly. Garlands of intestine spilled on the ground. I'd seen illustrations of the equine digestive system. I'd read there were one hundred feet of intestine, along with other organs, folded and enclosed in the abdominal cavity, but, the actuality of the lengthy coiled corridor, which food passes through in a horse, had never been real before. The visual would always inform my feeding and care practices afterwards.

Meanwhile, Dr. Marcia searched through the pile of internal organs, passing intestines through her hands like a butcher examining ropes of sausage. She paused and said, "Here it is."

She'd found a section of the intestine that was impacted with undigested food. The bowel had writhed and contorted at the site of the obstruction, cutting off blood flow, and the knotted intestine was turning black with gangrene.

"You made the right call," she said.

I'd never regretted the decision I'd made about Jake's post mortem exam. It provided information and peace of mind. But, faced with the same decision for Speedy, I hesitated. Would Dr. Penny think I was ruthless or uncaring? Would my friends, who'd gathered to help, be shocked or disgusted? If nothing were found, would I be left with the feeling I'd desecrated Speedy?

Dr. Penny said the words post mortem, as I was using the term, were merely a literal translation—after death. We might, indeed, find something. But a true post mortem, a necropsy in the medical and legal sense of the term, was an elaborate procedure that had to be done in a clinical setting. She could and would open Speedy's abdomen, but, whatever might be found, would not be conclusive.

Rather than opening up Speedy as Dr. Marcia had done, with a saber stroke, Dr. Penny used a scalpel to cut an eight-inch incision in Speedy's belly. The difference in approaches reinforced my view of her—calm, careful, conservative, and undramatic. In that procedure and in all that was to follow, she was on the side of good medicine and ethical practice, not to be swayed by emotions, or legal pressures, or even my sometime desire she support a position I favored. She was there for Speedy as an advocate for truth.

Reaching through the incision, Dr. Penny withdrew sections of intestine for examination. They were dark gray in color, suggesting a lack of blood to them. Dr. Penny stuffed the intestines back into the abdominal cavity and continued to search. That went on for some time, and I began to fret. Finally, Dr. Penny said, "We've got something here."

At the junction of the intestine and the cecum was a blockage. Dr. Penny opened the blockage and found a lesion, an ulcerated area, which would have caused pain every time Speedy ate, and perhaps even when he was exercised.

I recalled the research I'd been doing on the overuse of NSAIDs in horses and their potential for creating gastric ulcers. I asked Dr. Penny, "Could that lesion have been caused by all the Bute and Banamine and pain killers that were given to Speedy?"

She replied, "Yes, that might be the cause, but, that's an opinion. We don't have the medical evidence to rule out other causes."

Twilight was enveloping all of us by the time Dr. Penny stitched up the incision. My friends again expressed their sympathy. We were all covered with dirt and dried sweat from our exertions and exchanged funky hugs and farewells. Then, everyone left, and I was alone with Speedy.

My mind was numb as I sat next to him on the ground trailing my fingers through the damp dirty mane that had once been a silken banner. When I finally stood up and limped on cramped legs into the house, something inside me had changed. The Story would continue, I knew, but, my character had turned away from the insecurities, which had always defeated me.

A few months later, my father was nearing the end of his life. Doris phoned from Florida to say Dad had slipped into a coma. The family gathered for the deathwatch. We were advised there was no way of knowing how long he might linger in a comatose state. It could be quite a long time, or the end could come quickly. My father, never one to overstay his welcome or to inconvenience anyone, died within days.

Chapter 17

Among the papers in my legal file I retrieved from FeliceDeWinter, was an interesting two-page document, a curriculum vitae for Dr. Linus Weed. The first page was a brief resume of his college education and work experience.

The second page of his CV was intended to establish Dr. Weed's expertise in equine sports medicine, lameness issues, and his use of corticosteroids. The statistics he offered disturbed me.

In the year 2003, Dr. Weed stated he had seen 5,300 patients. Fifty three hundred!! The number astonished me. I located my calculator and began doing the math. If Dr. Weed worked a five-day week and took a two-week annual vacation, he would be examining twenty-one horses per day. Twenty one!

How did that translate into dollars and cents? Dr. Weed charged an exam fee of $40 per horse. At least, that's what he charged me. Multiplied by 5,300, that came to $212,000 per year just for examining the horses. (And, I couldn't help but recall the brief lameness exam for Speedy, which Dr. Weed described to Dr. Penny.)

Reading further in Dr. Weed's statistics, he stated he had injected 5,256 horse joints. His charge for an injection of Depo-Medrol™ on my bill was $50. Again I ran the numbers on the calculator. Fifty dollars times 5,256 came to $262,800. The two sets of figures added together came to $474,800 for the year 2003.

Dr. Weed also charged $40 per farm call, but, there was no way I could calculate from his CV how many farms he visited. Yet, it wasn't unreasonable to assume Dr. Linus Weed was raking in half a million dollars per year with his sports medicine and lameness business.

Nothing wrong with becoming a millionaire. This is America. The freedom to make a buck is a sacred right. So long as no one gets hurt. And, sometimes, even then—if you don't get caught. But was anyone getting hurt?

Assuming twenty minutes was a reasonable amount of time to examine, diagnose, prep, and sterilize an injection site, then twenty-one horses would require seven hours of exam time even before the tranquilization and injections began.

The injection process, if the manufacturer's instructions for Depo-Medrol™ were followed, involved shaving the hair from the injection site, inserting a needle into the joint, withdrawing a small amount of synovial joint fluid into a dry syringe, and assessing the volume in relation to the amount of corticosteroid to be injected. With the needle still in place, the aspirated fluid was to be disposed of, another syringe containing the corresponding amount of Depo-Medrol™ attached to the needle, and the injection could then proceed.

With an exam time of seven hours, plus injection time, the addition of travel time—well, that made for a pretty long work day, I thought. And, that was day after day for what Dr. Weed held out as a year, which was representative of his practice.

So where did all the horses come from? I remembered Tyler's excuse for not recalling what had been done to Speedy on September 23, 2002. He said, "We did a lot of horses that day."

Shannon Barlow mentioned seeing Dr. Weed inject a whole bunch of horses at Go 'n' Win Farm prior to a big show.

And, of course, Dr. Weed traveled to other states, to racetracks, and to hunter jumper barns, to practice his sports medicine. Perhaps at those places, large numbers of horses were also assembled for corticosteroids injections. Perhaps Dr. Weed did more than twenty-one horses per day. Perhaps he did forty or sixty per day.

How much quality control, how much attention to detail, how much good medicine, was a vet capable of with those kinds of numbers?

Dr. Weed's CV claimed he had injected 68,000 joints since starting his own practice five years earlier. Of those 68,000 injections, he stated, there had been only two adverse reactions, those being two joints, which went septic from bacteria introduced via needles, a possibility he said he explained to horseowners prior to injecting.

According to my research, there could be other adverse reactions besides septic infection from corticosteroids. Like deterioration of the cartilage. Like further damage to an injury when a horse that was relieved of pain by injections, was put back to work when it should be resting and recovering. And, of course, laminitis.

But Dr. Weed disavowed those three adverse reactions. He only acknowledged a possibility of sepsis. And, he'd only had two septic incidents out of 68,000 injections. But, how would Dr. Weed know?

He appeared to be a quick-fix guy, called in by trainers to inject groups of horses, then moving on to the next bunch. He wasn't around to see if any problems developed. He surely wasn't going to return to, say, Virginia, if a joint on one horse went septic. That would be a problem for a local veterinarian, who could devote time to the patient, wouldn't it?

Upjohn Pharmacia is the manufacturer of Depo-Medrol™, which is a synthetic formulation of *methylprednisolone acetate*. The medical literature for the use of Depo-Medrol™ contained numerous precautions, such as this one warning of infection:

"The suppression of inflammation may mask the signs of infection and tend to facilitate the spread of microorganisms. Hence, all patients receiving this drug should be watched for evidence of intercurrent infection."

The Depo-Medrol™ instructions also warned of systemic effects, a term that includes laminitis, and says the following:

"However, it is possible that mild systemic effects may occur following intrasynovial administration, and this possibility is greater the larger the number of structures injected and the higher the total dose employed."

Moreover, corticosteroids may continue to exert an effect sometimes for weeks. Again, Upjohn's instructions warned:

"Animals receiving methylprednisolone acetate [Depo-Medrol™], as with all corticoids, should be under close observation for possible untoward effects."

But, how could Dr. Weed observe anything? If he flew to Florida to inject who knows how many racehorses, then flew back home, he would be unavailable by the time any systemic or untoward effects appeared. Again, that would be a problem for a local vet to sort out, wouldn't it?

Such was the case when Speedy foundered. Dr. Weed, whose nomadic veterinary practice took him out of state, was not available. Dr. Albright had to be called.

But, Dr. Weed's CV noted, he'd only had two adverse reactions.

Obviously, my objections were not with Depo-Medrol™. Like the cortisone, which restored the use of my arm when all else failed, Depo-Medrol™ is a wonder drug, a modern day miracle. But, if it's used indiscriminately, or excessively, or when other milder therapies could be tried first, that, in my opinion, was a problem. And, clearly, Upjohn Pharmacia, the manufacturer, took pains to urge proper use of its product.

Why was so much Depo-Medrol™ used on Speedy? Had Tyler's training regimen and conditioning been so harsh he created severe lameness in Speedy's legs? Or were the injections meant to be a tune-up or a lubricant, like spraying WD–40™ on engine parts?

Why hadn't less aggressive therapies been tried first? Some answers would never come. But, discovering Dr. Weed's CV and running the numbers suggested my darling Speedy, my golden boy, was just another horse among a sea of horses, just another item on an assembly line, just another dollar sign, instead of what he was to me, a brief shining blessing.

In the late 1980s, I was working as a waitress at a cozy Italian restaurant in Bellingham, Washington. Among the regular customers was a Native American couple, husband and wife, who worked at the nearby Lummi Indian college, a teacher and a social worker, as I recall.

One day, they said to me, "We hear you have horses."

I replied that I did, and we conversed for a while. The coastal Indians of the Pacific Northwest do not have a horsemanship tradition like the Plains Indians. When our chat became awkward, I put it down to that. But, the couple seemed to be seeking affirmation of ideas they already held or to convey something I needed to know. Finally, the woman said, "So, do you feel the horse is the Spirit Messenger?"

I was confused. She continued, "According to Indian lore, the horse is the messenger between the Great Spirit and the People. Have you felt that?"

I couldn't speak for Native American beliefs, but, I knew from my own reading that mythology and literature are replete with the motif of the horse as a creature specially favored by the Divine. The ancient Greeks believed the sun was a chariot of fire drawn by horses only the god Apollo could control. The winged horse, Pegasus, carried the thunderbolts of Zeus and was subdued by Bellerophon with a golden bridle of the goddess Athena.

Even mortals could treat their horses as godsends. Alexander the Great's warhorse, Bucephalus, was the most famous horse of antiquity.

The mad emperor, Caligula, was so infatuated with his horse, Incitatus, he fed the animal oats dipped in gold and made the horse a Roman Senator.

In the 39th chapter of the Bible book of Job, Jehovah gives Job a tutorial of His creation of the heavens, the earth, and all its creatures. The Almighty references His creation of the horse and asks who else but a Divine Creator could have made something so special:

> 19 Hast thou given the horse strength? Hast thou clothed his neck with thunder?
>
> 20 Canst thou make him afraid as a grasshopper? The glory of his nostrils is terrible.
>
> 21 He paweth in the valley, and rejoiceth in his strength; he goeth on to meet the armed men.
>
> 22 He mocketh at fear, and is not affrighted; neither turneth he back from the sword.
>
> 23 The quiver rattleth against him, the glittering spear and the shield.
>
> 24 He swalloweth the ground with fierceness and rage; neither believeth he that it is the sound of the trumpet.
>
> 25 He saith among the trumpets, Ha ha; and he smelleth the battle afar off, the thunder of the captains, and the shouting.

A divinely ordained creation of the horse is assigned by the Koran. According to Islamic tradition, Allah fashioned the Arabian horse from the four winds as a gift to the Prophet Mohammed. The Koran contains some of the most rhapsodic verses ever written about the horse, including these:

"When God created the horse, he said to the magnificent creature: I have made thee as no other. All the treasures of the earth shall lie between thy eyes. Thou shalt carry my friends upon they back. Thy saddle shall be the seat of prayers to me. And thou fly without wings, and conquer without any sword. Oh horse…

"Thou shalt be for Man a source of happiness and wealth, thy back shall be a seat of great honour, and thy belly riches; every grain of barley given thee shall purchase indulgence for the sinner."

The theme of the horse's divine connections has been sounded even in popular entertainment, my favorite being the motion picture *Ben Hur*. When a sheik, played by actor Hugh Griffith, is convincing Ben Hur, played by Charlton Heston, to be his charioteer, the sheik takes Ben Hur into his tent where his four grays live with the family.

Of his horses, the sheik says, "I could sing you a song of the horse. I tell you, no other animal has descended so unscathed from the first innocence of the world."

What is the song of the horse? Those, who are unfamiliar with horses, or who haven't formed a deep attachment to them, may wonder. I could see the song of the horse between a tired old mare named Cocoa and a young woman named Caroline.

Cocoa belonged to a mutual friend of ours, Claude Bartley, a lifelong horseman, who, as an elderly fellow, still bought and sold a few horses. Whenever someone asked for a *bombproof* horse for their kids, Claude would sell them Cocoa. When the kids were ready to move up or lost interest in horses, Claude would buy back Cocoa.

She was a bay roan, who was not a well-made horse to begin with, and, at the age of twenty-five or so, she was, uh, not a pretty sight. The roaning process had turned her swayed back and sagging belly gray.

Only her head, shaped like a hammer, was still bay in color. A sparse black tail and scraggly mane completed the unlovely picture.

Cocoa's virtue was she could be depended upon to plod along dutifully in all circumstances. No one, no matter how green a rider, could possibly come out of the saddle while riding Cocoa unless they were hit by a meteorite. And no impudent beginner booting Cocoa in the ribs was going to persuade her to canter. Cocoa's robotic walk and occasional bone-shaking trot were all the old horse would give anyone—except Caroline.

During a rough childhood, her family could not fulfill Caroline's dreams of horses. But, Claude could. Caroline rode and trained the horses Claude collected from disinterested owners, disbanded rental strings, and kids going to college. In return, Claude provided Caroline with 4-H horses. Riding all kinds of horses made Caroline a skillful rider and one with a special touch, attributes that were delightfully apparent in the relationship between Caroline and Cocoa.

With Caroline on her back, the weary old mare was transformed. She would arch her stubby neck, tuck up her bulbous tummy, elevate her back, prance on her stiff legs, and caper with pride, as though she were a grand blue-blooded horse from the royal stables chosen as the Queen's parade horse.

There, in that reaching down inside themselves to give the best they have; there, in the inexplicable acts of generosity, which occur despite the great communication divide between the horse and human species; there in the virtues of beauty, courage, service, and grace that humans admire and horses are so good at; there in the magic of Caroline and Cocoa—there was the song of the horse.

Soon after Speedy's death, my horse began to appear in my dreams, what dreams there were. I had always enjoyed deep refreshing sleep. But, years of insomnia and night frights were instituted by Speedy's death, by my troubling investigations, by the wearisome judicial process, and by my growing fear of something apocalyptic lurching closer.

When Speedy appeared in my dreams, he was not the bright-eyed golden prankster he had been in life. He was ashen and sad-eyed. He did not gallop in verdant dreamscape pastures, but stood foursquare, affixing me with a look, which said, "Do not forget me. Do not let my death go unanswered."

One night as I tried to sleep, the weight of it all threatened to overwhelm the self-control I struggled to maintain. I couldn't curb my growing fear. I knew more hardships were headed toward me. Mike was away, out on some distant highway. I felt completely alone. I gave into despair.

I sobbed uncontrollably. The unfairness and finality of Speedy's death, all the sadness and frustration so long suppressed, poured out.

I wailed aloud in grief for my beautiful horse and for all the nameless gathering fears, "Speedy, Speedy, my boy, my darling boy. Why? Why?"

Salty tears scorched the skin of my cheeks. Snot ran out of my nose. My chest hurt. Still I cried and cried and asked, "Why? Why? Why did you have to go? Why did this happen?"

Gradually, I became aware that a silence was creeping in. The sounds of night, frog song, bird calls, whir of insects, diminished. The sound of my own voice receded. I could not hear my sobs. Could not hear the questions choked out of my raw throat. Could not hear anything anywhere.

The profound silence enveloped me. Was I still awake? Or was I dreaming of silence? I found myself listening intently to an utter blanketing silence. Listening and listening. Then, right above my head, words were clearly and authoritatively spoken:

"It is the story."

Like the reverberations of a bell, the words hung in the air. In the midst of my mental confusion, I could still hear them. *It is the story. It is the story.* Slowly, the words became fainter and normal night sounds resumed.

As a writer, I knew humankind has had a long problematic history with cryptic messages, going all the way back to the first innocence of the world when a hissing voice said, "Eve, go ahead. Eat the apple. What can go wrong?"

Advice-seekers, who visited the oracles of ancient Greece and Rome, were given esoteric answers that usually sent them on the wrong track. I had been asking questions, wrenching and painful questions. I'd gotten an answer. Could the message be trusted?

Part of me wanted to argue for the safety of a scientific explanation. What is it the brain specialists say about *déjà vu* and about hearing voices? Something about a communication lapse between the two lobes of the brain? Maybe it was a synaptic hiccup brought on by a late night crying jag.

Yet, I recalled the moment of clarity I felt in AinsleyKillbuck's office when I saw myself as a character in a story.

As I lay in a tangle of beds sheets, grappling with the perplexing words, I wanted to reject the idea a person like me, who had been a flop at just about everything, who made such disastrous choices for Speedy, who wasted time and money in a fruitless lawsuit, had any role to play in a larger story. How could I possibly be entrusted with another task?

On the other hand, I was still a writer. An under-performing one. A failed one. But, still a writer. Perhaps *It is the story* meant I was supposed to write Speedy's story. I had been keeping notes and records from the start of Speedy's life to his untimely death. But, Speedy's tale had turned out so badly.

Horse stories always had happy endings. Velvet Brown and Pie won the Grand National. The *King of the Wind* and his devoted handler suffered many hardships before the Arabian was purchased by Lord Godolphin and founded a dynasty. The Black Stallion won all his races. Seabiscuit inspired a nation during the Great Depression and beat his archrival, War Admiral.

I could see no way to write a horse story that didn't have a happy ending.

Chapter 18

Throughout the summer of 2005, various collections' attorneys representing Dr. Linus Weed sent notices demanding payment of $1,624.50 with interest. In each case, I responded the unpaid bill consisted of work Dr. Weed performed without my authorization; I blamed my horse's subsequent health and soundness problems on his unauthorized work; and I would not pay.

I withheld the fact Speedy had died. I doubted it would have deterred Dr. Weed in his quest for payment, and I thought it might be useful to make the announcement at another point in time.

On September 15, 2005, a collections' attorney from a nearby town filed a complaint on Dr. Weed's behalf in the municipal court of the county where I lived. I'd been waiting for that. I filed a counterclaim of veterinary malpractice and asked for $40,000 in compensatory damages, $40,000 in punitive damages, reimbursement of $3,000 for legal fees paid out in my first lawsuit, and court costs.

Dr. Weed must have been shocked when his legal hounding for sixteen hundred bucks produced that result. He hastily called in Brock Hightower.

The local court accepted my counterclaim, ordered Tyler Wragge be added as a Third Party Defendant, and sent the case back to Judge Barton Flint at Gordon County Court of Common Pleas. Celinda Knott returned as Tyler's lawyer. As a *pro se*, a Latin term for a self-represented lawyer, I would be facing the two lawyers, who seemed to have thwarted Felice DeWinter.

I had few illusions about a successful outcome. I presumed the complexity of the law and legal maneuverings would defeat me somewhere in the process. But, I was determined to use discovery to wring more information from the people whose actions, I believed, crippled and, ultimately, killed Speedy.

Early in the pleading process, the tactic, which had successfully demolished my case at the arbitration hearing in 2004, was attempted once more. In a sworn affidavit, Dr. Weed wrote:

"In 2002, Judy Berkley sued me for malpractice. I presented the issue to AVMA and they determined that my care of her horse was within the applicable standards of veterinary medicine and would therefore cover my attorney fees and take appropriate action regarding this case."

That didn't ring true. I had no luck finding any organization, which would take a stand on anything—ethically or legally. Why would American Veterinary Medical Association be any different?

I phoned AVMA's headquarters in Schaumberg, Illinois, and spoke to an official named Dr. Regina Blanco. I briefly outlined what had been done to Speedy, his death, the litigation which ensued, and the repeated claims by Attorney Hightower and Dr. Weed that AVMA approved Dr. Weed's actions.

Dr. Blanco seemed taken aback. She explained AVMA consisted of two divisions, membership services and insurance brokering, but neither division would have done what Dr. Weed claimed. In email verification, Dr. Blanco wrote:

"As we discussed…the AVMA has no knowledge of any details pertaining to any insurance claims that may be filed against our members, and therefore does not review claims. In addition, the AVMA does not offer or dispense legal advice."

There are legal terms for what Hightower and Dr. Weed's claims of AVMA approval represented, falsehoods, perjury, and suborning perjury. I called it damned lies. I seethed with resentment something so fishy I could sniff it out, had been accepted by a room full of lawyers at the arbitration hearing. But, all I could do with that spilt-milk-regret was to conclude I couldn't do much worse representing myself than the professionals had.

Michael Koepf is an old friend whose novels *Save the Whale* and *The Fisherman's Son* draw upon his younger days when he worked as a commercial salmon fisherman. I once asked Koepf about life on the water. He laughed and said, "Are you asking about the *romance of the sea*? Well, let me tell you about the romance of the sea on a fishing boat. It's hours and hours of monotony interspersed with moments of hideous terror."

Over the years, I've often recalled Koepf's description because it works so well for life around horses. Most of the time, the company of horses is pleasantly monotonous. But, the backfire of a car, sting of a hornet, or sudden appearance of something unfamiliar, can turn a snoozing horse into a half ton projectile.

Monotony. Hideous terror.

To cope with those extremes, I've tried to cultivate a state of mind, which is calm and comforting to the horses, but stays alert and ready to react quickly. I call it Pitchfork Zen. I do some of my best thinking when I'm not thinking—Pitchfork Zen.

One day, I was taking a break from writing legal documents, performing menial tasks in the barn, deep in the peaceful unfocused state of Pitchfork Zen. Into the blank space between my ears, came an abrupt and forceful thought:

"Check the x-rays."

Ridiculous, I thought.

Dr. Penny, J.T, and I had all looked at the radiographs many times. Dr. Weed's x-rays were problematical because they were unmarked, dark, and hard to read. Without proper identification, Dr. Weed's x-rays could be bogus copies fabricated from x-rays of a healthy horse's hooves. But, that was just speculation.

Dr. Albright's x-rays taken on September 30, 2002 were clear, well-exposed, and properly marked. And, Dr. Albright had no reason to tamper with the x-rays.

I was dismissive of the thought, which had interrupted my Pitchfork Zen. However, the thought came again with the strength of an order snapped by a drill sergeant: "CHECK THE X-RAYS!"

I dropped what I was doing in the barn and rushed into the house, propelled by the conviction I was going to find something I'd missed. First, I picked up the large manila envelope, which Dr. Albright had used to mail his radiographs of Speedy. Previously, whenever I looked at the x-rays, I reached into the envelope and carefully extracted the radiographs.

On that particular day, I felt excited and a bit exasperated. I quickly sat at my desk, held the envelope upside down, and just shook it. The x-rays spilled onto the desk. Following after them came a folded sheet of white paper, drifting down slowly in the wake of the tumbling x-rays. *What the heck was that?* Because of my previous careful handling, I hadn't seen the paper before.

I unfolded the paper, noted the letterhead of Dr. Albright's veterinary practice, and read his diagnosis of Speedy's condition on September 30, 2002—"Acute Laminitis, no rotation at this time."

I was dumbstruck. With all the activity surrounding Speedy's return home and his rapid progression to full-blown laminitis, I hadn't queried Dr. Albright extensively back in December 2002. We discussed that he tested Speedy for Cushing's, but, the actual diagnosis of laminitis had somehow passed over my head or had not been mentioned.

Dr. Albright's diagnosis pushed the laminitis closer to Dr. Weed's administration of corticosteroids on September 23, 2002, and demonstrated Dr. Weed's claim, in sworn testimony, that the onset of laminitis had occurred in December during Dr. Penny's treatment of Speedy, was a deliberate and contemptible falsehood.

With the directive to check the x-rays still ringing in my mind, I wondered if lightning could strike twice? I laid out the x-rays in two piles and began comparing. I wasn't seeing anything new. The lateral x-rays, whether Dr. Weed's or Dr. Albright's, didn't show rotation.

The dorsal views, which clearly showed the shape of the horseshoes, were not much different. Dr. Weed's showed no irregularities. Dr. Albright's showed cloudiness within the interior of the hooves, which could indicate the early stage disruption of the laminae. But it would take a topnotch expert witness, the kind I couldn't afford, to draw a convincing distinction between the two sets of dorsal x-rays.

I stared at the round horseshoes in Dr. Albright's x-rays, fondly remembering Speedy's beautiful round feet. Suddenly, my brain froze. My hands began to tremble. Round feet! Round shoes!

Was it possible? I put down Dr. Albright's x-rays and began rummaging through Dr. Weed's x-rays. *Where were his dorsal views? Oh, good heavens, could it be?*

Dr. Penny, J.T., and I had always concentrated on the lateral views looking for rotation or something in the nail placement, which would prove Dr. Weed's x-rays were fraudulent. We had consulted the dorsal views for problems in the hoof interiors. But we hadn't compared the shapes of the horseshoes in the two sets of dorsal views.

When I held one of Dr. Weed's dorsal views up to the light, I saw—an oval shoe. The other—an oval shoe.

I was incredulous. The shameless punk had the nerve to send phony x-rays! That was malpractice. That was tampering with records. That was Dr. Weed's ass in a sling.

I sat amid the welter of x-rays laughing at the unbelievability of the moment, the implausibility of the plot twist, and the sheer flamboyance of the story. As I returned the x-rays to their respective envelopes, still chuckling and shaking my head, I had my first writer-to-writer chat with The Author.

I said, "Author, you know that was over-the-top, don't you? The way that paper floated down—as though you tossed it to me—are you kidding?

"And finding those mismatched x-rays after all this time—unbelievable! It's hokey. It strains credulity. I'm sorry to have to say this, Author, but it's just plain bad writing."

As the gravity of the new developments settled in, my amusement gave way to comments that were heartfelt. I said, "I know you are near, Author. I know you want this story told. I will do everything I can and entrust the rest to You."

Taking depositions is an important but expensive tool of discovery that was going to drain my already depleted funds. The fee for a court reporter was $55 per hour and transcripts were $3.40 per page. So, I had to choose deponents, who would give the most bang for my buck. I decided to include Dr. Lance Albright and Shannon Barlow.

I chose a centrally-located town, reserved a conference room, notified attorneys Hightower and Knott, and sent subpoenas ordering Dr. Albright and Shannon to appear for deposition on May 26, 2006. Something about the date was bothersome, but, I couldn't figure out why and went on with my plans.

Dr. Albright, who had been accommodating initially, became a problem. He wanted to be paid, not the nominal deponent's fee, but $1,500 to appear and give testimony. I wanted to know what I would be getting for that amount. Twice, I asked Dr. Albright to confer with me or to submit a written statement. He ignored my requests for information. So, I sent him a subpoena with the standard deponent's fee attached.

My deposition of Dr. Albright went extremely well. He acknowledged the connection between corticosteroids and laminitis. He testified he diagnosed Speedy with laminitis on September 30, 2002, relayed the diagnosis to Tyler, and was replaced, without explanation, by Dr. Weed. Though he had to be prodded, he admitted Dr. Weed's x-rays of Speedy's hooves did not match his x-rays.

I thought Dr. Albright would be my star witness.

Apparently, Brock Hightower also thought my questioning of Dr. Albright went extremely well. After the veterinarian's deposition, Hightower waylaid Dr. Albright and steered the doctor from the conference room into the men's room. The lawyer's loud braying voice alerted me that Hightower was trying to influence the testimony of my star witness. When I broke up the confab, Hightower's parting words to Dr. Albright were, "I'll be talking to you."

Subsequently, I attempted to contact Dr. Albright for clarification of what I considered Hightower's witness tampering and to again solicit a prepared statement from him.

Dr. Albright refused to respond.

Shannon Barlow, after our conversation at the 2004 Buckeye, was on a back burner. I checked with her a couple of times to see if she was still willing to testify about Tyler Wragge. She was. But, when I sent her a subpoena, she vigorously objected to being deposed on May 26th.

The date coincided with the start of the 2006 Buckeye where she was entered and planning to show horses. (Aha! That's why the date I chose for depositions had been bothering me.) A pissed off youngster aching to be at a horseshow wasn't going to be cooperative.

So, we agreed to speak by phone as a means of generating an affidavit. I expected to revisit the episode at the Youth Nationals where Tyler inserted charcoal into Sultan's mouth and the disastrous aftermath.

However, Shannon's interaction with Tyler Wragge hadn't stop after the Youth Nationals' incident. She became the object of Tyler's spite, as did anyone who fell out with him. When Tyler learned from my first lawsuit that Shannon was on the witness list, she said he began to actively harass her at horseshows. Consequently, Shannon was ready to divulge much more than she had before.

At the beginning of our conversation, Shannon covered familiar ground. She related she spent a great deal of time at T&T Stables when Sultan was boarded with Tyler, she had been fond of Tyler as a big brother figure, and she saw and heard a lot about Speedy.

Tyler, she said, was telling all his clients Speedy was a horse who was going to win a national title and finally make him a star. In fact, Tyler approached her about purchasing Speedy, but, at $25,000, my horse was a bit pricey for the Barlows.

Then, Shannon's narrative veered into territory, which shocked and enraged me, that being, Tyler's standard training practices. He used a bit made of welded screws, she said. Such a bit was meant to rip the sensitive flesh of horses' mouths, to cause pain, to inspire fear, and to quickly achieve compliance to the mouthpiece.

To get horses to yield to leg cues, Shannon said Tyler used spurs, regularly, savagely, viciously, so the horses learned early and painfully to respond to the slightest touch of boot heels.

I was almost gasping at what I was hearing. I asked Shannon, "Do you mean he did that to all the horses? The young ones just starting their training? Speedy, too?"

Yes, she replied. All the horses got the same treatment.

While I struggled with grief and rage, I also had no doubt Shannon was telling the truth. The dots were there in my own experience and investigations. I just hadn't connected them. McKenna's stories of horses with blood dripping from their mouths.The raspberries at the corners of Speedy's mouth. The myriad spur wounds on the sides of Rock Steady Baby. The cancelled appointments—for what?—Tyler's supposed medical appointments or the healing of ripped gums and mouth tissue? The closing of bloody gashes on Speedy's golden flanks?

Another dot lined up. The brutality explained why Speedy rarely acknowledged me when Tyler was around. My horse knew he was in the presence of danger. His attention to Tyler, never taking his eyes off him, attention I mistook for devotion, was the look of a gazelle when the lions are hunting nearby.

My mind was overwhelmed with bloodlust. If I could have physically attacked Tyler in retribution for his infamy, I'd have done so without regard for my own safety. Through my rage, I was aware Shannon was still speaking. She related she often saw Dr. Samuel Hawkins at Tyler's stalls during major shows, and Tyler also used what he called an herbal remedy to, in his words, "help the horses get around the ring better."

That, too, connected the dots. I had marveled at Speedy's composure as a yearling at his first big show and again at the Nationals when my horse was so calm amid all the activity. Drugged! Not well-trained by a gifted horseman, as I thought. But drugged by a—a—what?

Suddenly, I fully understood the incoherence of McKenna's first attempt to warn me about Tyler. Indeed, there were almost no words to describe him.

The Nationals—Shannon was talking about the Nationals. Why would she have inside information about the Nationals?

I had to pull together my wildly scattered thoughts and concentrate. Shannon knew what went on at the Nationals because—why? Because she was the young woman helping Tyler to groom Speedy for the Western Pleasure class, the pretty blonde, who gave me a brief, icy greeting.

Speedy foundered before the Nationals, she said. But, Tyler planned to take Speedy anyway. By way of explanation to his other clients, Tyler claimed Speedy's owner was forcing him show the lame horse. That explained the cold shoulder I was given by Shannon and Tyler's other clients.

Speedy, however, did not, could not, cooperate with Tyler's lies. Shannon said Speedy was in too much pain to endure Tyler's attempts at training in Louisville. Indeed, he had bucked Tyler off at one point. I remembered seeing Speedy rear up, seemingly for no reason, when asked to lunge in the warm-up area. And, that explained why Tyler hadn't done any practice riding in the Main Ring in Freedom Hall.

So, Tyler called Dr. Sam with his syringes of ACTH and calcium for help. Help in disguising Speedy's pain. Help in bluffing the foolish woman, who placed her treasure in his hands. Help in covering his actions until he could concoct another lie. Help until he could dump Speedy and move on to the next owner with a Nationals' quality horse and start his ruthless climb toward stardom again.

The realization that May 26th coincided with the opening of The Buckeye suggested a daring move with regard to another person. Dr. Samuel Hawkins, who had injected Speedy at the Nationals, refused to send Speedy's x-rays to me, and stopped communicating when the questions got tough—would again be the official show vet for The

Buckeye. He would be in Ohio and within the jurisdiction of Judge Barton Flint's court.

I sent Dr. Hawkins a subpoena to appear for deposition using The Buckeye horseshow office at the Ohio Expo grounds as the address. I assumed a member of Franklin County sheriff's department would unobtrusively present Dr. Hawkins with the paperwork. But, an acquaintance called to say the horseshow was abuzz with the news Dr. Hawkins had been served.

I figured Dr. Hawkins would find a way to evade the subpoena and be a no-show at the deposition, which is what he did—with the assistance of Tyler's lawyer, Celinda Knott. She wrote a motion to quash the subpoena, claiming Dr. Hawkins hadn't received sufficient notice, and his responsibilities at the horseshow prevented his attendance at the deposition.

A statement signed by Dr. Hawkins accompanied the motion. In it, he stated he couldn't attend because of time constraints and because he had "previously contracted work to perform for clients."

Previously contracted work? Not that he had to be available for the horses in case of injury or illness but for previously contracted work. *What might that be,* I wondered. *Injections of calcium and ACTH?*

I considered briefly Celinda Knott's writing a motion on behalf of Dr. Hawkins might be a conflict of interest. Hawkins was not her client, and I had sought information from him about Tyler. But, I was buried in paperwork and didn't have time to take up the matter with Judge Flint.

In response to the Court's order that Tyler Wragge be added to my lawsuit as a Third Party Defendant, Attorney Knott filed a counterclaim of defamation against me. Her claims on behalf of her client were laughable. She wrote:

"Tyler Wragge [TW] and Tyler Wragge Elite Horses [TWEH] are well known and highly respected in the circles of horse owners, horse show sponsors, stewards, judges and other participants in the highest caliber horse shows and sales which occur not only throughout the entire United States, but also throughout the entire world."

Entire world? By his own admission, Tyler hadn't been able to break out of the ranks of run-of-the-mill trainers and into the domain of big name trainers.

And, according to Attorney Knott, interpreting her client's version of events, Tyler had nothing to do with Speedy's laminitis and the resultant cover-up. She wrote:

"Judy Berkley became disenchanted with TW and TWEH when Speedy became lame and unable to perform to her expectations, blaming all of Speedy's problems on TW and TWEH and the veterinarians to whom they entrusted the horse's care…Since experiencing the disappointment of a horse gone lame and a dire financial circumstance become more dismal, Judy Berkley steadfastly set out to ruin the reputation of TW and TWEH throughout the entire horse world."

Entire horse world, again? It seemed Attorney Knott's vocabulary would have been severely stunted without the word *entire* attached to her absurd claims. But how, according to Tyler and Knott, had I defamed Tyler throughout the entire world?

By speaking to his former clients and by filing a complaint with IAHA, which caused him mental anguish, humiliation, and loss of reputation and business, he said.

A suit for damages must be stated with specificity and Tyler's wasn't. Without names, dates, and dollar amounts, to demonstrate lost clients and lost revenue, a defamation countersuit was just legally-sanctioned blackmail, as Tyler's lawyer certainly knew.

But, it represented the world lawyers seek to create for the rest of us, one that suppresses the right to complain about injustice, harmful practices, and shoddy performance. One that makes the reporting of misdeeds the problem, not the misdeeds themselves. One that seeks to shut down free speech.

The more I read of Attorney Knott's preposterous claims, the more I was plagued by the notion I'd heard her name before. I put aside Knott's legal brief and began searching through the box that contained papers and memorabilia of Speedy. Finally, I found it.

There, in my notes, made during a conversation with Rick Sims, who sued Tyler Wragge; there where Sims said I should call his lawyer if I wanted more information; there was the name of the lawyer, who built a case against Tyler and his parents citing Tyler's lies, phony medical billings, unauthorized veterinary work, botched sales, and confiscated horses. There was the name of Rick Sims' lawyer: Celinda Knott.

My opinion of lawyers, which I thought was already at rock bottom, managed to drop another notch.

An affidavit from Tyler, written in his own words, accompanied the defamation counterclaim. It was disturbing to read his account, and his contempt for former clients and their horses. He wrote:

"Ms. Berkley, Ms. Jamison, and Ms. Barlow have become horse trainers and veterinarians par excellence since each of them has manufactured in their own minds some sense of having been wronged by me; and that their claims are merely those of 'wannabes' who fail to understand good and commonly accepted methods of training, some of which may not appear pretty, but all of which are necessary; and that each of them failed to understand the length of time it takes to properly train a fine horse—each hoping for overnight success—each becoming what is known in my business as 'barn hoppers' and each placing blame wherever necessary to avoid acknowledging that their own horse had not yet risen to the level of their expectations and perhaps never would..."

Imperial Echo+, Kiss Me Kate, Sultan, Speedy—the horses that belonged to each of us *wannabes*—had put Tyler in the winner's circle and moved him toward his personal goals, only to be denigrated in such a shameful way.

What caught my attention, however, was the cold-blooded phrase *good and commonly accepted methods of training, some of which may not appear pretty, but all of which are necessary.*

Tyler's good and commonly accepted methods of training, I assumed, also covered methods I had recently learned of, drawing blood with screw bits, flaying with spurs, and drugging. To be sure, those methods did not appear pretty or necessary.

In sneering at Shannon Barlow, Tyler wrote:

"The substance Ms. Barlow refers to in her Affidavit as 'charcoal' was not charcoal at all, but a product known as Wonder Dust produced by Farnam Animal Health and is a non-harmful method of helping a horse close down on a bit and is commonly used by trainers..."

The statement reeked of I'm-so-smart and you're-so-dumb cockiness. But was it smart? I consulted the ingredients' label for Wonder Dust™, a product that's applied externally to staunch blood flow of wounds and to reduce proud flesh in scars. Wonder Dust™ contains activated charcoal, alum, tannic acid, and hydrated lime, elements, which are well-known caustics.

I phoned Farnam corporate headquarters and spoke to a representative, who was aghast at the internal application of Wonder Dust™. The rep said Farnam certainly didn't endorse the use of its product in a horse's mouth.

Commonly used by trainers, Tyler said, good and accepted methods...

How was Speedy depicted in Tyler's defamation countersuit? Attorney Knott wrote:

"From the beginning of her relationship with TW and TWEH, Judy Berkley had notions of grandeur regarding the show quality and monetary value...of Speedy."

Tyler's affidavit claimed:

"Speedy arrived at my facility with an awful hair coat, 225-300 pounds underweight, and with poorly maintained hooves."

So, a scraggly scarecrow with bad feet arrived on Tyler's doorstep in March 2002, and what did Tyler do? Fall on the ground laughing at my notions of grandeur? Or, did Tyler, as Shannon Barlow and I both recalled, begin talking of Speedy as the horse, who was going to make him a star?

I relished the thought of questioning Tyler at trial about his affidavit claims.

Mr. Wragge, were you hard up for clients in 2002? No? Then why did you accept a scraggly, underweight horse as a candidate for a national championship when you must have had other clients with better horses?

Mr. Wragge, if Speedy was 225-300 pounds underweight, how did you overcome that deficit? With anabolic steroids? With an excessive feeding program, which set up the horse for laminitis?

Mr. Wragge, you have claimed Speedy's bloodline has a propensity for faulty hooves, so why did you accept a horse of that bloodline, which already had poorly maintained hooves?

Yes, I relished the thought of asking those questions and more, but the judicial process I experienced, was about deleting the truth, not finding it.

On February 26, 2007, I was in Judge Barton Flint's courtroom for a Trial Management Conference, which would sort out procedural matters and particulars for a trial, which was scheduled for April 2, 2007. During the preceding seventeen months, I'd assembled documentation and witnesses that could tell a jury the compelling story of what had happened to my horse. But, I had a serious problem. I didn't have an expert witness, who could testify to Speedy's value.

My plan had been to contact Phoebe Fowler. I assumed her previous evaluation of Speedy was on file, and she could just update the paperwork. I hoped her evasions and foot-dragging, as reported by Felice-DeWinter, were just a personality conflict between an equine professional and an arrogant lawyer.

I was wrong.

Fowler began by ignoring a certified letter from me for weeks. When I finally located an email for her and pressed for the appraisal, a real commotion erupted. She suggested I misrepresented Speedy's show record and questioned whether Speedy was actually dead. She said Attorney DeWinter never followed up with her or paid her. Worst of all, Fowler threatened to change the $25,000 amount of her original evaluation.

When I got irate, she called her attorney for assistance. That attorney was Mark Rinaldi.

Who? I recognized the name but had to sift back through the years to nail it down. Hmm, Mark Rinaldi. Oh yeah, he was the lawyer, who was very involved in the Ohio horse scene, who wanted to know the details of my case and the names of the participants, and, who recommended Felice DeWinter.

Knowing I was short of time and needed Phoebe Fowler, Attorney Rinaldi claimed he would try to broker the situation between Fowler and myself. Instead, he ran out the clock so I wouldn't have Fowler as an expert appraiser at trial. Then, he contacted Samantha Barlow and claimed I planned to question Shannon on the stand about Dr. Weed, an allegation, which got the Barlows all riled up, as it was intended.

Rinaldi's intrusion into my case and Fowler's unaccountable resistance to doing the job of a horse appraiser were perplexing and infuriating. Though I could scarcely spare the time to take detours from the grueling legal process, I decided to work my writing contacts in the horse community to see if I could learn anything about Fowler, which might shed light on her conduct.

"Steer clear of her," was the advice of one of my contacts.

"Too late for that," I replied, "Why do you say so?"

The answer was jaw-dropping.

A while back, said my informant, Fowler had a new pickup truck and a fancy new horse trailer—then she didn't. It was rumored she'd embezzled thousands of dollars from a veterinarian she'd been working for. To escape prosecution, she had to return the truck and trailer and pay back the money.

I was stunned at the possibilities. How many veterinarians generate so much money that thousands could be diverted without immediately being missed? Who accepts a give back in lieu of prosecution nowadays? Perhaps a family member? Or someone, who wished to avoid the publicity of a trial?

I didn't have time to investigate a fragment of gossip, which might or might not be true. But the absence of an expert appraiser to appear in Court was just one of several huge problems that came out of the Trial Management Conference.

For starters, Judge Flint decreed Dr. Lance Albright had not been designated an expert witness, therefore, his testimony would be severely curtailed. Dr. Albright would not be allowed to divulge that Speedy had laminitis on September 30, 2002. Nor could I use his written diagnosis of laminitis as documentary evidence. Nor would Dr. Albright be allowed to comment on the discrepancy between his x-rays and Dr. Weed's x-rays.

However, I would have to pay Dr. Albright a hefty fee for appearing at trial. (I assumed my payment arrangements with Dr. Albright would only be known to Judge Flint if Dr. Albright, on his own or advised by Hightower, had complained to the judge.)

Additionally, I would have to write out the questions for my own testimony on the witness stand and provide someone to read those questions to me at trial. Worse yet, I would have to submit the questions, in writing, to the other lawyers PRIOR to the trial.

I was fuming at what I felt was denial of due process, equal protection under the law, and my freedom of speech, but, there was one more serious setback.

Attorney Hightower dropped Dr. Weed's demand for payment, the legal complaint, which had initiated the second round of litigation. Dr. Weed was no longer a Plaintiff, said Hightower. The lawyer requested the case be *flipped*, that is, I would become the Plaintiff owing to my counterclaim of veterinary malpractice. Judge Flint granted Hightower's request.

The flipping move raised a frightening possibility. If plaintiffs are unsuccessful in making their cases, they can be assessed attorneys' fees and court costs. It seemed so unfair to be thrust into that position. Dr. Weed, out of greed and revenge, I believed, had pursued me with a bill for services to Speedy, unauthorized services, which brought heartbreak and financial ruin. Because I fought back, I might, as a newly flipped Plaintiff, incur incalculable debts.

The opposing counsels sought to move me toward dismissing the lawsuit by offering deals. Hightower said Dr. Weed's demand for payment would never be renewed. Tyler's lawyer offered to drop the defamation counterclaim. All Tyler's mental anguish, humiliation, and purported loss of reputation and loss of business, unspecified though it was, would just evaporate.

The lawsuit I worked on so diligently was in tatters. So many important elements, documents, and witnesses were disallowed by Judge Flint, there wasn't enough left to convey a coherent narrative to a jury. I had no choice but to dismiss my case on March 7, 2007.

Litigation was over. Justice for Speedy was not. With the termination of legal proceedings, I could pursue my complaint against Tyler Wragge and Dr. Samuel Hawkins with Arabian Horse Association.

Chapter 19

Five years had passed since my original complaint to IAHA was delayed by the start of my first lawsuit, and more time was lost to the second round of litigation. Following dismissal of my case, I again petitioned Ethical Practice Review Board for a hearing. A date had been set, February 2, 2008, at AHA headquarters in Aurora, Colorado.

By that time, my financial situation was so dire, I could barely afford a cheap plane fare to Denver. Money for a hotel room, meals, and a rental car, was not to be had. I couldn't have contemplated attending the meeting I had sought for so long, except for events, which happened years earlier.

Isabel Greenway was my oldest friend. We met in elementary school as third-graders and sustained our friendship for more than fifty years, despite contrasting personalities, differing lifestyles, and geographic separation.

I'd spent most of my adult life in the West. Isabel, who lived in New York City, was an Easterner through and through. Her husband, Frank, was an executive at a prestigious New York ad agency. Their comfortable, well-established life included a city apartment in an upscale neighborhood, a second home in Connecticut, her career, and the perks of Frank's position.

Then tragedy struck. In 1989, Isabel's beloved Frank was diagnosed with brain cancer and died the following year. I sent condolences from

California and privately wondered how my friend would cope with such a loss. Her eventual solution surprised me.

The confirmed New Yorker wanted to move out West. Knowing I had lived in Aspen, Isabel telephoned and said, "Help me decide if I should move to Boulder, Colorado."

I enthusiastically endorsed the change. I believed everyone should experience the grandeur of the West. Isabel relocated. My friend, who I associated with art gallery openings, Broadway plays, and snooty soirees, became a skier and a hiker.

Years later, Isabel's residency in the Denver area and her offer of help were what made it possible for me to attend the AHA hearing. She volunteered to provide lodging, meals, and transportation to get me to the Denver suburb of Aurora for the Feb. 2nd hearing.

I was reluctant to ask for any more favors, but, I thought I could use her assistance with the presentation. Without hesitation, she agreed.

Isabel's assurance she would take care of everything in Colorado, allowed me to concentrate on preparations for the hearing. If I knew one thing about Isabel, after a lifetime of friendship, it was that her word was an immovable rock.

In gearing up to write my presentation to AHA's Ethical Practice Review Board, I revisited all the materials I had collected. The stuff had long since outgrown the shoebox marked Speedy and filled two large plastic storage totes. I dug out the AHA Handbook to re-read the section on the complaint process, and studied the history of my contact with AHA.

After my complaint was filed in April 2003, the Probable Cause Panel, the first hurdle in filing a complaint with AHA, decided to *stay all proceedings* because litigation was pending. At the conclusion of the first lawsuit, I renewed the complaint in 2005. Then, Dr. Weed's demand for payment of his bill touched off another round of litigation, and AHA's stay order was again implemented.

Irritably, I wondered, "Why must everything and everyone kowtow to lawyers? They are becoming an un-elected ruling class. They're trying to fit us with a one-size-fits-all straitjacket."

I could imagine AHA hoped my complaint had gone away. But, I had made a promise to The Author and to a golden horse that I would persevere. After I renewed the complaint again in 2007, the process seemed to move slowly.

At one point, I called AHA to check on the status of my complaint. A representative said the show season was underway and gathering together Ethical Practice Review Board members for a hearing was not likely to happen until afterwards.

I urged the rep to consider the liability the organization might incur by delaying with regard to the people named in my complaint. If another episode such as happened to Speedy were to be repeated and the victim discovered AHA was *on notice*, that is, had foreknowledge of previous misconduct, the resultant lawsuit could be humungous.

Apparently, that was not of concern to AHA as the process plunked along for months until I received devastating news: EPRB would not hear my complaint against Tyler Wragge.

Would not hear my complaint against Tyler? Why the hell not? The answer was infuriating: Because the arbitration panel in Chastain, Ohio, had ruled against me in December 2004, EPRB was going to accept that as a favorable decision for Tyler.

The arbitration hearing three years earlier—the arbitration that was rotten with perjury and misrepresentation—was to determine AHA's decision? A flawed decision by lackadaisical lawyers was to supersede AHA's own rules?

I begged EPRB to reconsider. I explained I had won an appeal because of fraudulent presentations. I expressed my concern for the safety of other horses and their owners.

Surely, EPRB could find a way to do something if it wanted to. AHA had a provision for exceptional circumstances in Article 308.1(d) which stated:

"A determination of whether exceptional circumstances exist shall be made by the PCP and shall be based on whether the charges raise substantial issues relating to the care and welfare of Arabian, Half-Arabian, or Anglo-Arabian Horses or will substantially affect the AHA and its operations and events."

Despite my plea, EPRB found nothing exceptional in my circumstances and again declined to hear my complaint against Tyler Wragge.

I wept with anguish. There would be no justice for Speedy from the instigator of his ruin. No justice for torment Speedy suffered from drugs, spurs, and bits. No justice for his brief life. No justice for Sultan with his scarred mouth and split tongue. No justice for Rock Steady Baby with his slashed sides. No justice for nameless horses hidden from view, their mouths streaming blood.

Tyler was beyond the reach of justice. He could fade back into the horseshow industry where he would lure new clients with his slippery woe-is-me lies and would continue, I believed, to torture horses instead of training them.

How happy Tyler must have been to receive EPRB's decision. He'd finally gotten rid of me. He could confidently relive that moment outside the arbitration conference room when he and Dr. Weed stood shoulder-to-shoulder, waggled the fingers of their hands at me, and sang out, "Bye bye Judy. Bye bye."

While EPRB excused Tyler, it found no way to excuse Dr. Samuel Hawkins. Did I wish to pursue my complaint against Dr. Hawkins, AHA asked. Yes, indeed, I did.

But, why would I bother? That AHA already knew of the practices of trainers like Tyler Wragge, I felt sure. That AHA already knew of the activities of Dr. Samuel Hawkins, I felt sure. That AHA already knew about chemical warfare, I also felt sure. Why then, would I undertake yet another wild goose chase?

In spite of much evidence to the contrary, I still believed Truth had power. That words could compel. That a story rationally presented and properly substantiated could persuade.

But, if that isn't the case, if Truth no longer has a place in our society, if all of agencies, which govern us have become papier-mache structures, if all the officials are paper-shuffling puppets, if the rules do not apply to favored classes, I needed to know the reality and extent of that phony landscape. Because the flimsy illusion would inevitably collapse and what might follow could be chaos.

So, I spent the early part of 2008 selecting items from the big plastic totes, which spoke to Dr. Hawkins' role in Speedy's story, and organizing the materials into a presentation. A friend of mine, who is a graphics' artist, constructed an exhibit, which reinforced my verbal presentation (we called it idiot-proofing) so there could be no way to misunderstand the facts.

The AHA Handbook described the hearing this way:

"At the hearing, common law and statutory rules of evidence shall not apply, and the admissibility of evidence shall be determined by the EPRB. All evidence that is relevant and has probative value shall generally be admitted."

I managed to let myself think that sounded like a plaintiff-friendly, informal atmosphere, which would be a welcome change from the fussy intricacies and truth-squelching of litigation.

As I combed through the contents of the plastic totes, I came across the dark blue pamphlet published by United States Equestrian Federation (USEF), which outlined the Drugs and Medications rules. I reviewed Article 409, the "No Foreign Substances Provision" and Article 410, the "Therapeutic Substance Provision."

It seemed clear to me the injections of calcium and ACTH that Dr. Samuel Hawkins gave Speedy at the 2002 Nationals violated the spirit of both provisions. Yes, calcium and ACTH are present in the equine body, and thus, are not *foreign* substances—and not being foreign, don't show up on a drug screen. But, the lack of medicinal value and potential harm of calcium and ACTH might qualify as foreign.

As to Article 410, calcium and ACTH have no therapeutic application and must have been used to affect performance.

I remembered Dr. Paul Shepherd, who headed up the Drugs and Meds sector of USEF at the beginning of my ordeal, had grasped the situation perfectly. He offered information, which enlarged my understanding. He was generous with his time and deplored what had happened to Speedy. He provided names of prominent veterinarians I might approach as expert witnesses. He checked records for me to see if any drug reports had been filed. He seemed to be that rarity of modern times, an official doing his job.

Since Dr. Paul Shepherd had been so accommodating in the past, I hated to impose further on his time. But, I had to do a lot of things I hated in seeking justice for Speedy. And, it occurred to me if Dr. Shepherd would supply a statement, which I could take to the AHA hearing, it might carry a lot of weight.

On January 4, 2008, I phoned USEF and asked for Dr. Paul Shepherd. I was informed Dr. Shepherd had retired and someone else was heading up the drugs and meds sector. My heart sank.

While I was experiencing a funk at the news of Dr. Shepherd's retirement, the receptionist transferred my call to a person named Martha Crutchfield. She repeated Dr. Shepherd had retired and inquired if she could be of assistance.

I took a deep breath in order to tell Speedy's story again, as I had so many times before to people, who were professionally involved with animal protection. I explained I was leaving in one month for an AHA hearing and had hoped Dr. Shepherd would supply a statement regarding calcium and ACTH.

Crutchfield said, "They're not on the list."

What's not on the list? What list? Crutchfield had interrupted me, and I was confused at the sudden insertion of *The List*.

I started to talk about the No Foreign Substances and Therapeutic Substances Provisions, and again, Crutchfield cut me off, saying, "They're not on the list."

After those disruptions, it dawned on me Crutchfield was referring to the list of forbidden substances in the blue pamphlet, which included such disgraceful items as arsenic, cocaine, LSD, nitroglycerine, methadone, and strychnine. But, the pamphlet said, "These are only examples...there are thousands of forbidden substances."

Surely, calcium and ACTH violate the spirit of USEF drug rules, I argued to Crutchfield. Over and over the pamphlet said any substance used as a stimulant, depressant, tranquilizer, performance enhancement, etc. was forbidden.

"They're not on the list," said Crutchfield.

Then, Martha Crutchfield invited me to submit my documentation to the new head of Drugs and Meds. With only one month left to prepare for the AHA hearing, I didn't have the time or desire to generate any more paperwork for feckless officials.

I did, however, take time out to send Crutchfield an email, which expressed my frustration. I wrote:

"I have pursued this matter, virtually by myself for five years. Time and again I have been disappointed by the failure of equine organizations to confront the out-of-control drugging situation in the Arabian horse industry that insiders call 'chemical warfare.' Now I finally have the person who I believe is the architect of that chemical warfare in a position where he might be held accountable, and still, it seems, no help will be forthcoming.

"My long ordeal will finally conclude after the hearing. I don't anticipate a positive outcome. I've done everything that a lone individual can do to try to protect other horseowners from a similar fate. But, what's really needed is for veterinary licensing boards to stop protecting this kind of activity and for equine organizations to stop giving lip-service to horse protection and to boldly address the systematic drug abuse that showhorses are subjected to. My circumstances offer what may be a once-in-an-era opportunity to act boldly. I'm sorry that wasn't on The List."

Chapter 20

My first view of Isabel's home was through a snow globe whirl created by an unexpected blizzard that dropped heaps of snow as we made our way from Denver's International Airport to Boulder. Her multi-level house suggested a Frank Lloyd Wright interpretation of a Japanese teahouse and reflected Isabel's taste for simple elegance and interest in Eastern religion and philosophy.

Inside, our first order of business was to open a bottle of chardonnay and unwind from the tension of white-knuckle driving at slow speeds, sliding and skittering across frozen roads. While Isabel organized a few munchies in the kitchen, I looked around.

The spacious living room was furnished with sleek expensive furniture. A few large modern paintings hung on the walls. The only other concessions to décor were a bronze Buddha atop a bookcase and a statue of the goddess Kuan Yin on a pedestal. Through the French doors that led to a fenced backyard, I could see a smiling Buddha with a cone of snow on his bald head, sitting amid a rock garden.

Over the rim of the wineglass, I savored my friend's enduring beauty. It was the first time I could regard her lovely face without the gremlin of envy lurking at the back of my mind. In fact, I rejoiced that her beauty and regal bearing would provide a much-needed counterbalance to the way I looked.

The grueling ordeal of the past six years had robbed me of peace of mind and whatever was left of my looks. My hair was gray, streaked with white. I couldn't remember the last time my skin had been moisturized. My cheeks were splashed with red from a stress-related condition called Rosacea. I was out of shape and overweight from years spent sitting at a desk and writing interminably.

Concerns about how I appeared to others were part of a previous life, before seeking justice for Speedy took precedence over everything else. But, I could imagine the impression my rundown appearance might inspire in the EPRB members. I looked like one of the Crazy Cat Lady types, who feed a hundred strays and kick up a fuss when the local humane society intervenes.

But, Isabel's beauty and composure comforted me. No one so attractive and well-groomed would be hanging out with a Crazy Cat Lady. Surely the Board members would see that.

When we finished the wine, it was late. We hauled my baggage up the stairs to the guestroom. Handily for my purposes, the guestroom adjoined Isabel's home office. She had cleared all her belongings off the computer desk and bookshelves to make room for me to work. Hung across the doorway to the office was a string of Tibetan prayer flags, each stamped with the image of a horse.

According to Buddhist tradition, the Tibetan *wind horse* combined the strength of the horse and the swiftness of the wind, and was believed to be the fastest way to carry prayers to heaven. How remarkable, I thought, to arrive at my friend's home and find the Spirit Messenger hovering nearby.

I'd hoped to have the presentation finalized before I arrived, but I still had much to do. I was looking forward to Isabel's out-of-towner's tour of Boulder, the scenic Flatirons, and old mining towns on the

Eastern slopes of the Rockies, but, I couldn't slack off on preparation. Isabel, who was a perfectionist, understood my need for diligence.

But, she didn't hang a Do Not Disturb sign on my doorknob and disappear. Instead, she dug into the paperwork with me and handled innumerable tasks. The tedium and repetition of working on someone else's obsession would have driven a lesser person nuts.

On the evening of February 1st, we'd done all we could do. I packed the presentation back into a wheeled suitcase. Isabel printed out the Mapquest directions for the drive to AHA headquarters at 10805 East Bethany Drive in Aurora. And, we said goodnight.

Wearily, I crawled into the guestroom bed, pulled the blankets up to my chin, and tried to sleep. But, my brain wouldn't shut down, and my eyes wouldn't close. I stared at the Tibetan prayer flags with the wind horse images, which hung above the door. Instead of dozing off, I had a growing feeling of panic. I realized the AHA hearing was the last stop in, what had so far been, a futile quest to fulfill my promise to Speedy.

But, even more worrisome was the fusion in my mind of Speedy's fate with the peril I felt for my country. If the 40,000 members of Arabian Horse Association couldn't set aside petty bickering and self-interest to rally around their passion for the breed in order to uproot horseshow industry abuses, then, how could a much larger entity, the citizenry of the United States, possibly pull together to save the country?

I had to sleep. I fought the panic. I prayed the 23rd Psalm over and over.

"He maketh me to lie down in green pastures. He leadeth me beside the still waters."

I prayed, as had become my custom, only for courage and integrity. I did not pray for a specific outcome. Only The Author knew how the story would end.

As I prayed and struggled to fall asleep, the prayer flags above the door began to shimmer. I saw the wind horse flags garlanding exotic temples and fluttering in the breeze with Himalayan peaks in the background. I seemed to hear the deep-throated gong of huge temple bells. Drowsily, I continued to pray the 23rd Psalm.

Finally, the words of the age-old psalm for God's safe passage, mingling with the images of pristine mountain landscapes and heaven-bound horses, lulled me to sleep.

"I will fear no evil, for Thou art with me."

The next morning, Saturday, February 2, 2008, Isabel and I were up before dawn. The hearing was scheduled for eight in the morning, and we had an hour-long drive. We dressed hurriedly, loaded our coffee mugs, and climbed into Isabel's SUV for the drive from Boulder past Denver to Aurora.

Isabel drove the interstates confidently, changing lanes and highways efficiently, until we were in the immediate vicinity of AHA headquarters. It was situated within one of those areas that are conglomerates of office buildings, executive parks, or whatever they're called. But, we couldn't find AHA. Couldn't find East Bethany Drive.

We stopped several times to ask directions. We got I-don't-knows or directions that put us right back where we started. The executive park was deserted for the weekend, which made it difficult to find anyone we hadn't already asked for directions.

I felt myself slipping back into the panic mode that gripped me the night before. We couldn't find AHA headquarters! It was right there—somewhere.

Isabel gunned the SUV up and down the empty streets of the executive park with a look of determination on her face.We were not going to be defeated or be late if she had anything to do with it.

Finally, we saw several hotel vans unloading passengers with luggage in front of a building on—oh, thank goodness—East Bethany Drive. As we followed the new arrivals up the front stairs, I was only dimly aware of the building's dark gray stone exterior landscaped with conifers. It was an incongruous setting, I thought briefly, for a breed that originated in the desert.

Upstairs, a young woman, who I'd been communicating with for several months, greeted me and Isabel. She pointed out the restrooms, a conference room where the hearing was to take place, and a table I could use for my materials. In an adjoining room, EPRB members, eight of them from around the country, were assembling. The ninth member, said the liaison, had booked a flight but was snowed in at a Midwest airport.

Hmmm, I thought. A quorum of five members was the minimum required for a hearing. Six members decided the Boggs' case. But, all nine EPRB members had planned to attend. Was that a good sign?

As I surveyed the room, I didn't see a seat reserved for Dr. Samuel Hawkins. For years, I'd been anticipating a confrontation with Dr. Hawkins. Wondering if I would be allowed to question him. Wondering how he would explain himself.

I asked the young woman, "Is Dr. Hawkins here?"

"No," she replied, handing me an informational packet with a spiral binding, "But, his defense and reasons for not attending are in here. You and all the EPRB members have copies."

So, Dr. Hawkins was a no-show again. I was peeved and disappointed, but somehow not surprised.

I tossed the packet on the table, pulled up a chair, and began quickly scanning the enclosed papers. Essentially, Dr. Hawkins claimed Speedy had a *previous* history of laminitis, but did not arrive at the Nationals with laminitis.

Dr. Hawkins also claimed, "The coding of an exam as a lameness examination does not imply that the horse is lame," an assertion, which was inconsistent with his medical notes from the Nationals, when he wrote, "Increased pulse both front feet, turns sore both ways…"

He acknowledged taking Speedy off all medications, drugs for laminitis that he categorized as *anti-inflammatories.*

Referencing the injections he gave of ACTH and calcium, he wrote, "The medications used were prescribed and administered by me."

Medications? Dammit. What disease is treated with ACTH and calcium? What condition?

Well, Dr. Hawkins had an answer for that. He wrote, "The medications that were administered by me are naturally occurring substances in the blood and hardly constitute drugging."

When I recalled those naturally occurring substances in the blood had the potential to kill or to blind or to alter the body's hormonal balance, I could almost agree *drugging* was not the right word. I thought a better term might be *criminal negligence.*

Dr. Hawkins claimed we actually met and discussed Speedy's condition at the Nationals. (Lie) That he was only following AVMA and AAEP guidelines in refusing to send Speedy's x-rays to me. (Lie) And, that he advised me of the interpretation of the x-rays. (Lie)

Dr. Hawkins wrote, "I have been an equine veterinarian for 24 years and this is the first complaint that I have received."

He then went on to list all the shows for which he had been the official veterinarian: twenty-two consecutive Egyptian Events, nineteen consecutive Region 14 shows, seven consecutive U.S. Arabian Nationals, six consecutive Region 12 shows, two consecutive Ohio Buckeye shows, and he would be starting a new association with Region 15.

Dr. Hawkins' involvement with AHA was much more extensive than I realized.

But, he wrote, "I am not in attendance at this hearing because I am a solo practitioner with patients under my care."

Did I get that right? Would the EPRB note the contradiction? Dr. Hawkins could be away frequently from the patients under his care for long stretches of time to attend numerous horseshows every year, but, he couldn't find time to attend a hearing, which might affect his relationship with AHA, the entity that put on those shows. Amazing!

Unless, Dr. Hawkins believed he had nothing to fear.

While I was speed-reading Dr. Hawkins' portion of the informational packet, Isabel was arranging the presentation on the table. A tall blond man, who was mingling with the Board members, left that group and approached us. In the dead of winter, when nearly everyone else had pale or pasty complexions, his skin was tanned to the color of peanut brittle.

He clasped his hands together as he stood before us. He glanced hopefully at my beautiful friend, Isabel, with a look that a wolf would direct towards a pork chop, and said, "Ms. Berkley?"

I introduced myself and watched a look of disappointment flit quickly across the caramel-colored face as he turned to me.

"I'm Thad Farquhar, chairman of the EPRB," said the tall man, "May I speak to you privately, Ms. Berkley?"

We adjourned to a small room where Farquhar expressed his prefrences for how the hearing was to be handled. He said, "Since Tyler Wragge has been excused from this proceeding, I don't think you should refer to his role in this matter."

Farquhar had a few other suggestions that were thinly disguised orders. It all sounded so familiar: Suppress the truth, edit the content, withhold evidence, and try to affect the outcome.

"You're a lawyer, aren't you?" I said.

He seemed surprised by the question. But, yes, he was a lawyer.

"Well, counselor," I said, "I haven't waited all these years and traveled all these miles to do a last minute editorial job on what I have to say. Nor am I going to place all the blame on Dr. Hawkins by omitting any reference to Tyler Wragge's role."

Farquhar stared at me. A little frown, shaped like the letter W, appeared on the orange skin between his eyebrows and stayed there. He started to repeat himself, but, I held up my hand in a dismissive gesture.

We returned to the conference room where Farquhar joined the rest of the EPRB members, who had taken their seats in a long line facing the table where Isabel and I sat.

Each of the Ethical Practice Review Board members was introduced. Rather than a panel of impartial judges, all of them were involved in the industry as breeders and trainers and such. However, two of them were introduced as doctors. I asked if they were doctors of veterinary medicine. They were.

I allowed myself a moment of optimism. Perhaps the veterinarians would stand with me against the misuse of drugs on showhorses and against the insidious chemical warfare, which made a mockery of sportsmanship.

I introduced Isabel and made it clear she had no stake in the proceeding. She was not a lawyer, not a horse person, or in any way an interested party, just a helpful friend. With the preliminaries completed, I started the presentation.

I stuck closely to the script Isabel and I had worked on. In preparation for the hearing, I didn't know whether the event would be recorded or videotaped, so the script was to be my record of the proceedings. As it turned out, AHA had engaged a stenographer. I didn't plan to spend any more money on transcripts, particularly since my presentation, timed by Isabel, ran about three hours.

I knew reading from a script during a presentation is not advisable. But getting off script, getting into my disgust at the characters who, I believed, had brought down Speedy, also wasn't advisable. So, I read. I tried to vary the cadence of my voice. Tried not to rush. Tried not to dawdle.Tried to look up from the script frequently to make eye contact.

And, when I did look up, I saw eight people looking back at me with blank emotionless faces.

Isabel got up from the table frequently to place information on the graphic exhibit, which was placed on an easel facing the Board members. The exhibit was a timeline of the critical months of September through December 2002. My narrative, supplemented by the timeline, demonstrated Dr. Weed's unauthorized corticosteroid injections, Dr. Hawkins' injections of ACTH and calcium at the Nationals, the unsuccessful struggle to get medical records from Drs. Weed and Hawkins, and the flood of drugs given to Speedy after the Nationals under Tyler Wragge's supervision.

Copies of documents, medical records, and affidavits, which substantiated my claims, had been submitted to AHA prior to the hearing and were included in the informational packet that was distributed to the Board. I referenced the evidentiary documents and held up my copies as I made my allegations.

I was allowed to present a videotape of Speedy in the qualifying class of the Western Pleasure class from the 2002 Nationals. Its very existence was incredible. Before I left Louisville, I asked Tyler if I could obtain a tape of the class. He claimed all the videocameras had been reserved by individual competitors, so, no, there was nothing to see. Years later, in another moment of Pitchfork Zen, I was told: "Get the videotape."

I phoned the video company and was informed one camera was always reserved for an overview of the class, something Tyler probably knew. However, the digital recordings were only kept for a couple of years, then, destroyed. They would have to check their inventory.

Amazingly, the tape, which featured Speedy in a number of sequences, had managed to survive. More amazing, Speedy's breakdown apparently caught the videographer's attention as the tape recorded the moments immediately afterwards. It showed Tyler leaning over in the saddle to look down at Speedy's right leg as they joined the lineup for final judging.

However miraculous the existence of the tape and its contents were to me, I had to argue with Farquhar for its inclusion in the hearing. He finally agreed, but ordered me to refrain from making any comment while the tape played. I should have taken the opportunity to ask a question, which I was constantly asking myself: "Why is everyone so afraid of freedom of speech?"

When my presentation proceeded, I noted Dr. Hawkins took Speedy off all medications after the first exam at the Nationals. His records did not indicate the medications were resumed, leaving open the possibility Speedy was left untreated and in pain for six days. And, the Board had Shannon's affidavit attesting to Speedy's pain.

I argued strenuously against the use of ACTH and calcium on Speedy and claimed USEF Drugs and Meds Article 410, the Therapeutic Substances rule, had been violated by Dr. Hawkins.

As I neared the conclusion, the closing remarks I'd prepared ahead of time seemed inadequate. Nothing I had said to that point elicited any change in the expressionless faces of the EPRB members. In hopes of inspiring some reaction among the stone-faced officials, who were to pass judgment on Speedy's fate, I went off-script at the end to make an impassioned plea that AHA rectify abuses in the industry and become true stewards of the Arabian breed. The eight blank faces remained unchanged.

Obviously, the Ethical Practice Review Board would confer and come to a decision on February 2, 2008, after which the eight members would leave the Denver area and return to their homes. Since I was spending a few more days with Isabel, I expected the decision would be waiting for me when I got back to Ohio.

It wasn't.

I waited until February 22nd for official notification before emailing the young woman, who had been the liason. The decision was supposed to have been mailed to me, she said, and apologized for the oversight. She sent the verdict via email attachment. My capacity for disbelief had been strained so often, I could only feel a dull sense of astonishment at the Board's decision: Dr. Samuel Hawkins had done nothing wrong.

In order to exonerate, Dr. Hawkins, my evidence had to be misrepresented and ignored. For example, the EPRB decision claimed I had argued USEF's Foreign Substances Provision, when, in fact, I had argued theTherapeutic Substances Provision.

As to the general spirit of USEF policy, that the use of foreign or therapeutic substances as stimulants, depressants, or local anesthetics to affect performance made them forbidden substances, well, the EPRB found that I'd presented insufficient evidence that ACTH and calcium were forbidden substances.

Moreover, the Board's decision said I failed to establish Speedy was unsound and in pain at the Nationals, despite Dr. Hawkins' own lameness exam, which noted my horse "turned sore both ways" and Shannon's affidavit attesting to Speedy's pain.

If either of the two veterianarians, who were present at the hearing, dissented on behalf of my horse or objected to chemical warfare or testified to the health risks of ACTH and calcium, their objections were not mentioned in the Board's decision.

The plaintiff-friendly atmosphere of the hearing that was suggestion in the AHA Handbook, turned out to be, what too often passes for justice in our country, an unproductive Shell Game, just another exercise in lawyer-ish sleight of hand.

Words like *cover-up, sham*, *farce*, and *whitewash* passed through my mind. I recalled the words Rick Sims used to describe how his complaint to AHA was handled—*a joke*.

All the words were inadequate to describe what I believed EPRB's decision represented: Maintenance of the status quo. Endorsement of chemical warfare. Support for Big Name Trainers, Big Money Breeders, and cut-throat competitors, those who want the un-level playing field created by performance-enhancing substances.

Worst of all, I believed the decision illustrated the degraded position the Arabian horse actually occupied in AHA. Behind all the flowery rhetoric about the breed's exotic history, behind all the professed reverence for the horse, which AHA's very existence was built upon, the Arabian was, for official purposes, merely a commodity for generating money for a powerful horseshow oligarchy within the organization.

And, the membership of AHA, the majority of horseowners who, I believed, loved the breed, but wanted changes, was expected to put up and shut up, that is, put up their money for sweepstakes programs, registrations, show fees, and countless revenue streams, and shut up about how they wanted things done.

Chemical warfare, it seemed, was not going to change. Like so much in the Arabian horseshow industry, it was part of the Way Things Are Done. Thus, other changes, which might reduce horseshow abuses, changes like a designated veterinary area policed by show stewards, changes like rotating veterinarians for major shows, changes like the elimination of stall drapes, changes like immediate disqualification for physical abuse of horses at showgrounds, changes like a truly ethical complaint process, were not likely to be adopted.

Soon after I was advised of EPRB's decision, the program for the 2008 Buckeye arrived. Listed among the judges for the show was Thad Farquhar. It was a slap-in-the-face reminder of the conflicts of interest and inbred cronyism of AHA.

Chapter 21

The curious conduct of Felice DeWinter was a mystery I figured would never be explained. Three years after I dismissed my case, my lawyer's unaccountable hostility toward me, her bogus claim about a $5,000 expert witness, and her failure to aggressively pursue my lawsuit, were irritants, which had receded in my mind.

But, one day in 2008, a forceful thought about DeWinter interrupted my Pitchfork Zen state of mind with the words:

"Google DeWinter"

By then, I had learned to comply without hesitation to those sudden messages. I was astonished at what an Internet search produced. On that very day, my former lawyer was up before the Disciplinary Counsel of the Ohio Supreme Court on charges, which could result in disbarment. The three-count complaint against DeWinter alleged she mishandled three separate lawsuits.

Two of the lawsuits were race discrimination actions. In one of them, DeWinter was seeking $10 million in compensatory and punitive damages for fourteen African-American plaintiffs, who had worked at a county agency.

A lower court held that no evidence and, in some instances, insufficient evidence, was presented to support the claims of racially-motivated employment discrimination. In addition, the Court said DeWinter's case also suffered because she failed to hire an expert witness as she claimed she planned to do. (Still didn't have time to be chasing expert witnesses, it seemed.)

Along with the race discrimination actions, DeWinter was pursuing a lawsuit for sexual harassment, which had descended into an unseemly brawl in the local legal community. DeWinter had wrongfully accused and sued two defense lawyers for defamation. The fracas personally cost her $4,000 in reimbursements to the lawyers and their legal counsel.

In all three cases, DeWinter was unwilling to accept the adverse decisions of the Courts. She filed affidavits against judges and public officials alleging bias, misconduct, and racial prejudice. She requested the dismissal of one judge claiming he was possibly a racist and was under investigation by the FBI for criminal conduct. She took one case to the Court of Appeals and lost. Her legal flailing suggested she was having some kind of meltdown.

The Supreme Court considered the matter for two days and recommended disbarment for an indefinite period of time. Moreover, as penalty for filing a frivolous workplace discrimination lawsuit, which ran up a legal tab of more than half a million dollars, DeWinter and twelve of the African-American plaintiffs were collectively liable for $660,000 in attorneys' fees.

Although the Supreme Court was hearing the matter in 2008, I had a hunch about the timeline. Sure enough, all three of the problematic lawsuits filed by DeWinter were concurrent with her handling of my case. I thought, "How piddling my $50,000 litigation must have seemed compared to ten million dollars!"

But, was that just guesswork or sour grapes on my part? I pulled the court dockets on all the cases and checked the dates when DeWinter's cases started to blow up. There, clustered around the time frame when DeWinter's behavior toward me became intolerable, were bomb craters of DeWinter's other exploding lawsuits.

Small wonder DeWinter had no patience or time for me. She was juggling live hand grenades—and dropping them. And, if her arrogance and secrecy with me were any indication, she was probably trying to keep her clients from knowing how badly things were going. It looked to me as though DeWinter wasn't defeated by attorneys Hightower and Knott or by weaknesses in my lawsuit. She was looking for a way to bail out.

The unexpected directive to *Google DeWinter* at the very time the Supreme Court was considering DeWinter's disbarment and the subsequent revelations gave me some peace of mind about decisions I'd made. I was right to dismiss my lawsuit rather than go to court with a lawyer whose conduct was so erratic. And, it was prudent to dismiss my second lawsuit rather than risk liability for attorneys' costs if my case, weakened by all the disallowed evidence, was deemed frivolous.

DeWinter's fate was sealed, I suspected, because she had attacked judges and other lawyers. I wondered if the Supreme Court would be concerned about a former self-represented lawyer, who had grievances with lawyer misconduct.

My lawsuits were damaged by two attorneys. Brock Hightower's false claim of AVMA approval scuttled the arbitration hearing. I had letters and court-filed documents signed by Hightower, which made the claim. Additionally, I believed, he tampered with my witness, Dr. Lance Albright. I filed a complaint against Hightower with the Disciplinary Counsel of the Supreme Court of Ohio, charging perjury, suborning perjury, and obstruction of justice.

Hightower offered a couple of limp denials and no evidence to refute my claims, but, that was sufficient for the Ohio Disciplinary Counsel to dismiss my complaint.

Mark Rinaldi was licensed to practice law in Ohio and in Tennessee. I filed complaints with the Supreme Courts of both states, citing

Rinaldi's intrusion into my lawsuit, his attempts to intimidate me, his waffling with regard to Phoebe Fowler, which intentionally left me without an appraiser, and his meddlesome conduct aimed at upsetting Samantha Barlow and my witness Shannon Barlow.

The Disciplinary Counsel of Ohio immediately declined to pursue the matter. However, Tennessee's Board of Professional Responsibility undertook an inquiry that spanned several months. The outcome was the same, the Board found no fault, but, during the process, Attorney Rinaldi seemed to be rattled. He made admissions in his defense, which added a little to my understanding.

His statements included the following:

"I did know some of the actors in Berkley's case; I know many of the facts in her case...I had conversations with other attorneys familiar with the case in hopes of gleaning insight...The only discussion I had with Samantha Barlow, regarding said testimony was merely to ask if she knew why Shannon was being called as a witness...I have taken some criticism among colleagues with whom I have shared this current predicament and it is not unreasonable to expect that some members of this Board will share some of their same thoughts."

Did Rinaldi's *conversations with other attorneys* include conspiring with them to harm my case? I had no evidence to support that. But, my own opinion of the legal profession didn't preclude it.

In another statement, Rinaldi made the astonishing claim that his interference in my lawsuit proceeded from good intentions, that he didn't want to see me "blind-sided in the middle of a trial."

That blind-siding would have come about through Phoebe Fowler, he said, "whose testimony regarding the value of Berkley's horse would only be a fraction of what [Berkley] is anticipating, and if believed, would wipe out most of her damage prayer and injure her credibility with the Court..."

While Rinaldi's admissions didn't fill in all the blanks of the strange episode, I was left with one uncomfortable thought: The age-old chicanery of horse tradin' now has a new element, the shrinking, flip flopping, here-today-gone-tomorrow, horse appraisal.

My concern that the integrity of veterinary medicine was being compromised by the activities of a few unethical vets, caused me to reapproach Ohio Veterinary Medical Licensing Board with evidence from the second lawsuit of Dr. Weed's perjured testimony and falsified x-rays.

The Board found no fault with Dr. Weed.

I phoned OVMLB's office and demanded to know how the Board arrived at such a decision. A representative told me the Board felt my complaint, despite new evidence, had been dispensed with in 2003.

I argued with the rep, "I sent the Board two sets of x-rays from Dr. Albright and Dr. Weed that didn't match. The horseshoes were different. How did the Board explain that?"

The OVMLB rep replied, "One of the Board members [a veterinarian] said the x-rays didn't match because two different processes were used to take them."

Two different processes? Wearily, I started to object, but, then I finally recalled Dr. Penny's advice from years earlier: Don't expect much. It's just a Good Old Boys Club.

Sometime that year, J.T. came to my farm to do some work. As he was laying out his tools and strapping on his leather apron, he looked at me with mischief in his eyes, and said, "Guess who I met up with."

"Who?" I asked. He grinned and said, "C'mon, guess."

From his impish manner, I was getting a clue. I said, "You're kidding! Dr. Weed?"

"Yup," said J.T., "I was at a show barn shoeing a horse in one set of cross-ties. This guy in the cross-ties beside me was feeling around on a horse's legs and back. I thought he was doing equine massage. Next thing I know he's having his assistant scrub up some injection sites. I asked the barn staff and they confirmed who he was."

"When you say feeling the horse's legs and back, do you mean no flexion test, no x-rays?" I asked.

"Nope. Nothing."

For a couple of years, I tracked Tyler Wragge's career via published horseshow results. Occasionally, he rode a horse to a Top Ten, less frequently a Reserve Championship. But, it appeared he hadn't advanced to the top tier of trainers, and a National title still eluded him.

Did he ever reflect upon Speedy? Amid all his lies, I believed Tyler told one truth. That was his wistful remark about Speedy at the Nationals when he said, "He's the best horse I've ever ridden."

Did Tyler regret his actions? Did he ever feel remorse for Speedy? I was doubtful. Mine was not an isolated case. Tyler had damaged horses and alienated clients over and over, exhibiting the dangerous pathology of a person, who doesn't learn from mistakes.

Therefore, it came as a surprise that Tyler was not completely unteachable. He had learned one thing very well. That was to cover his butt by requiring his clients to sign a ruthless written contract. The contract's provisions granted Tyler absolute control over a horse's training, health, veterinary care, and show career, and insulated Tyler from any liability if he screwed up.

Would potential signers read between the contract's lines? Would they understand they were relinquishing all their property rights to the conduct and whims of another person? Or would they be blinded by stars in their eyes?

That McKenna Jamison would own another showhorse was never in question. As Gigi and all of McKenna's friends were sure, her heart and mind and lifestyle were so entwined with Arabian horses she would eventually move past her grief over Imperial Echo+ and buy a horse. However, she was to take quite awhile.

McKenna wanted a particular bloodline. She wanted a certain look. She wanted a Western Pleasure prospect, which had already been started under saddle so she could get back to showing. And, she applied her usual experience, knowledge, and thoroughness to the search.

Eventually, she located a stunning bay gelding, paid an undisclosed amount, and brought the horse home. As soon as the new purchase was settled in, training began—and trouble soon followed. The bay was flighty and unpredictable. It seemed to be dealing with past trauma or painful experiences it couldn't move beyond. And, there were health issues. The horse was not going to be a second-best replacement for Imperial Echo+ or even a reliable showhorse.

Using her contacts, McKenna located a groom, who had worked around the horse and was willing to talk to her. The bay had been drugged and subjected to physical abuse.

As the year 2008 progressed, my apprehension persisted. The failed AHA hearing, my abortive complaints to OVMLB, and the nonchalance of the legal establishment regarding lawyer misconduct, were months earlier. Yet, I couldn't disconnect from the feeling of dread I'd lived with for years.

But, events in September and October of 2008, clarified my anxieties. Officials of the federal government announced the United States of America was bankrupt. Not just bankrupt, flat broke, and busted, but trillions of dollars in debt.

The economic state of affairs, the worst financial crisis since the Great Depression, soon spread bankruptcy, job loss, intractable unemployment, decimated retirement accounts, home foreclosures, evictions, misery, uncertainty, and distress, to millions of Americans.

The causes of so much havoc, I recognized from my own experiences: Ineffective officials. Inept bureaucracies. Rampant greed. Flagrant dishonesty. Unchecked corruption. Lies. Betrayal. Villainy.

Three years have elapsed since the sellout and impoverishment of the American people were announced and the completion of this book. Little has been done to address the gargantuan problems or to reverse the calamitous course we're on. And, no sense of urgency is discernible. Where I once hesitated to write Speeedy's story because it didn't have a happy ending, I now fear the story of my country will end disastrously.

The decline in the economy, coupled with our own mistakes, brought tremendous hardship to Mike and me. I blame myself for much of the damage. Over and over, I spent Mike's hard-earned money trying to get a broken system to yield a positive result. By 2008, there were no options left—and no money.

With the assistance of the only commendable lawyer I met along the way, we filed for bankruptcy. Our home and farm, which we'd hoped to turn into our private little heaven, was sold to satisfy our creditors. As painful as it was to part with our dream, the only possessions I agonized about were the horses. I dreaded they would be taken from me and wind up being sold for slaughter.

I needn't have worried. The horse market was glutted, the accumulation of unwanted, abandoned, and no longer affordable horses so great, the administrator of our bankruptcy didn't have the slightest interest in trying to sell them. I leased five acres of land with a simple shelter for Queenie and Sugar and our other horses, and vowed they would not suffer from my misplaced trust in the system.

They live without the frills I wish I could give them, but, they have everything that matters to horses, plenty of feed, fresh water, and the enjoyment of horse companions. Their health and hooves are still cared for by Dr. Penny and J.T. Laney.

Speedy no longer haunts my dreams. His ribbons, trophies, photos, and videotapes, are packed away, too painful to look at. But, memories of Speedy come often— and always with piercing sadness.

Given hard times and human incompetence, prospects for the Arabian horse are not encouraging. But, the time is ripe for a membership revolution to shake up AHA.

In 2007, there had been one tentative step forward.The revulsion for the abuses associated with the hard stand-up reached a critical point, as did frustration and discontent about arbitrary, undocumented decisions by showring judges.

Thus, changes in halter classes and a scorecard system were suggested. Horses would be shown in more natural poses, which would be less stressful to the animals, and less alarming to knowledgeable spectators. Judges would have to evaluate tangible attributes of the horses on a point scale and commit the numbers to a scorecard.

Despite the opposition of some prominent halter trainers, a resolution was proposed at an AHA Convention, and the scorecard system was finally passed. However, the Scottsdale Arabian horseshow, which did not operate under AHA auspices, promptly announced it had no plans to abandon the hard stand-up in its halter classes. And, the continued resistance within AHA to the scorecard system and to the elimination of the hard stand-up suggests nothing is set in stone. And, without a cornerstone, what else can be built?

In 2009, Arabian Horse Association enraged many horse-lovers and AHA members when it unexpectedly came out in favor of horse slaughter and supported the reopening of meat processing plants. The slaughter industry, which processed up to 100,000 horses annually, had been suspended for several years by an act of Congress in response to the revulsion of the general public to inhumane transport and wanton disposal of horses.

Within the Arabian horse community, as elsewhere, there was disagreement between anti-slaughter advocates and those who viewed the horse meat industy as a necessary evil. Despite the lack of consensus, the governing board of AHA did not poll its membership to determine if the endorsement represented a majority opinion, before issuing a proclamation in the name of Arabian horse enthusiasts.

Moreover, the controversial endorsement conjured up the worst transgressions of the 1980s.The new business model, which I was on the lookout for, still appears to be a lot like the old business model. It's still on a track of misunderstanding the market, creating unrealistic expectations, encouraging over-breeding, and, when that doesn't work—sending its mistakes to slaughter.

How long will the industry's silent majority of true horse-lovers endure such atrocities? When Speedy was born, AHA's membership was said to be 45,000. A decade later, AHA was reporting membership of 33,000. If the numbers plummet way down to, say, 10,000, will a heroic few summon the courage to throw off fear of litigation and the stranglehold of a power-wielding minority in the horseshow industry and go to battle for the Arabian horse?

It can be saved. Careful breeding could reverse much of the conformational damage within several generations. Abolishing chemical warfare and cleansing horseshows of those who use performance-enhancing drugs, could restore confidence in sportsmanship. Ejecting those who abuse Arabians, would demonstrate true respect for the breed.

But, the mission would require long-term commitment, clear standards of Right and Wrong, dedication, perseverance, and love for the task—the same kind of battle that is needed to save America.

Epilogue

It is the story.

On a sleepless night, when I felt lonely and abandoned, when I wept uncontrollably, and asked *Why? Why?,* those puzzling words were spoken. I've come to a fuller understanding of them.

Yes, it is Speedy's story: A beautiful, innocent creature performs brilliantly before it is tormented and meets an untimely death at the hands of villains within a corrupt system.

But, the resonance of Speedy's story with the central event of the Christian faith, the sacrifice of a blameless human being for the redemption of humanity, helped me to appreciate the words I heard referred to a greater story and a much older one. And, I found it in The Author's bestseller, the Bible.

Humankind's failures, the ruination of what is good and beautiful, the ascendancy of greed and corruption—all those events have been foretold. The mess we find ourselves in and the failure of human governments are not news to The Author. But, the way out is also foretold. Time and again, The Author has forgiven and embraced individuals and societies, which turn away from false idols and godless pursuits and return to scriptural guidance.

And, for those who follow His guidelines, He offers the greatest reward, everlasting life in a place we already know and love. Our beloved earth, cleansed of sin and evildoers, a paradise regained, will be our eternal home.

In that heaven—not the heaven of white robes, golden harps, and fluffy clouds—but the heaven of fertile soil, abundant grass, pure water, plentiful harvests, peace and tranquility, will there be horses? Will horse-lovers be blessed in the afterlife with the companions that enriched our lives while on this earth?

The Old Testament prophet, Isaiah, foretold a renewed earth so idyllic that wolf and lamb, kid goat and leopard, calf and lion will dwell together peacefully. (Isaiah 11:6)

The Author's faithful servant, Job, believed His Creator would wish to see him again, that he would be resurrected because his Maker would yearn for the work of His hand. (Job 14:15)

My prayer is for the fulfillment of Isaiah's vision, and that The Creator will also yearn for the creature He made and described in such glowing terms to Job—the magnificent horse.

My hope is the spirit messengers, who have served throughout the ages as emissaries between The Author and humankind, will be rewarded with a place in the new heaven.

My joy would be to see Speedy again.

About the Author

Judy Berkley has been a published writer since 1984. Her freelance work was featured in numerous publications including *San Francisco Examiner, California Living, San Francisco Magazine, Equus, Horsemen's Corral,* and *Driving Digest.*

In 1992, she became a regular columnist at the four newspapers, which comprised the Alameda Newspaper Group (ANG) in the East Bay of the San Francisco area. When ANG purchased the *Oakland Tribune,* Berkley became the news group's most visible columnist, writing five columns per week that appeared in all five newspapers.

Eventually, Berkley found political correctness in the news business so restrictive and damaging to freedom of speech, she resigned from her columnist position. In 1995, seeking respite from an increasingly stressful world, Berkley and her husband moved to the Midwest and bought a farm in rural Ohio.

Berkley planned to turn her lifelong love of horses into the focus of her writing and activities. From what she thought would be a tranquil lifestyle, came the most dramatic and demanding episodes of her life, which she chronicles in *Justice for Speedy: A True Horse Story.*

Made in United States
Troutdale, OR
11/03/2026

56845385R00166